MONTAIGNE'S UNRULY BROOD

MONTAIGNE'S UNRULY BROOD

Textual Engendering
and the Challenge to
Paternal Authority

RICHARD L. REGOSIN

University of California Press

Berkeley · Los Angeles · London

University of California Press
Berkeley and Los Angeles, California

University of California Press, Ltd.
London, England

© 1996 by
The Regents of the University of California

Library of Congress Cataloging-in-Publication Data

Regosin, Richard L., 1937–
    Montaigne's unruly brood : textual engendering and the
challenge to paternal authority / Richard L. Regosin.
        p.   cm.
    Includes bibliographical references and index.
    ISBN 0-520-20194-9 (alk. paper)
        1. Montaigne, Michel de. 1533–1592. Essais.
2. Intertextuality.   I. Title.
    PQ1643.R395   1996
    844'.3—dc20   95-6077
                                                               CIP

Printed in the United States of America
9 8 7 6 5 4 3 2 1

For Barbara, and for our own unruly and wonderful brood: Deborah, Elizabeth, Rebekah, and Sophia

Contents

Acknowledgments ix

Introduction 1

1. Textual Progeny 13

2. Montaigne's Dutiful Daughter 48

3. The Imposing Text and the Obtrusive Reader 80

4. The Presumption of Writing: Between Ovid's Children 119

5. Monstrous Progeny 152

6. Fathering the Text: The Woman in Man 183

Notes 225

Bibliography 243

Index of Essays 249

General Index 251

Acknowledgments

I owe a special debt to Patricia Donahue and David Carroll whose thoughtful comments and difficult questions helped me to gain a better understanding both of Montaigne's textual engendering and of my own. In many ways they played "sage femme" and "sage homme" to the birth of this book. I am also particularly grateful to Steven Rendall for his generous support and helpful assistance.

A portion of chapter 1 appeared in slightly different form as "Montaigne's Child of the Mind" in *Writing the Renaissance: Essays on Sixteenth-Century French Literature in Honor of Floyd Gray*, ed. Raymond La Charité (Lexington, Ky.: French Forum Publishers, 1992). A section of chapter 2 was previously published as "Montaigne's Dutiful Daughter," *Montaigne Studies* 3, no. 1 (1991). Portions of chapter 4 appear in different form as "Nemo's Descent: The Rhetoric of Presence in Montaigne's *Essais*," *French Forum* 13, no. 2 (1984). Part of chapter 5 appeared earlier as "Montaigne's Monstrous Confession," *Montaigne Studies* 1 (1989).

Introduction

Among the precocious children Montaigne evokes in his *Essais*—
children intelligent and dull, faithful and rebellious, strange and
wondrous children such as the Siamese monster and the young girl
who turns into a boy—the figurative child of the mind stands apart,
not only as the essayist's own progeny, his book, but as the unimag-
inable body bearing all these other, natural children within itself as
constituents of its very being. As if the book were not an only child,
not, for example, only a reasonable and obedient son who dutifully
carried his father's hopes for immortality into the world, but a hybrid corpus of siblings, multiform, variegated, conflicted, like a
strange and unruly brood pulling their parent in different directions.
Traditionally, the metaphor of the book as child has single-mindedly
and openly expressed the fidelity of textual progeny, its capacity to
represent its author and to assure the integrity of his name. But the
hybrid figure of the *Essais* discloses the many faces of textuality, the
complex nature of its internal contradictions, its competing inclinations to truth and dissimulation, to faithfulness and betrayal, to form
and to deformation. And it exposes as well what the metaphor has
also traditionally expressed, single-mindedly but insidiously: the fiction that male sexuality is the origin of literary authority, that to write
is to father the book, and to produce a male lineage.

The figure of an authentic and natural literary paternity, of a perfect and coherent filial text, and of the immortality it properly confers
is almost as old as Western literature and philosophy itself.[1] It finds
early, and legitimizing, expression in the *Symposium* where Diotima
teaches the doctrine of Eros to Socrates, explaining that love is the
longing for immortality man seeks to realize through procreation
(207a–209e). Those who generate through the body turn to woman
as the object of their love, she says, and raise a family, but there are
those who conceive in the spirit rather than in the flesh, and they
create children "lovelier and less mortal than human seed." Every
poet, every creative artist, Diotima insists, has the responsibility to

1

beget these spiritual children. "Who would not prefer such father-hood to merely human propagation," she asks rhetorically, "if he stopped to think of Homer, and Hesiod, and all the greatest of our poets? Who would not envy them their immortal progeny, their claim upon the admiration of posterity?" Think of Lycurgus, she says, and the offspring he left behind in his laws; think of Solon, the father of Athenian law; and, finally, think of all those remembered for their noble deeds and for the diverse virtues they fathered. "Tell me if you can of anyone whose mortal children have brought him so much fame."

Although freed from its philosophical moorings by Montaigne's time, the trope returns to his text in its traditional form as the noble, faithful, perfect child of the mind. There it assumes its place as the privileged sibling among the essayist's many children, the child de-sired and blessed by the father, given fullest expression in order to stifle its motley rivals. This reassuring figure of writing, this child alone, is explicitly centered in the *Essais*, and it is doted upon in "De l'affection des peres aux enfans" (II,8,399–402).[2] Like Diotima, Mon-taigne distinguishes in this essay between the generation of physical children and those begotten by the more noble spirit, those especially prized offspring, he adds, that most faithfully represent their author and immortalize him. Rather than focusing on the Platonic love for a beautiful person that produces the spiritual child, the essayist ex-presses the intense feeling these highborn offspring inspire in their authors and the willingness of these fathers to sacrifice all for them, including life itself. There was the bishop Heliodorus who preferred to lose the benefits of his office rather than see his child—the romance *Theagenes and Chariclea*—burned by synodal decree. There were La-bienus and Greuntius Cordus who killed themselves when their tex-tual children were condemned and destroyed. Montaigne multiplies his examples of paternal affection, cites Aristotle to claim that of all artists the poets are most in love with their own work, and concludes with a reference to the "vicious and inflamed" passion of Pygmalion for his beautiful, lifelike statue—as if this case confirmed once and for all the validity of the analogy between natural and spiritual progeny. "And I do not know," the essayist asks, and not entirely rhetorically, "whether I would not like much better to have produced one per-fectly formed child by intercourse with the muses [*de l'acointance des muses*] than by intercourse with my wife" (II,8,401).

Montaigne thus reworks and elaborates the Platonic undertext and its conventional topos, lending to spiritual paternity an intensity and passion that confirms that writing is indeed the highest form of conception. He represents a text that, as writer, he has generated as his child, both the expression of his paternal affection and its object, and he portrays the child returning that love by carrying the father's name into the world and ensuring his fame. Everything in this confident presentation, especially in its hyperbolic expression, appears to affirm the integrity of artistic ambition, the promise of literary conception, the reality of paternal expectation and of filial responsiveness. Even when he evokes (and condemns) Pygmalion's excessive, incestuous love, the essayist does not make anything of its troubling implications, nor does he allow it to disturb his lavish praise of paternal affection. To conclude his discussion he quotes Ovid's description of the statue softening under the caress of its passionate creator and coming to life, as if to imply that, for him, as apparently for the gods who assured Pygmalion's immortality, what matters is only the perfection of the sculptor's art and the intensity of his love for Galatea. And even when Montaigne suggests that textual progeny can be misread and mistreated, as were those of Heliodorus and Labienus, he indicates that the writer and his text can be redeemed by posterity and their fame ultimately ensured. From the desire for immortality to its attainment, from the love of beauty to its embrace, the line apparently passes directly and unambiguously through the generation of the children of the mind. There appears to be no question of paternal insecurity or of filial perfidy, no question of misrepresentation by the child or ultimately of its being misunderstood in the world, no question of unrealized aspirations. And no questioning of the concept of paternal conception. In this traditional family portrait, the artist, the writer, is always and unproblematically a father, the mother is excluded, and the only child is always, or preferably, a son.

But this traditional father, and his faithful son, cannot obscure the faces of the more problematical siblings who vie for attention throughout Montaigne's text. In the essay on the education of children (I,26), an essay motivated by the impending birth of the child of Diane de Foix, Montaigne seeks to mold a thoughtful child that is also his text. But, alongside the child who learns to be virtuous and to speak meaningfully, there emerge other children who elude paternal authority and appear ignorant and empty. Montaigne's essay on the resemblance of children to their fathers (II,37), in which he marvels at the power of the seed to imprint the image of the father on the child, also generates images of children marked by difference, children who misrepresent and by misrepresenting betray the father. In a world where paternity can be assured only by resemblance between father and child, the "different" child always bears the stigma of illegitimacy and of monstrousness.

There are other, and stranger, faces of textual children that must be brought to light. When Montaigne tries out the subject of the monstrous child to situate it within the natural order of things (II,30), the lexical and semantic network that exists in the *Essais* forcefully indicates that he is speaking implicitly of his own text as a deformed child, natural perhaps, but imperfect, excessive, disturbing. And when he writes of literary creation and of the creation of his essays in "Of Idleness" (I,8), he also admits to the generation of monsters and chimeras as the children of his mind. In this essay about the engendering mind, conception is figured not as male but as female, as nature and as earth, as if to imply that Montaigne's own literary "paternity" must be bracketed, that it can never be other than a form of maternal reproduction, displaced, repressed. Montaigne has perhaps been a literary mother all along.

The force of this challenge to the patriarchal model of generation is heightened by the appearance of daughters as artistic and textual progeny and as rightful heirs, daughters who contest the exclusivity of the filial text. Heliodorus's text was a daughter, Montaigne says in "De l'affection des peres aux enfans," Epaminondas's victories were daughters, and daughters, as the story of Pygmalion and Galatea reveals, demand at the very least that the traditional relation between parent and offspring be reconsidered. Marie Germain is another of Montaigne's children, a girl child of the essayist's writing (about imagination) who represents a link between textuality and sexuality and upsets all notions of gender determination by turning into a boy. And, most prominent, Marie de Gournay, the essayist's "fille d'alliance," is generated as a child of Montaigne's writing in "De la praesumption" (II,17), the daughter whom he loves "plus que paternellement" and who will be called upon to fulfill the representative role traditionally played by the textual son.[3]

Since my purpose in this book is to analyze the topos of textual progeny in Montaigne's *Essais* to disclose how it bears on our understanding of writing, textuality, and reading, I will contend with a hybrid corpus of siblings with multiple faces and competing voices. The *Essais* offer particularly fertile ground for study, not only because of the seminal place the metaphor occupies in this lexical, semantic, rhetorical, and structural complex, but precisely because of the diversity and complexity of forms in which it appears. Significant aspects of Montaigne's writing compellingly invite the reader to question the traditional and reassuring metaphor of paternal conception and spiritual offspring and to challenge its assumptions and implications. The essayist himself at times encourages readers to read against the grain by his restless questioning of his own writing and his interrogation of the nature and status of his book, but the reader must also take into account what the text expresses obliquely and what it often discloses in spite of itself, paying particular attention to its unexamined and unspoken assumptions and implications. At the intersection of Montaigne's self-reflexive commentary and what I will call the reader's necessarily obtrusive reading, the *Essais* express and enact scenes of writing, of textual and sexual generation and filiation, and of reading marked by paternal anxiety, monstrous birth, betrayal, and misreading and misrepresentation. And, most dramatic of all, the text performs scenes of literary conception that disrupt the "logic" and status of male generation and of the filial text.

·   ·   ·   ·   ·   ·   ·

In the *Phaedrus*, where Socrates presents his account of the invention of writing (274b–279c), we encounter another genealogical tale of literary conception and of textual progeny, but this one is fraught with the conflicting desires and competing aspirations that characterize the most engaging family dramas. Here again we have a traditional patriarchal narrative of fathers and sons whose limitations must be addressed, but it can serve nonetheless to gloss what I read as powerful and opposing inclinations of the *Essais*. Reading the *Phaedrus*, we can see that to speak of discursive and textual progeny is to speak of rivalry, unruliness, and the complex relations between the generations; it is to speak of legitimate and illegitimate birth, of affection and abandonment, of faithfulness and betrayal, and of death.[4]

Socrates develops his tale as the story of two brothers. The myth and the king himself speak exclusively of Theuth's only son, writing, but the philosopher explicitly introduces a second son, speech, who had, of course, been there all along. The two siblings, who resemble each other as what we might call the twin forms of the logos, are in fact rivals, and their rivalry demands that a choice be made between them in which Truth itself is at stake. Socrates discloses that the spoken son is the chosen one, chosen for the purity of his origin in the soul, for the truth and faithfulness of his discourse, the knowledge he embodies, and the lively, active way in which he defends himself and chooses to whom he should speak. This is the loyal son who always accompanies the father, who is heard only in his presence, the true and legitimate son who properly speaks for the father. The written son turns out to be the bastard brother, just as Thamus had intimated, the illegitimate son who speaks only in the absence of the father and who conveys only the semblance of truth. This disloyal son betrays the father, fails to defend him, falls into the hands of readers who misread and mistreat him, and in his inability to respond actively and intelligently always needs his parent to come to his rescue and speak for him.

What Socrates takes for the differences between speech and writing in the representation of the logos I will recast within textuality itself as its opposing tendencies and as the dynamic tension that defines it. The absolute hierarchy of values that privileges speech over writing in the *Phaedrus* becomes a more complex and conflicted relation within writing itself, for it is not always easy to tell whether authorial authority is the guarantor of truth or merely its figuration, whether the errant text is the obstacle to meaning or the means of its production, whether the reader is the faithful friend of writing or its adversary. Can the writer master writing so that it represents him and speaks truthfully in his stead, or must it always evade his grasp like an errant child? Does the text remain silent in the face of questioning or foolishly repeat the same thing, as Socrates indicated, or can it react like the spoken word, responding either in its author's name or for itself? Can the reader master the text, or is misreading always in some sense the condition of reading itself? I use a reductive either / or formulation in these questions to foreground the opposing tendencies of textuality, but the effort to engage these issues will demonstrate that they are inextricably linked and interdependent. The desire for mastery and totalization—of being, of truth, of language itself—is what motivates the conception of writing and the generation of reading. But there is always another side to the story of writing, textuality, and reading that must accompany and affect it—what I have called the family drama of conflict, anxiety, and subversion—that is played out in the figures of the diverse textual siblings.

I locate Montaigne's *Essais* in the interstices between these conflicting tendencies of writing, textuality, and reading, between the essayist's aspiration to being, truth, and presence and his encounter with absence, appearance, and art, between his longing for the fullness of language and the experience of its emptiness, between his desire as an author to impose his portrait unequivocally as his "self" and the inevitable misreadings of that portrait. And because I see Montaigne's text, and ultimately all writing, as both performing and concealing what conflicts with and subverts its program, I emphasize the side of unresolvable tensions, of anxiety and deception, of unfulfilled desires, of texts and readers that both fall short and go too far. Neither side tells the whole story, and neither side can be told alone. The essayist might not achieve stasis of Being but he does define being in time, a coherent though fragmented self. He might not embody himself fully in his language, but he does not fully lose himself there either. What I have called the aspiration of writing—Truth, Being, the immortality represented by Socrates's "legitimate" son and by Diotima's immortal son—is present at the beginning of writing as its impetus, and it is also there at the end, but in a different form, one conditioned by the presence and influence of other siblings, the "illegitimate" and errant children who populate what we can call the realization of writing and reading.

Textuality, then, appears to be diverse and different from itself, yet its sides are bound to each other, bear upon each other, like the Siamese twins Montaigne presents in "D'un enfant monstrueux" (II,30), the perfect and imperfect bodies joined together to form the monstrous child that can serve as an emblem of the deformed and divided body of the writing. Montaigne readily, even eagerly, accepts the mixed, the conflictual, the hybrid, in a word, the monstrous, as his own personal mark and as the form of his writing, as if to signal his singularity and originality. But the *Essais* reveal that he is not alone, that the monstrous is in fact a constituent of the human itself, that it lies not outside but within nature and man. And the writing also reveals that the monstrous is not only an anthropological and a moral category but an aesthetic category as well and that the categories are inseparably linked. Thus, Montaigne's text also discloses that the monstrous is a constituent of writing, that it lies within writing as the product of its necessary ambiguities and complexities, its inevitable tensions and contradictions, its unavoidable and conflicting inclinations toward truth and dissimulation, toward order and formlessness, toward clarity of meaning and its opacity.

Where Western art has traditionally constituted itself by concealing, ignoring, and repressing the monstrous and its own monstrous nature, Montaigne professes it and makes it the ground for his writing. But this admission of diversity and of difference does not admit all. Nor can it. This explains why I said earlier that I seek to articulate that which in writing is unspoken, unavowed, muffled, or marginalized, why I foreground the disparate and the disruptive as well as the consistent and the unified, why I seek coherence and also bring out that which is indeterminate, that which eludes inclusion and mastery. Art lives, one critic has said, by resisting interpretation as well as by inviting it, and it is this double movement, he adds, that is figured in the grotesque, or what I am calling the monstrous.[5] It is this double movement that is *in* art as its monstrous other that I read in this book.

One diverse and potentially disruptive element that the *Essais* cannot fully admit nor fully master, that it both muffles and articulates, denies and reveals, is the presence and integrity of the feminine.[6] In large measure Montaigne perpetuates misogynist attitudes and marginalizes women and the feminine. As an authorial father giving birth to a textual son, he too appropriates conception, displaces the female body, and marginalizes feminine discourse. Yet, as I suggested, the essayist also makes occasional but significant countermoves that can be read against literary paternity and its imposition of conventionally gendered roles.

My reading of the *Essais* consists of further countermoves to extend and develop that interrogation and that challenge. At specific moments when Montaigne treats the composition of his text, he addresses women readers as if to implicate the female in its conception. In a richly suggestive formulation that contains conflicting figurative implications, he says that we are both father and mother in the generation of the child of the mind. When he establishes Marie de Gournay as his adoptive daughter, he positions her to become the guardian of his writing, as if the daughter could (or must) supplement the son and even supplant him. When the essayist suggests that his language and writing contain qualities traditionally ascribed to women, he undermines accepted notions of literary paternity and of the text as son. I move between analyses of textual and sexual production and progeny in order to bring to light the important implications of gender for our understanding of writing and reading.

·   ·   ·   ·   ·   ·   ·

In studies that seek to combine broad and pervasive theoretical questions that preoccupy modern readers with their grounding in a single text from the past, it is not always easy to avoid anachronistic or ahistorical generalizations about writing and reading. There is an undeniable attraction to interpreting "back" to Montaigne from contemporary theory and its concerns, just as there is an almost irresistible lure to reading "out" from the *Essais* to questions of writing and reading "in general." The critic can and should attempt to be faithful to the intellectual, cultural, and literary context within which Montaigne wrote, to the ideas that shaped his attitudes toward writing, to his own readings, and to the contemporary meanings of words and concepts. Yet there are no means for recuperating the past in any absolute sense, no means for engaging it that are not themselves readings and interpretations incapable of fully overcoming the gap of historical difference. One important reason for taking Montaigne seriously today is the striking way in which his conception of problems of reading and writing, and those of his contemporaries, converge with the formulations of modern theorists and literary critics. Then as now there were disputes about the nature of language, the relation of words to things, the status of representation and of imitation, the place of tradition, the function of rhetoric, the capacity of the written work to embody truth, being, plenitude, and presence. In Montaigne's self-reflexive and encyclopedic text we find ourselves before a distant yet pertinent textual expression that allows us as modern readers to gain understanding of our own critical activity and to situate ourselves theoretically.

Inevitably "misreading" Montaigne, I will seek to give him his due while responding to our own interests as twentieth-century readers. It cannot be otherwise. The fortuitous similarities that might link past and present (or that we ourselves "read into" the past and present), the unbridgeable differences that separate them—these are the very conditions of reading, what allow us to hazard interpretation and generalization, however tentative they must remain. Montaigne sensed this; he understood that similarity and difference were relational rather than absolute terms, that one could not be conceived without the other, or outside it, and that this complex and conflicted relation was the opening to vigorous and persistent essaying, testing, trying out, weighing, rather than their closing off. To say that interpretation or generalization is tentative is to say that it is also an experiment, an essay, a form of active, even at times obtrusive, reading and writing that, like a face (as Montaigne says with characteristic irony), is no guarantee of the truth of what it signifies but deserves some consideration.

Each of the chapters of this book uses the metaphor of textual progeny as it occurs in Montaigne's *Essais* to provide a perspective on problems of writing, textuality, and reading. Beginning with the essayist's concern with education as the acquisition of language for both child and text, chapter 1 addresses the authorial desire that the textual progeny faithfully represent him and contain his truth, that it embody his image and convey his meaning. The analysis delineates how the problematic figure of the father-author shapes our understanding of authority and intent and how that of the child both opens and limits the possibilities of representation and communication, how textual progeny is at once responsive and errant. Chapter 2 explores the implications of textual errancy for both author and reader and analyzes Montaigne's own response to the dangers of being misread and misrepresented. The pages of his essay "De la praesumption" (II,17) beget a textual child who will speak for the father and be the guarantor of his writing and his meaning, a dutiful daughter who will lovingly represent him and seek to assure his truth. But my reading of the historical and the textual figures of Montaigne's "fille d'alliance," Marie de Gournay, reveals the problematic position of the daughter who cannot speak for the father without also speaking for herself, who threatens in her faithfulness to displace and to betray him. As an author writing in her own name, as a woman speaking out specifically, and self-consciously, in the name of woman, Marie de Gournay challenges the model of literary paternity. Her voice reminds us that all considerations of authorial intent and its legacy, of meaning and its integrity, and of reading and misreading are also subject to the irrepressible presence of the feminine.

Implicit in both the performance of the errant text and in the dutiful daughter's inability to guarantee textual integrity is the figure of an active, even obtrusive, reader who reads against authorial intention or in spite of it, against the grain of pervasive textual norms and values that the author or the daughter (or the critic as guarantor) designates as textual intention. The metaphor of the book as child suggests that the writer seeks to dominate and to persuade the reader and to impose meaning, but readers do not necessarily submit —nor should they. As its title suggests ("The Imposing Text and the Obtrusive Reader"), chapter 3 argues that reading represents an agonistic relation between author and reader for "control" of the text and of its "meaning," a relation that divides the loyalty of the textual progeny, both faithful to the author and complicitous with the reader. The discussion of how reading takes place, or might take place, involves my own obtrusive reading of several recent theorists on the subject and indicates how literature can inform theory and be its corrective as well as its illustration.

Chapter 4 returns to the subject of authorship, to the relation between author and textual progeny, and specifically to Montaigne's concern that by writing about himself, by projecting his child as his self-image, he be thought presumptuous, guilty of *philautia,* vain self-love. Montaigne presents himself, and desires that his readers see him, as modest and humble; he professes his ignorance and his vanity as moral, epistemological, and aesthetic imperatives so that, like Socrates, he and his textual progeny will be (thought) both virtuous and wise. But a reading of the essayist's revered Ovid, and the two seminal stories concerned with images and self-images, Narcissus and Pygmalion, discloses that excessive self-love and erotic, even incestuous infatuation lie at the heart of literary conception and are the very conditions of Montaigne's own writing project.

The discussion of a textual child that is both presumptuous and self-denying, that is thus divided and discordant, raises in chapter 5 the question of literary conception and the birth of the monstrous text to which I referred earlier. Pursuing the lexical and semantic implications of Montaigne's essays on the monstrous child and on deformity, the discussion situates difference within textuality and discloses the decentered and deformed nature of writing and its implications for reading. Finally, in chapter 6, I draw together the various threads concerning gender and sexuality that have emerged through the book and engage them extensively as they pertain to the writing subject and its progeny. A reading of Montaigne enlightened by recent feminist criticism reveals a richer and more conflicted sexual and textual complex at work in his writing—and, by extension, in writing in general—than the overdetermined metaphor of literary paternity and the filial text allows.

Thus, Montaigne's unruly brood: the unanticipated emblem of a multiform textuality marked by competing inclinations, conflicting desires, and incongruous interests and figured by the diverse faces of progeny who both represent and mislead; a brood of dutiful sons and daughters, errant and rebellious siblings, offspring well-formed and monstrous. The task of the reader will be to engage the complex drama played out in this dynamic family, what we can call the family drama of authorship and of textuality, which is also the drama of reading itself.

1

Textual Progeny

*Car ce que nous engendrons par l'ame, les enfantemens de
notre esprit, de nostre courage et suffisance, sont produicts
par une plus noble partie que la corporelle, et sont plus
nostres.* (II, 8, 400)

For what we engender by the soul, the children of our mind,
of our heart and our ability, are produced by a nobler part
than the body and are more our own.

translated by Donald Frame

One of the thorniest interpretive problems posed for modern readers
of Montaigne's *Essais* is to determine the value of its discursive content. This was not always the case because historically the content
has been accepted at face value, the essayist's words taken literally to
mean what they say. Although apparently not always appropriately
titled, most often digressive and aleatory in form, each of the essays
seemed to contain two parallel strands meant to be read in conjunction and always literally, with a modest allowance made for the essayist's gentle irony: a discourse on a given topic of philosophical,
historical, political, or social interest and a series of intercalated personal reflections about the essayist himself, his attitudes, character,
and writing. The self-portrait or presentation of the writer—which
Montaigne claimed in his prefatory "Au lecteur" as his goal—
emerged from each of the strands: from the topical discourse as the
"trial" of the writer's judgment, from the reflexive commentary that
was both "trial" and explicit self-revelation, and from the twining of
the strands. The essayist's comments on his subject matter and his
efforts to elucidate his meaning and intention served as a privileged
metatext, the text of insight in which Montaigne came to know himself and the reader to know Montaigne. And on those occasions
when this literal reading of Montaigne's ideas and of the idea of a
literal Montaigne encountered specific rhetorical figures or flour-
ishes, it tended either to ignore them or to ascribe to them a literal

function. Montaigne writes as he thinks, we were told; rather than elements operating within a rhetorical or literary construct, figures are the literal and concrete manifestation of the essayist's mental processes, the unmediated expression of the mind's own discourse. The essayist's outspoken preference for a plain, direct, and unadorned style, and his explicit antirhetorical stance, lent confidence to such a reading, in spite of, or because of, the evidence of Montaigne's own practice.[1]

What has provoked the interpretive issue I raise has been a challenge to explicitness that has motivated a host of contemporary readings of the *Essais*.[2] The apparently straightforward elements of the content—the subject matters of the essays, the writer's commentary on himself and his writing—and the supposedly transparent elements of form have been given significance as components of a vast and complex textual system. The *Essais*—as the direct representation of the attitudes and characteristics of an individual subject prior to and outside of the writing—have been textualized, that is, opened to the invitation that aspects of content, and most centrally the writing subject himself, be interpreted as figurative elements *in* the writing and often, most strikingly, as figures *of* the writing. Thus, for example, the literal terms of Montaigne's friendship with La Boétie and the death of the friend presented in "De l'amitié" are read metaphorically as the loss of the sense of a self possessed and used to explain what occasions the writing and how it attempts to recuperate that self and to make it known.

This emphasis on the rhetorical, or figurative, however, has its own pitfalls. The *Essais* can become something resembling a self-enclosed play of figures if form is dogmatically or exclusively given priority. Or they can be reduced to a vast allegory (of writing, for example) if the letter is effaced and subjects such as friendship, or education, or vanity, or sincerity relinquish their experiential significance. In both cases Montaigne's text suffers a weakening of its links to that existential life that appears so forcefully and centrally to generate the writing and to be its ultimate creation as well. But while the risk of overemphasizing the figurative is real, we have gained from this perspective a stronger sense of the presence and operation of rhetorical elements within a discourse that has traditionally been treated as primarily, and even exclusively, philosophical and autobiographical; and we have gained a better understanding of how writing can be said to mirror its own functioning.

The story of our understanding of the *Essais* seems to be traced by this opposition of the literal and the figurative and by the tendency of each to eliminate, reduce, or ignore the other. The task before us is to attempt to overcome the choices imposed by the competing polarities and their corresponding values. One of the important contributions of contemporary critical theory has been the challenge to traditional binary oppositions and the suggestion that they be seen as fluid, unstable, dynamic, and interactive rather than as separate and exclusive. Here the *Essais* themselves can provide an important perspective. Although Montaigne explicitly affirms the literal emphasis and disdains what he considers the figurative excess of rhetoric, he also discloses how language, its forms, and its figures allow the reader to produce meaning. The essays draw our attention to the way essential literal elements of its discourse—the voyage, for example, or the child—are meant at the same time to function figuratively. Both levels or meanings maintain their integrity, so that the literal retains its proper experiential value and also acquires value as a trope.

In order for the *Essais* to function simultaneously as self-portrait and the means to self-knowledge, as memory and as essays of judgment, as personal commentary and as the effort to construct a self, both the literal and the figurative—or what might be transposed as the historical and the literary, or the existential and the rhetorical— must interact and overlap. For example, Montaigne's "voyage" is literally his trip to Italy and other travels, all of which provide the basis for essaying judgment through reflections that are cultural, moral, social, and political. But it is also the passage through time that is the life lived, in the world and in the book, as it moves toward death. And in that self-reflexivity that makes Montaigne's writing its own subject, the voyage is also that movement of or through the writing that is his essays, the writing and rewriting of the evolving and elusive self that is the unfolding of his text. All of these meanings exist at once, so that when one reads "voyage" the meanings slide into each other, are simultaneous, mutually intrusive, and never without some tension among them. It is only in this overlapping of terms, without privilege and without priority, that we can appreciate the complexity of Montaigne's project and understand his claim that he and his book are one, that things and words, life and text, coincide. We might want to recall here that traditional biblical exegesis aimed to preserve the literality of the letter and at the same time sought to coax forth truths that were also, and simultaneously, allegorical, tropological, and anagogical. While Montaigne's *Essais* obviously cannot share the metaphysical status of scripture or yield its truths (nor do they seek to), they aspire on their own secular terms to knowledge, truth, presence, and being. In a way that could be said to depend on the interrelationship of history and writing, the letter and the figure.

·   ·   ·   ·   ·   ·   ·

In the closing pages of "De l'affection des peres aux enfans" (II, 8) Montaigne turns from the affection of fathers for their literal, physical offspring to the love of authors for their writing and to his own feelings for his *Essais*. Writings are like children, he says as he works the traditional trope, productions of the mind more worthy than those of the flesh, and more the effect of their progenitor: "Ce que nous engendrons par l'ame, les enfantemens de notre esprit, de nostre courage et suffisance, sont produicts par une plus noble partie que la corporelle, et sont plus nostres; nous sommes pere et mere ensemble en cette generation" (400a) ("For what we engender by the soul, the children of our mind, of our heart and our ability, are produced by a nobler part than the body and are more our own. We are father and mother both in this generation" [291]). To their authors, whom they more vividly represent than progeny of flesh and blood, these children of the mind bring honor, Montaigne claims, if they are well formed, and immortality.

We thus encounter in the child a textual subject that Montaigne himself treats both as letter and figure and that has been ignored by most readers of the *Essais*.[3] And this is so in spite of the facts that the literal child is pervasive in Montaigne's text and that the figurative child of the mind is a powerful emblem of his own writing. Perhaps we have overlooked the literal because Montaigne's own child is conspicuously absent from the *Essais*. I sense that we have undervalued the force of the figure because it is, and was, a literary commonplace, less original and therefore, perhaps, less revealing or representative than other images of Montaigne's thought. Yet both the letter and the figure, and their relationship, compellingly invite interpretation because their complex status allows us to raise concerns central to our understanding of authorship, textuality, and writing and in the process to shed light on the *Essais* themselves.

Let us begin to restore the child, both literal and figurative, to its rightful place by remarking that the absence of Montaigne's own children from the *Essais* seems to create a space in which textual children proliferate. With the exception of one surviving daughter, they were also absent from his life: "[b] ils meurent tous en nourrisse; mais [c] Leonor, [b] une seule fille . . . est eschappée à cette infortune" (II, 8, 389) ("They all die on me at nurse; . . . Leonor, one single daughter . . . escaped that misfortune" [281]). But children are everywhere in the *Essais:* "enfants" is the eighteenth most frequently used noun in the work, appearing 237 times in 56 of the 107 essays; other forms such as "enfance," "enfant," "enfanter," "enfantement," and so on appear another 147 times.[4] Four essays contain the word "enfant" in one of its forms and directly address issues in which children are central: "De l'institution des enfans" (I, 26), "De l'affection des peres aux enfans" (II, 8), "D'un enfant monstrueux" (II, 30), and "De la ressemblance des enfans aux peres" (II, 37). Montaigne's children are both classical and modern, they appear in essays treating subjects as diverse as affections (I, 3), custom (I, 23), solitude (I, 39), drunkenness (II, 2), cowardice (II, 27), and vanity (III, 9) and are evoked 18 times in the "Apologie de Raimond Sebond" (II, 12) alone. They are successively heroes, victims, or fools, either models of a natural wisdom or examples of a stupid simplicity. At times children represent continuity with the past and at other times they allow the essayist to speak about the future. And, most striking, they are both literal, physical children and figurative children of the mind as well. Leonor is Montaigne's only surviving child, but the *Essais* is also his child; the essayist identifies his two children in "De l'affection des peres aux enfans" (II, 8).

In this abundant talk of offspring—historical and fictional, real and metaphorical—the central irony is that of talk itself. The essayist who could not (or would not) keep his text from spilling over between the lines and into the margins, and onto additional slips of paper, who after the publication of the *Essais* in 1580 and 1588 went back to his writing to amend, to revise, to make additions, this verbose writer speaks repeatedly of the enfant, that which by its etymological nature is unable to speak (*in* + *fans*, present participle of *fari*, to speak). Montaigne himself is above all he who speaks, who speaks in order to speak exclusively of himself ("parler seulement de moy" [II, 8, 942]), and who seeks to write as he speaks ("je parle au papier comme je parle au premier que je rencontre" [III, 1, 790]). The *Essais* are the "confession" of his ignorance and his vanity, he claims —that is, a form of speaking that is thought to derive from the same root as *fari*. But what does it mean to speak in the *Essais?* What is the significance of these children, literal or figurative, who by their very nature cannot yet speak? What does it mean to say that the *Essais* are Montaigne's child, a child who does indeed speak, and who speaks so copiously? In whose voice and for whom does it speak? And to whom? In addressing these questions let us keep in mind that, because Montaigne intends that his writing be taken for speech, he treats the one as if it were the other and necessarily blurs differences between them. The lessons for proper speaking in "De l'institution des enfans," for example, are most profoundly those for the proper writing of essays; the student of that essay is above all the essayist himself. Later in this chapter I will come back to examine the implications of Montaigne's conversational style.

These questions might once have seemed inappropriate because they appear to obscure the distinction between what is to be taken literally and what figuratively. The recourse to the etymology of "enfant," for example, resurrects a long-forgotten, perhaps even dead, meaning whose own status is not entirely clear (was it to be taken literally that children did not speak or was this a figure for an early stage of physical, moral, or linguistic development?) in order to apply it with apparent recklessness both to "real" children and to tropes. But isn't that precisely the point? We should seek to upset comfortable distinctions, to open up the literal to its figurative possibilities and the figurative to its literal potential. Under this kind of pressure, and in the dynamic interplay it generates, the letter and the figure (of the child) both produce and reflect the image of writing itself, its construction and its operations, its aspiration to be more than it is (like life, for example), and the limitations that make it less. Within and between Montaigne's narratives and examples of literal children and the functioning of the traditional trope of the child of the mind lie central issues of the use of language, authorship and origin, textuality and representation, and reading and interpretation.

·   ·   ·   ·   ·   ·   ·

Referring to his own childhood experience in "De l'institution des enfans" (I, 26), Montaigne implies that the infant is born "tongue-

tied" and that the acquisition of language is the equivalent of loosen-
ing or unknotting the tongue. In order to learn Latin as his mother
tongue, the essayist tells us, he was placed in the care of Latin speak-
ers "avant le premier desnouement de (sa) langue" (173). (Or perhaps it is language that is tied up or bound in the child and subse-
quently unleashed.) Once untied, the tongue (or its language) can
speak wisely or foolishly, depending on how it is educated. There is
language acquisition in the literal, physical sense and, I would suggest, language learning in the figurative or moral sense. In the *Essais*,
until the child learns the second "language" it remains true to its
name, unable to speak. The pedagogical program of the *Essais*—
although there is little that is programmatic about it—consists above
all in giving the child the right language, in teaching him *how* to
speak.

In one of the important paradoxes of the *Essais*, Montaigne represents the uninstructed masses as the model of proper speaking. He
depicts them engaged in discussion that is spontaneous, forceful,
and true to its purpose in "De l'art de conferer" (III, 8). In "De la
phisionomie" (III, 12) they provide Socrates with his own exemplary
speech: "[b] Ainsi dict un paysan, ainsi dict une femme. [c] Il n'a
jamais en la bouche que cochers, menuisiers, savetiers et maçons. [b]
Ce sont inductions et similitudes tirées des plus vulgaires et cog-
neues actions des hommes" (1,037) ("So says a peasant, so says a
woman. His mouth is full of nothing but carters, joiners, cobblers,
and masons. His are inductions and similes drawn from the com-
monest and best-known actions of men" [793]). But untutored
speech in itself cannot directly and immediately serve the child of the
noble Madame Diane de Foix, comtesse de Gurson, to whom "De
l'institution des enfans" is written, just as it could not serve Montaigne himself. Proper language acquisition is a matter of proper
schooling, of tutored speech, which requires that the essayist indeed
set a curriculum in place (a course, a literal and figurative career,
from Latin *currere*, to run) to guarantee that what came "naturally" to
Socrates, or was posited as "natural" for the coachmen and masons,
can indeed be learned. Schooling is necessary, one might say, because
the coachman and the mason who speak this authentic speech are
not historical realities but literary figures who can be found only in
books.

Paradox thus abounds: the uneducated embody the ideal of education, the natural must be mediated and acquired. I thus bracket "natural" speech in the *Essais* as a figure by which Montaigne intends to represent the expression of thought and judgment evidently unmediated by a traditional high culture that distorts and perverts. We might hear in his "natural" language, in its idealized simplicity and spontaneity and thus its truth and authenticity, a distant echo of Plato's characterization in the *Phaedrus* of oral discourse as "living speech," "written in the soul of the learner," the untrammeled expression of interiority. The letter and the figure of "unnatural" language, in Montaigne's terms, is rhetoric, which he treats as a dominant aspect of traditional learning. This tutored speech, with its emphasis on form, participates in the major structuring opposition in the *Essais* that operates between inside and outside, and, like the outside itself as surface or appearance, it becomes the site of untruth and artifice, suspect because of its potential for deception. The goal of Montaigne's pedagogy is to anchor language inside, in mind and judgment, so that words coincide with thought and express the truthfulness and sincerity he pretends they have in their "natural," spoken usage. "Que les mots aillent où va la pensée," he says in "De l'art de conferer" (III, 8, 924b), an essay in which one might see him instructing adults how to speak.

As a figure of the text, "natural" speech participates in a vast fable of nature and the natural that includes not only coachmen and masons, peasants and children, but animals, cannibals, and the whole New World as well. The essayist tropes on the natural in order to argue against all forms of cultural and intellectual artifice, against its hegemonic practices, against all surfaces that might mask and distort, and, in a further paradoxical turn, against rhetoric itself as a most pernicious deception. Rhetoric suffers Montaigne's scathing attack because it shamelessly and effortlessly exploits the "natural" and dangerous disparity between words and things and because, as part of the institutional, curricular program, it corrupts the innate naiveté (and goodness?) of the child learning how to speak. Montaigne's own rhetoric thus serves ironically as a way both of showing up the facticity of culture and all that is artful—including rhetoric itself—and of affirming positive values such as simplicity, spontaneity, and humility.[5]

But this (rhetorical) strategy, which turns rhetoric against itself, is risky business because it cannot clear a space in which the natural exists absolutely as itself; nor can it absolve the writer of complicity. In fact, what rhetoric's "suicidal" gesture announces is precisely the victim's survival and its persistent presence at the very foundations of discourse itself, both oral and written. Perhaps we can see this most clearly if we consider Montaigne's status as essayist. As a writer, the essayist cannot literally "speak," he cannot participate directly in the (alleged) immediacy and authenticity of natural (oral) language, even though he acts as if this possibility were self-evident: "Le parler que j'ayme," he says in "De l'institution des enfans," "c'est un parler simple et naïf, tel sur le papier qu'à la bouche" (I, 26, 171a) ("The speech I love is a simple, natural speech, the same on paper as it is in the mouth" [127]). But the lesson of Montaigne's writing, and the lesson of our reading, is that while he can write *about* a nonrhetorical, "natural," language, he cannot *write* it in any absolute sense. At best, he can only represent spoken language in his essays, he can only imitate it, and to do so he must have recourse to the rich resources of rhetoric, to its forms and figures. And, in the process, he must himself irresistibly perform the disparity that he seeks most ardently to avoid in teaching the child how to speak, the disparity between "authentic" or "natural" judgment and thought and its necessarily mediated expression. Montaigne's *Essais* cast judgment and thought as language, they reveal that judging and thinking *are* language, and, in the unavoidable gap between desire ("le parler que j'ayme") and its fulfillment ("sur le papier"), rhetoric repeatedly shows its telltale and subversive face.

Montaigne's own writing practice thus confirms the need to bracket the "natural" of language, both because the "natural" shows itself up as a trope and the trope discloses that it is "natural" to language. Discourse (even or especially his own) cannot realize itself without enacting the factitious and the artful that it harbors within. When the essayist expresses his desire that "les mots aillent où va la pensée," he reminds his reader that words and thought do not "naturally" coincide and that some effort of will or habit is required, some effect of education.

Ideally, then, Montaigne seeks to teach a "natural" language that would overcome its own "unnatural" failings, a language that expresses correct judgment, corresponds faithfully to thought and is sincere, and at the same time actively shapes and forms that judgment by its practice. And he teaches not only Mme Diane de Foix and the reader but the child and his tutor as well, speaking to the tutor and in his place, to demonstrate that proper teaching is most centrally a question of proper speaking. It is a question of speaking and allowing the student to speak, as Socrates did (I, 26, 150); of asking for the recitation of what has been learned rather than memorized (151); of wisely warning (*advertir*, 155), conversing (*entretenir*, 155), saying (*dire*, 160, 161), communicating (163). The essayist as master tutor indicates how the child is to speak the words of others in quotation and paraphrase, citing his own work as example: "Je ne dis les autres, sinon pour d'autant plus me dire" (148c) ("I do not speak the minds of others except to speak my own mind better" [108]). He teaches how it is to speak the language of self-correction and confession (154–55), how to learn the language that is written in the book of the world (158), and that of philosophy as well (160–61).

.   .   .   .

In all of this talk about language, in the copious articulation of this essay in which the essayist, the tutor, and the child all speak, a striking irony of what I am calling "proper language" (which is always synonymous with "proper judgment") is that it is as much a question of not speaking as of speaking itself. There is always the danger of saying too much, even when one has something worthwhile to say, as Plutarch knew: "Il sçavoit qu'és choses bonnes mesmes on peut trop dire" (157a) ("He knew that even of good things one may say too much" [115]). There is also the danger of speaking to the wrong people: "On luy apprendra de n'entrer en discours ou contestation que où il verra un champion digne de sa luite" (154a) ("He will be taught not to enter in discussion or argument except when he sees a champion worth wrestling with" [114]). In the school that Montaigne calls "cette eschole du commerce des hommes," children should be learning to listen to others: "Le silence et la modestie sont qualitez tres-commodes à la conversation" (154a) ("Silence and modesty are very good qualities for social intercourse" [113]), that is, in both social relationships and in speech. Watching and listening silently, being what the essayist calls a "spectateur(s) de la vie des autres hommes" (158c), ideally allows one to judge the life observed and order one's own. The world, figured in the essay as a mirror, requires (in)sight rather than speech; and the image of the world as book requires reading that by Montaigne's time has become predominantly silent.

Language, then, cannot be expressed in an unbridled, unlimited manner but must be withheld, denied, and negated if it is to function meaningfully, that is, truthfully represent proper judgment and shape judgment to make it proper. Silence thus functions as a language just as language itself could be said to realize its true "nature" when it functions as silence. And what should be said of that language that *is* expressed? In order that it function properly, language must be transparent, a window to be seen through or a mirror (as one appears to look *through* the mirror at what it reflects). Speaking of the best poetry in "Sur des vers de Virgile," Montaigne characterizes aesthetic expression in a way that makes form a vehicle for content: "Quand je voy ces braves formes de s'expliquer, si vifves, si profondes, je ne dicts pas que c'est bien dire, je dicts que c'est bien penser. . . . Nos gens appellent jugement, langage; et beaux mots, les plaines conceptions" (III, 5, 873b) ("When I see these brave forms of expression, so alive, so profound, I do not say 'This is well said,' I say, 'This is well thought.' . . . Our people call judgment language and fine words full conceptions" [665b]). If the language draws attention to its own operation, it gets in the way of its purely expressive or communicative function and inhibits the powerful effect of its content. Montaigne's references to "penser" and "jugement" suggest that what I might call "moral" expression functions in the same way. This echoes what is frequently in the *Essais* a fundamental critique of rhetoric: in its loud and ostentatious trumpeting of form, it perversely betrays language's proper role as the "soft-spoken" medium of judgment's noble aspiration to virtue.

The ideal language then would show nothing of itself, or, put another way, would be nothing in itself. The nothingness of language of course has nothing to do with the vacuousness of vain speech. It is rather the self-effacing quality of a paradoxically substantial language that reveals judgment without revealing itself, that expresses thought without itself being expressed. In his desire for pure signifieds, Montaigne demonstrates his distrust of the signifier that must inevitably contaminate truth by its own presence. My own analytical (rhetorical) strategy has sought to represent this ideal language through a vocabulary drawn from the visual, referring to invisibility, transparency, showing, revealing, and effacing in order to emphasize both this language's paradoxical silence and the way it is both present and absent. Here I would harken back to Ramus, whose misgivings about rhetoric and voice led to the recommendation of a plain, unadorned style whose "perspecuity" or translucency derives from the analogy with visual apprehension. Montaigne too, I would say, longs for discourse—both oral and written—that would function like the invisible, and silent, medium that transmits light.[6]

One of the most striking examples of Montaigne's efforts to make voice and speech function as if they were not there, or not themselves, is his insistence that *dire* become *faire*. In "Du pedantisme" he compares the educational programs of Athens and Lacedaemon with a paradoxically rhetorical flourish that aims at the elimination of rhetoric and of language itself:

> A Athenes on aprenoit à bien dire, et icy, à bien faire; là, à se desmeler d'un argument sophistiqüe, et à rabattre l'imposture des mots captieusement entrelassez; icy, à se desmeler des appats de la volupté, et à rabatre d'un grand courage les menasses de la fortune et de la mort; ceux-là s'embesongnoient apres les parolles; ceux-cy apres les choses; là, c'estoit une continuelle exercitation de la langue; icy, une continuelle exercitation de l'ame. (I, 25, 143a)

> At Athens they learned to speak well, here to do well; there to disentangle themselves from a sophistical argument and to overthrow the imposture of words captiously interlaced, here to disentangle themselves from the lures of sensual pleasure, and with great courage to overthrow the threats of fortune and death; those men busied themselves with words, these with things; there it was a continual exercise of the tongue, here a continual exercise of the soul. (105)

The comparison operates a series of displacements by which "dire," "mots," "paroles," and "langue" are purged from education. In the parallel structure of the crafted period Montaigne transmutes verbal action into moral action; the predicates that enclose the student in the vacuousness of language in Athens are transformed by the substantial complements of virtue in Lacedaemon. Language, I would say, paradoxically turns against itself, brings the force of both grammar and rhetoric to silence itself. Education is no longer a question of weaning the child in any simple way from its inability to speak, of untying its tongue and giving it voice. The child does not learn how to speak but how to do. In the binary opposition that structures the comparison, moral action (*faire*) and speaking (*dire*) appear to be mutually exclusive, although I might want to put the issue another way and say that here actions are meant to speak in a figurative sense, and to speak louder than words.[7]

The paradoxical gesture of using the very medium, agent, or faculty one seeks to destroy to destroy itself, of forcing a kind of suicidal self-reflexivity, is a familiar Montaignian move in the *Essais*. Not only does he turn language against language and use rhetoric to undermine rhetoric, he reasons to challenge reason and quotes to criticize what he calls borrowing flowers from others. What are the implications of such a strategy, and what can its effects possibly be? Can it escape its tautological enclosure and achieve its ends? What are the consequences for the one who challenges or attacks from "within," who provokes the suicidal reversal? I will have to return to these questions. For now let us explore some of the ramifications in the *Essais* of this language that apparently seeks to transcend its own limitations, to be other than what it is.

    .   .   .   .

It is a supreme irony of the *Essais* that the imperative of *faire* requires the practice of *dire*, that what the essayist *does* must also be taken literally as "une continuelle exercitation de la langue." He who says in "De la ressemblance des enfans aux peres" that, whatever he is, "je le veux estre ailleurs qu'en papier" (II, 37, 784a) ("I want to be elsewhere than on paper" [596]), must admit as de does in "De la vanité" that he is most prominently on paper: "Qui ne voit que j'ay pris une route par laquelle, sans cesse et sans travail, j'iray autant qu'il y aura d'ancre et de papier au monde?" (III, 9, 945b) ("Who does not see that I have taken a road along which I shall go, without stopping and without effort, as long as there is ink and paper in the world?" [721]). Montaigne himself often claims, as in the closing pages of "De la ressemblance des enfans aux peres" (II, 37), that *his* writing is not just writing but a form of virtuous action, or at least an action that seeks to reflect and shape virtuous judgment. Here he appears to reverse the widely accepted Renaissance practice that applied criteria drawn from rhetorical discourse—gravity, decorum, harmony—to the judgment of moral action so that his writing (and its inevitable and inadmissible rhetoric) can acquire moral substance. In terms that evoke the educational program of "Du pedantisme" and "De l'institution des enfans" he insists that his study ("mes estudes") has been used "à m'apprendre à faire, non pas à escrire. J'ay mis tous mes efforts à former ma vie. Voylà mon mestier et mon ouvrage. Je suis moins faiseur de livres que de nulle autre besoigne" (784a) ("in teaching me to do, not to write. I have put all my efforts into forming my life. That is my trade and my work. I am less a maker of books than of anything else" [596]). But the substitution by which the work of life ("ouvrage," "besoigne")—both the writing and the book—becomes life itself ("ma vie," "mon mestier") reveals itself in the syntax of his discourse as a metonymic structure, a contingent and relational association rather than a necessary identification. And while the rhetorical figure is intended to distinguish Montaigne from those "faiseurs de livres," as he pejoratively calls them, those who write for personal gain, to seek renown or material reward, and who produce *only* a book, it also implicates him in making a book. Literally speaking, and in the presence of the powerful metonymy, we are reminded that the literal cannot simply be dispensed with or ignored, that no writing is possible without *dire* and *escrire*. All writers are contaminated by this literal truth, all writers are always and in some sense also faiseurs de livres.

Because on the face of things Montaigne cannot simply make his language be his thought or his life, because he is drawn in spite of himself into the potentially vacuous realm of *langue, mots,* and *parolles*, he insists that speaking/writing be transformed into what it is not, into something else, into doing, making. Repeatedly the essayist attempts to differentiate his book from all others, stressing its originality ("C'est [c] le seul livre au monde de son espece" [II, 8, 385]) primarily in terms of the novelty, or the stupidity ("cette sotte entreprise," "un dessein farouche et extravagant" [385a]), of the project of making himself the primary matter of his book and also, perhaps, in terms of its nontraditional, apparently unfinished form as "essays." But Montaigne's writing is perhaps most wild and extravagant in its effort to make *dire* into *faire* and to make *langue, mots,* and *parolles* be what they are not. Words, he implies again and again, must become things (*choses*), they must be transformed from the inherently airy medium that he evokes in "De l'exercitation" (II, 6, 379) and made substantial. The ephemeral word, projected as it were into the air to fly off in the very instance it is articulated (*verba volant*), the vain word, semantically as empty as wind (*flatus*), this common, pervasive language must acquire the materiality of things. But what does Montaigne mean by "things"?

The primary "things" for Montaigne are ideas, concepts in the mind; these are always referred to as "choses" in his text, as "res" in the Latin he quotes. Words, he insists, can become secondary "things," they can follow and can gain substance as they express substantial matter of the mind. This appears to run counter to what I posited earlier as the transparency of "proper" language, the self-effacing quality of a language that was most natural when it was nothing in itself, when it let the light shine through. Here language must be capable of literally embodying thought. Speaking of the best poets in "Sur des vers de Virgile" (III, 5, 873b), Montaigne describes language that is "tout plein et gros d'une vigueur naturelle et constante" ("full and copious with a natural and constant vigor" [665]); he speaks also of words "enflées" by imagination, and in other essays of words that are "remplies," "farcies," "vives." These are writings in which "le sens esclaire et produict les parolles; non plus de vent, ains de chair et d'os" (873b) ("the sense illuminates and brings out the words, which are no longer wind, but flesh and bone" [665]). In a literal sense Montaigne would be "fleshing out" his writing, making the *Essais* a kind of secular (and parodic) incarnation. When language is semantically and morally impoverished, when it fails to embody thought, it is nothing but words, and he speaks about it as if it were bloodless, fleshless, what I might call death itself. "J'avois trainé languissant apres des parolles Françoises, si exangues, si descharnées et si vuides de matiere et de sens, que ce n'estoient voirement que paroles Françoises" he says, describing his reaction to reading borrowed words in "De l'institution des enfans" (I, 26, 147a) ("I had dragged along languidly after French words so bloodless, fleshless, and empty of matter and sense that they really were nothing but French words" [108]).

Montaigne is thus concerned to write a substantial prose, to express the abstract in concrete terms, to present the *Essais* as a textual body, and as his own incarnation: the writing appears as a "skeletos" in "De l'exercitation," a "livre consubstantiel à son autheur" in "Du desmentir," the "excremens d'un vieil esprit" in "De la vanité." This is both a moral and a rhetorical issue that expresses yet another effort to transcend contingent and factitious language.[8] As in the case of language that must deny itself in transparency, or of language that negates itself in silence, or language that longs to become pure substance (*faire*), we once again have language that must be transformed into something other than itself. My discussion has revealed that these are not consistent strategies, related systematically to each other; rather they are the diverse and conflicting expressions of Montaigne's desire for unmediated and stable truth. But we have seen that postlapsarian language resists such stabilizing gestures; it shifts and turns semantically, disturbing its signifying habits and straining its referential links. The limitations of language cannot be transcended from within language itself, as language itself constantly reminds us.

For my purposes, the unsettled name of the child as "enfant" can serve as an emblem of linguistic instability, of the restless displacement of signs and meaning, a sign itself at once lexical and semantic, developmental and social. Philippe Ariès has shown that at a time in Western history when most people still had only an approximate idea of their age the concepts of child and of childhood, and their corresponding vocabularies, remained equally imprecise.[9] The periodization of human life that was called "les âges de la vie" varied in number in medieval treatises, corresponding to the four temperaments, the seven planets, or to the twelve signs of the zodiac. Released from its etymological mooring, "enfant" became a fluid expression that referred to very young children as well as to young people in their teens and even twenties,[10] subsuming a broad range of terms that included *puer, adolescens, valet, garçon, fils,* and *beau-fils.* Rather than a prelinguistic state, "infancy" designated a condition of dependency. In a formal or legal sense the offspring were "enfants" as long as they were under the authority of the father, although I might want to say that as long as they depended on that authority and were not authorized to speak for themselves, in their own names, they did exist, in a certain sense, in a "prelinguistic" state. That authority could also be exercised by a metaphorical father, as in the extended, and popular, usage of *enfant* to refer to members of the lower social class, those in household service, and those in the military (cf. the etymology of *infantry,* from the Latin *infans,* child). Montaigne may found his pedagogical project on the premise that proper language learning provides the child the stable foundation for a moral life, but language itself, as the very example of the child shows, in its imprecise and problematical signifying function reminds us that it can never serve as a firm, fixed ground.

.   .   .   .

One might argue that the *Essais'* preoccupation with the child betrays its own concern with learning how to speak, that the writing situates itself anxiously between the initial unloosening of the tongue (language) and the mature moral expression (action) toward which it strives. To write is of course literally to "dénouer la langue," to loosen the tongue and to let language loose, and I think it not amiss to speak of the anxiety of writing, even (or especially) in the case of Montaigne, allegedly so settled and serene. What talking about the child has uncovered so far is precisely the presence of elements that disturb, displace, unsettle, and destabilize from within comfortable, conventional notions of speaking, writing, and language itself. What disturbs is not that Montaigne attacks accepted rhetorical practice or upsets a traditional curriculum in which it plays a part but that even in his attack he himself is always implicated in its use, in its excess and artifice. What destabilizes is not that he seeks a direct, immediate moral expression but that in this effort he forces language into paradoxical postures it cannot sustain: silence, invisibility, substantiality. And what is unsettling about silence and invisibility is not that they are intended as the guarantees of truth and the authenticity of being but that they can also be emptiness, vacuity, as I suggested, nonbeing that proclaims itself as loudly as if it spoke for itself. The word made flesh? Montaigne's attempt to transcend language through language itself can only parody incarnation as the impossible (and scandalous) object of his desire, can only temporarily muzzle the irrepressible voice of the trope that pushes forth to speak in the name of its own factitiousness.

If Montaigne *could* have realized the intentions of his writing project, it would have signaled the end of writing, the end of language, for being would have been wholly present in all its plenitude and no longer needed to be spoken. Paradoxically, these are the terms of Montaigne's friendship with La Boétie, which the *Essais* situate *before* the writing and which obviated the need for writing, as numerous critics have pointed out.[11] When the death of the friend shatters the ideal of presence it creates a void that the writing project can (must) fill. But what the complex status of the child reveals, as it strives to be what it cannot logically be—simultaneously a child and a speaker—is that the project cannot entirely "be" either, that the writer must continually write, must continually urge language toward that which *it* can never be or do.

> Et quand seray-je à bout de representer une continuelle agitation et mutation de mes pensées, en quelque matiere qu'elles tombent, puisque Diomedes remplit six mille livres du seul subject de la grammaire? Que doit produire le babil, puisque le begaiement et desnouement de la langue estouffa le monde d'une si horrible charge de volumes? Tant de paroles pour les paroles seules! (III, 9, 946)

> And when shall I make an end of describing the continual agitation and changes of my thoughts, whatever subject they light on, since Didymus filled six thousand books with the sole subject of grammar? What must prattle produce, when the stammering and loosening of the tongue smothered the world with such a horrible load of volumes? So many words for the sake of words alone! (721])

"What can the child's prattle produce?" Montaigne asks of his own writing. The *Essais* are always in some sense "babil," "begaiement," the not yet fully formed speech of the child of the mind. They also bear in some sense the trace of Babel, that originary "desnouement de la langue" that indeed threatened to suffocate the world with words. When the tongues of both essayist *and* child are loosened, when the language of the essayist *as* child is unleashed, only empty speech is produced unless proper instruction intervenes. But the formation of the child and the development of substantial speech can only represent an ideal toward which the child, like the essayist, endlessly strives and whose conclusion remains endlessly beyond reach. Montaigne imagines his text as a child who does not (will not or cannot) grow up, the very performance of inadequacy, of limitation, the enactment of the shortcomings of language and of the essayist / child coming up short of his own ends.

Given this inevitable situation, one might ask not only, "Why the compulsion to write?" or put the other way, "to beget a child?" but also, "Why continue to write?" If the loss of the perfect friendship represented in "De l'amitié" (I, 28) and the consequent loss of the sense of self ("luy seul jouyssoit de ma vraye image, et l'emporta" [III, 9, 983b]) ("he alone enjoyed my true image, and carried it away" [752]) serve as figures of an alterity that defines Montaigne's relationship to himself and to others, what motivates the writing, and makes of Montaigne an essayist, is the effort to overcome difference both within himself and between self and other. The desire to know and to possess himself is accompanied by the poignant call to the absent other ("O un amy" [III, 9, 981b]), by the need for a friend like La Boétie, and by the need to be known by others as he is and for what he is: "Je suis affamé de me faire connoistre; et ne me chaut à combien, pourveu que ce soit veritablement; ou, pour dire mieux, je n'ay faim de rien, mais je crains mortellement d'estre pris en eschange par ceux à qui il arrive de connoistre mon nom" (III, 5, 847b) ("I am hungry to make myself known, and I care not to how many, provided it be truly. Or to put it better, I am hungry for nothing, but I have a mortal fear of being taken to be other than I am by those who come to know my name" [643]). With striking intensity Montaigne reaches out; the *Essais*, the child of his mind, are conceived to allow him to be known and to guarantee that he will not be taken amiss.

Eminent people, Montaigne says as he begins his discussion of presumptuousness (II, 17), those whom fortune has made famous, are known by the public actions that bear witness to what they are: "ils peuvent par leurs actions publiques tesmoigner quels ils sont" (632a). But those others, like himself, who have been relegated by fortune to anonymity, those people will only be known for what they are if they speak of (for) themselves. Montaigne thus speaks out about himself, he writes as a public act by publishing his discourse, so that his actions too will speak for him and bear witness to what *he* is. Justifying his project, he defends himself and others who talk about themselves and seeks to deflect the charge of presumptuousness: "ils sont excusables s'ils prennent la hardiesse de parler d'eux mesmes envers ceux qui ont interest de les connoistre" (ibid.) ("they may be excused if they have the temerity to speak of themselves to those who have in interest in knowing them" [479]). What does it mean to be known by speaking of oneself, to bear witness to what one is?

Claiming not to be a famous person, Montaigne considers that his private action, by itself, would not (or could not) have borne witness to what he was, although he did indeed act on the public stage as he reminds us periodically in the *Essais*. The figure of the modest unknown is thus a pose, a rhetorical persona that ironically serves the writer in two ways: it allows him (or it requires him) to talk about himself (and so be a writer, an author), and it obliges him to excuse talking about himself (as he does in "De la praesumption"), but of course this is another excuse to continue speaking about himself. What would have been the consequence had he not written of himself? A reading of "De l'oisiveté" (I, 8), which evokes the time of his retirement prior to the *Essais,* suggests that he would have produced ideas and imaginings like an unfertilized woman who produces formless and purposeless "amas et pieces de chair" or like fallow land that teems with wild and useless weeds. Only through speaking/writing can he acquire the form that makes him what he "is"; only in this way can he situate himself and thus avoid the pitfall he recognizes, that to be everywhere is to be nowhere.

The figure of the writer bearing public witness to himself provides yet another perspective on the need to speak. If Montaigne had not spoken/written, he would have been silent about himself and everyone else would have been silent about him. No one, including Montaigne himself, would have said what he is ("quel il est"), and that is another way of saying that no one would have said *that* he is. He would have remained "private" in its several senses: withdrawn from the public body, not holding public office, removed from public knowledge, and, most striking, deprived (Latin *privare,* to deprive), deprived of self-knowledge, and in a profound sense deprived of life. Earlier we saw that a certain silent and invisible language is required if the essential and authentic self is to be known. In "Consideration sur Cicéron" Montaigne claims that he prefers to remain silent so that his true intentions can be read in his heart: "[c] Et me presente moins à qui je me suis le plus donné: [b] il me semble qu'ils le doivent lire en mon coeur, et que l'expression de mes paroles fait tort à ma conception" (I, 40, 253) ("And I tender myself least to those to whom I have given myself most; it seems to me that they should read my feelings in my heart, and see that what my words express does an injustice to my thought" [186]). In the context of the private person who does not speak about himself, however, we see another face of silence. Not to speak and not to be spoken of: silence, nonbeing, death. To speak of (for) oneself, I would argue, is to save oneself from nothingness, from death. I will come back to this in the course of my discussion.

Neither exclusively private nor entirely public, Montaigne will both enjoy the prerogative of the famous and have his public act, his essays, speak for him and remain at the same time a private person, away from the public eye, in retirement. In fact, to bear witness is always in some sense a public act since it always needs to be witnessed in turn by another in order to be what it is. In the self-reflexive gesture of writing about himself Montaigne becomes both the subject and object of his judgment and testimony, he begins by being his own witness: "et n'est aucun si asseuré tesmoing comme chacun à soy-mesme" (II, 16, 626a) ("and there is no witness so sure as each man to himself" [474]). He also imagines his distant and anonymous public to be his witness, seeing his readers in his mind's eye reading and seeing him in his text. Beholding and beheld in this way, Montaigne self-consciously engages in his reflexive performance, but he holds in fact that all writers write themselves into their texts, represent themselves, regardless of whatever else their writing represents. This is the lesson of the closing pages of "De l'affection des peres aux enfans" (II, 8) in which a broad range of writing—literary, historical, philosophical, religious, and confessional—as well as the work of sculptors, and even the heroic deeds of Epaminondas, are characterized as children of the mind, as "autres nous-mesmes," as images of the "father" that bear witness to him. Montaigne recognized the generative power of writing for the writer, a power that he expresses through the figure of generation itself—the production of the child—and the act through which the father (re)produces himself.

At this point an essential tension in Montaigne's work begins to emerge clearly. On the one hand, in his quest for self and self-knowledge the essayist needs to be concerned only with himself in order to write himself into his text and to be both its producer and its product. This self-reflexive preoccupation has long been considered the focal point of the *Essais*. On the other hand, I have been insisting on Montaigne's public concern, on his need to bear public witness and to engage the "other" who must respond to this need. The *Essais* express these conflicting inclinations in the opposition between figures of interiority and exteriority. We encounter a centripetal tendency that translates the dominant emphasis on self and a centrifugal force that leads out toward the other. But while each is necessary, each also has its dangers. The need to move inward toward the self raises the possibility of a solipsistic enclosure, a circle within which text and self endlessly (and presumptuously) mirror each other. The drive to move out creates the real possibility of wandering off and getting lost in otherness. Since the natural urge appears to be outward and away, the *Essais* seek both to call man back to himself and to respond themselves to that call. "De la solitude" (I, 39) and "De la gloire" (II, 16) simultaneously issue that call to turn away from the outside world and address what is personal, interior. The oft-cited closing passage of "De la vanité" (III, 9) again summons man (and the essayist himself) from the outside, citing the Delphic oracle to exhort him to look within: "Regardez dans vous, reconnoissez vous, tenez vous à vous" (1,001b).

The project of self-knowledge, and self-recovery, depends for its realization on the movement back and into the self, and it is equally and paradoxically true that it depends as well on its countermovement. Montaigne will thus seek himself by moving toward the other, with all the risks of losing himself that such a movement entails. He will express this need for the other in his need to bear witness and in the need for the discourse of bearing witness to be a form of *interlocution*. It is apparently not enough for him simply to show himself; nor is it enough simply to be acknowledged, once and for all, as if that were possible. A sustained linkage appears necessary, one that connects the self to the other, that allows exchange to affirm the sense of self, as the self speaks its subjectivity through the projection of an "I" and as it is addressed and recognized as the subject "you." But it is important to stress that, however much Montaigne's text longs for something like a dialogue, and however much we as readers subscribe to the conventional impression that the essayist "dialogues" with us and we with him—that we are in the presence of each other— the *Essais* remain in a profound and literal sense a monologue.

Both the link between self and other, between monologue and dialogue, and their opposition operate within Montaigne's use of the term *conversation*, which in sixteenth-century usage expresses personal contact or intercourse with others. I have intimated that the *Essais* are a form of "conversation" (from the Latin *conversari*, to turn oneself about, to frequent) as they turn to contact or frequent the other. But by making *his* "conversation" a mode of verbal intercourse Montaigne also anticipates its modern usage, drawing attention not only to its oral dimension but in this case to its textual dimension as well, to his writing as the incorporation and imitation of dialogue. The text assumes the task of making self and other present to each other but what I might call discursively present as *je, tu, vous,* and *nous* inscribed in the instance of written discourse. What *conversation* also reveals, however, is that this textual turn toward the other, this inscribed frequenting of the other, is also and most profoundly the turn toward and the frequenting of the self. It is particularly revealing that *to converse* derives originally from the middle voice of the rare Latin verb *conversare*, because it is precisely in the verbs of middle voice that Benveniste shows the subject to be inside the process of which it is the agent. Barthes claims that *to write* is a modern verb of middle voice that operates in this way—in an analysis that he derives from Benveniste—and we can see that Montaigne's use of the verb *to converse* functions in similar fashion. Modern literature, Barthes says, is trying to establish a new status in writing for the agent of writing, a status where the subject is immediately contemporary with the action, being effected and affected by it.[12] One might say that in the context of the *Essais* the family resemblance of *to converse* and *to write* speaks volumes; it discloses that in the act of interlocution where Montaigne turns toward the other he does effect and affect himself as he speaks—that is, as he writes.

This then is what motivates the so-called conversational style of the *Essais,* so-called because it can only resemble oral discourse and imitate dialogue and conversation through the addresses, questions, and responses that operate within itself. This style is also the motive (the motor or the mover) for a writing that cannot end, and it is its product as well, for dialogue, like the self hungry to make itself known, can never definitively realize itself or absolutely conclude. It seems particularly significant that in the three direct conversations with historical readers—Diane de Foix in "De l'institution des enfans," Mme d'Estissac in "De l'affection des peres aux enfans," and Mme de Duras in "De la ressemblance des enfans aux peres"—Montaigne speaks to them of children. In the first two cases, the dialogue engages the other as "mother" and speaks with her of her child and, by extension, of the essayist's own.[13] Conversing with the mother, Montaigne bears witness to himself, and he bears the child that makes him what he "is," a father (and a mother as well?), an essayist. He frequents the community of child-bearers who can (should) acknowledge him for what he is, and as one of their own.

The paradox of reaching out to come back to the self is thus only one of several profound incongruencies I have raised in this discussion. The confusion of gender, of Montaigne's gender as childbearer, and the place of the feminine and the masculine in literary conception are other curious and thorny questions to which I will also have to return. In fact, in my reading, the place of the feminine in Montaigne's text appears to be no place at all, for while the mothers to whom he writes are inscribed as such *in* the writing, it appears as if the essayist writes them *out* of his text, subsumes or sublimates them in the paternity / maternity that appears to be his and is reflected in the unique status given in his titles to "pères." This displacement of mothers to the background both announces and reflects the status of daughters, for Montaigne's writing explicitly perpetuates a patriarchal ideology that privileges both conception of the male child and its role as heir. Offering his essay on education as a gift to the "little man who threatens to come out so bravely from within" Diane de Foix, Montaigne explains parenthetically (but not inadvertently) that he considers her "too noble-spirited to begin otherwise than with a male." For these reasons I have begun my reading by treating textual progeny as a son and by analyzing the relation between author and text in terms of male lineage. But Montaigne's text will also serve in later chapters to reveal the limitations of this reading and the necessity of bringing the feminine back from the margins to which it had been relegated.[14] For the moment, let us leave these issues aside and turn to another paradox directly related to the question of Montaigne's writing as dialogue: that of absence.

·   ·   ·   ·   ·   ·   ·

In spite of Montaigne's textual strategies designed to create the impression of conversation and to heighten the sense of presence and proximity, what the essayist's testimony bears witness to is that both writer and reader, as witnesses, are absent to each other. The separation between author and audience, experienced in Montaigne's time in the still-recent advent of printing, and by the sense of an enormous physical and psychological distance created by an anonymous, dispersed readership, cannot be concealed or overcome by what I might call the stylistics or the rhetoric of dialogue. There remains a tension between literal absence and discursive presence, a necessary and inevitable tension that both generates literature and is its creation. Facing the blank page that mirrors his own nothingness—his absent self—and the nothingness of silence and of death, and in the face of an absent and mute public, the writer writes himself as testimony to himself. And in this language in which he is written, he writes his reader, his interlocutor, the witness who testifies to his presence. The book printed, published, circulates in public bearing his name and in the hands of his readers, before their eyes, in its materiality, claims to be Montaigne's child, the generation of self that overcomes nothingness and death itself.

This is a function of children, and particularly of the children of the mind ("les enfantemens de nostre esprit") who are evoked in the closing pages of "De l'affection des peres aux enfans" (II, 8, 399–400). All progeny, Montaigne infers, "nous representent et nous rapportent" and the spiritual children "bien plus vivement que les autres." These children's role is to represent, to be the agent or surrogate who speaks in the father's place, or name, who "speaks" the father ("nous rapporter"). Thus, the *Essais,* and all writing, I might suggest, fulfill their role as children able paradoxically to speak, but perhaps the child also speaks the absence of the father. In sixteenth-century France, only when the father no longer exercised his authority, when he died or otherwise was absent, was the child legally authorized to speak in his place and in its own name. And it is so linguistically as well, for the book is both the sign of the author and of his absence itself, both mediator and substitute.

Thus far I have been using the notion of absence in two complementary ways, as that physical disappearance caused by death (the dead are spoken of in French as *disparus*) and also as physical nonpresence, as when the writer is not present to the reader. But there is another form of absence that also compels the kind of production that the child of the mind represents. I would call this the absence from oneself, the deficiency, the gap, that is one's alienation from oneself, the sense that one does not wholly possess oneself or, in Montaigne's case, know himself in the fullness and plenitude of his being. In personal terms, the death of La Boétie and Montaigne's consequent feeling of loss, of being only half of his former self, figure this condition. Historically speaking, the Delphic injunction "Know thyself," as it comes to be understood in the Western literary and philosophical tradition, implies that the self is not already known, that man is in fact separated from himself. As Montaigne reads that injunction and as it motivates the *Essais,* the writing becomes the means through which that absent knowledge and with it the self will be (might be) restored, made manifest. In or through the writing as the child who speaks, Montaigne the father/writer might come to know and thus recuperate himself.

The production of writing reveals, however, that writing does not restore the self to its plenitude. This is perhaps why Montaigne's project can never conclude in any absolute way. What the essayist comes to know in his absence to himself is that the self he seeks to recover always remains in some sense absent. It cannot be totally mastered or possessed, and what can be known of it is overwhelming in its negativity, in the emptiness, vanity, and ignorance that predominate and in the variety, diversity, and difference that characterize both Montaigne (in his relation to himself) and the human condition in general. He who knows himself in his imperfection and weakness and knows the *nihilité* of the human condition, Montaigne says at the end of "De l'exercitation" (II, 6, 380), let him, like Socrates, boldly make himself known by his own mouth. Here the essayist conceives of his vocation as writer and as father. In the space created by the absence of self-knowledge, by the lack that is ignorance itself, the child of the mind is born as testimony to the father's ignorance and to its own.

The concept of absence in its various manifestations helps to explain the ubiquitous and central presence of death in the *Essais* by reminding us that all absence to some degree evokes, recalls, or represents death. All that is missing, that is no longer in place or simply no longer, all that wears down or wears away and so announces its own demise, all that is not yet foregrounds our own temporality, our mortality. In "De l'experience" (III, 13) Montaigne imagines life as successive losses, successive deaths of which Death is only the last: "La derniere mort en sera d'autant moins plaine et nuisible: elle ne tuera plus qu'un demy ou un quart d'homme" (1,101b) ("The last death will be all the less complete and painful; by then it will kill only a half or quarter of a man" [845]). Death inhabits life as a series of subtractions: "Dieu faict grace à ceux à qui il soustrait la vie par le menu" ("God is merciful to those whose life he takes away bit by bit"); as progressive failings or fallings (like Montaigne's tooth, "qui me vient de choir" [fall out]), as a kind of physical (and spiritual) melting away so that one is no longer what one was: "C'est ainsi que je fons et eschape à moy" ("Thus do I melt and slip away from myself"). Death also inhabits life as the absence of one's true self possessed and known, represented in the *Essais* by the absence of La Boétie, who, as Montaigne says, possessed his true image and "carried it away." And finally, I might add that death intrudes into life in the image of the future, in the future as an abyss from which the self will ultimately and eternally be absent. In his liminary address to the reader Montaigne imagines himself writing from beyond the grave so that having lost him, he says, his friends and family will have something to keep their knowledge of him more complete and alive.

If we conceive of absence in this metonymic relation to death, we might say that Montaigne always writes in the face of death, that whatever else he is writing about—friendship, self-knowledge or ignorance, children, or writing itself—he is always writing to face up to death in the form of absence and in a sense to face it down. I am reminded in this context of Scheherazade, for whom speaking alone forestalled death. As long as there were words there was breath, and the teller of tales—both speaker and writer—was able to postpone the inevitable silence and nothingness of the end. In an essay entitled "Language to Infinity" Foucault saw the self-reflexive nature of language itself as the hedge against death: "Headed toward death, language turns back upon itself; it encounters something like a mirror; and to stop this death which would stop it, it possesses but a single power: that of giving birth to its own image in a play of mirrors that has no limits."[15] The figure of language giving birth to a self-reflexive image as the way to defer death strikingly echoes the lexicon of production, of procreation in the *Essais,* of children as "autres nous mesmes" (II, 8, 399a), of children of the mind who effectively become "enfans immortels, qui immortalisent leurs peres, voire et les deïfient" (400c) (immortal children, who immortalize their fathers, and even deify them [291]). This is not the immortality sought after by some, the hollow and superficial glory conferred by public approbation that Montaigne eschews in "De la gloire" (II, 16), what I might call the child of fame or destiny that is always in the keeping of others. Something much more profound and profoundly personal is at stake here than a reputation that might survive on the lips (in the words) of others. Only Montaigne's own voice can postpone death, only the essayist speaking about himself and himself speaking, in language turned back upon itself in an endless play of mirrors, only that procreation that re-creates the self, that generates the child of the mind who continues to speak in the father's name, in his absence. In the void of the future, even and especially after death, the text will endlessly repeat what / that Montaigne (still) is.

But the effort to stave off death by conceiving of writing in this way entraps the writer in a double bind. The child is the source of the father's life as such: in the most literal sense, without the child there is no father, just as there is no survival. But the child is also the source of the father's death, as Montaigne reminds us in "De l'affection des peres aux enfans" (II, 8). Evoking the jealousy of those whose children assume a place in the world just as the parent is about to take his leave, "[a] il nous fache," he says in the first person plural, which includes himself among the envious fathers, "qu'ils [the children] nous marchent sur les talons, [c] comme pour nous solliciter de sortir. [a] Et, si nous avions à craindre cela, puis que l'ordre des choses porte qu'ils ne peuvent, à dire verité, estre ny vivre qu'aux despens de nostre estre et de nostre vie, nous ne devions pas nous mesler d'estre peres" (387) ("it vexes us that they are treading on our heels, as if to solicit us to leave. And if we had that to fear, then since in the nature of things they cannot in truth either be or live except at the expense of our being and our life, we should not have meddled with being fathers" [280]). To be a father means to begin to take one's leave, to relinquish one's place, to give up one's authority and one's voice since the child's life and being can *only* occur at the expense of the life and being of the father. This is not some contingency but the very order of things from which there is no escape. The irony here is overwhelming. The father seeks to save himself by becoming a father, and he condemns himself; he begins to absent himself before his death, when the child learns to speak and speaks for the father. Once the child is given the proper language and takes its place in the world, it does not wait for the father to disappear of his own accord. The child speaks, and its voice displaces and replaces that of the father and the father himself. Even though it purports to represent the paternal, the child draws attention to its own voice and to itself.

That the child inevitably supplants the father it meant to save is not the only irony of conception (writing). The child (as the text) cannot fulfill the ardent desire of its progenitor for protection; it cannot guarantee the father's integrity, no matter what the father does or how hard the child tries. Circulating out in the world in the father's name, inscribed with his signature as author, the child of the mind cannot completely impose its authority. The faithful repetition of the authoritative words of the father, the loyal effort to secure his intention, to assert his meaning, must ultimately fail to guarantee that the father will be taken for what he is once and for all. Speaking to represent the father and to assure his place, the child inadvertently opens up the possibility of violent displacement. And this opening reveals that there is always a gap in the way representation functions, a gap that is the insurmountable difference between the signified and the signifier, and it exposes as well the aporia that lies between intention and interpretation, between what is meant and what is understood.

Montaigne recounts his own concern in "De l'amitié" that La Boétie's *La servitude volontaire* has been misread and has thus misrepresented his friend. Used by the Protestants for political purposes for which it was not intended, the text has communicated a false image of its author. This of course is Montaigne's reading, and he asserts for himself the privileged position of the friend who, like the child, would be "autre nous mesmes" and thus able to express La Boétie's true intention, his will, and his meaning. And also like the child, the friend will speak for the other who is also himself, he will stand in for his friend to maintain him as he was: "Et si à toute force je n'eusse maintenu un amy que j'ay perdu, on me l'eust deschiré en mille contraires visages" (III, 9, 983b) ("And if I had not supported with all my strength a friend that I lost, they would have torn him into a thousand contrasting appearances" [752]). The violence of the figure is striking. The voice of the child, La Boétie's writing, does not suffice to safeguard the integrity of its father and the wholeness of his presence that purports to reside within it. A second surrogate is needed, a guardian for the child as well as for the father, one whose own voice supplements that of the child and prevents the father, the model, the original, the signified, from being torn asunder, fragmented into a thousand contrasting appearances.

In "De l'amitié," as a sign of friendship and to fulfill its obligation, Montaigne becomes that surrogate, he explains and justifies La Boétie's motives and his meaning: "Et affin que la memoire de l'auteur n'en soit interessée en l'endroit de ceux qui n'ont peu connoistre de pres ses opinions et ses actions, je les advise que" (I, 28, 194a) ("And so that the memory of the author may not be damaged in the eyes of those who could not know his opinions and actions at close hand, I beg to advise them" [144]). But who will speak for La Boétie after Montaigne is silent? And who for Montaigne himself? "Je reviendrois volontiers de l'autre monde pour démentir celuy qui me formeroit autre que je n'estois, fut ce pour m'honorer" (983b) ("I would willingly come back from the other world to give the lie to any man who portrayed me other than I was, even if it were to honor me" [751]), the essayist says, not entirely facetiously. The text will be left alone, on its own, to speak the intention of the father, to represent him. But this dynamic demonstrates that representation is never self-sufficient, it never can say all that it has to say, or that must be said, once and for all, so that nothing else need be said. The representative does not have final authority, it cannot speak so as to silence the voices of others who impose upon it and thus have the last word. Representation is not closure but the opening to others to speak in its place.

.   .   .   .

The reading that puts pressure on both the letter and the figure of the child in Montaigne's *Essais* thus reveals the inability of any authority, intention, or will to impose itself absolutely, to close itself off and to remain impervious to the outside. And this is because the challenge from without is always in response to the openings and gaps that already inhabit the inside. In the case of reading and interpretation, the opening that produces or allows them resides deep within writing itself, regardless of any specific text's desire to open itself up or to close itself off. The opening is, however, not a space of free and unimpeded passage but an arena of confrontation and of tension in which reading must negotiate between the writer's intention and its unrealizable textual expression, between the constraints of the textual matter and form and their inevitable and necessary misreading, between the irreconcilable demands of the historicity of both text and of reader.

In the *Phaedrus* Socrates belittled writing for drifting and wandering about like an errant son, getting into the wrong hands, addressing the wrong people, both mindlessly repeating the same thing forever and, in the analogy he draws with painting, maintaining a silence that discloses both its stupidity and its treachery. But the genealogical tales I have been telling reveal that the text does not always and everywhere say the same thing and is never really silent, even in the face of unexpected questions. Nor can it be said to fall entirely in the "wrong hands." Textuality always speaks in the different voices of its own unruly brood, it responds by opening itself up to the different possibilities of what it (or the parent) is saying,

even (or especially) when it responds in ways that were not anticipated. In fact, we are ultimately unable to determine if the response is
that of the text as child speaking for its parent or as child speaking for
itself. Nor can we confirm with absolute assurance that what we as
readers are hearing is anything more than our own ventriloquized
voice. Perhaps it is the nature of writing always to be made to speak
the words of others, as Socrates feared, words that are attributed to it
as if they were its own. These are not questions that I ask in the hope
of resolving the problematical status of spiritual parenthood and the
complex relationship among writer, text, and reader. They are, rather,
questions that define and delineate the space of textuality, the unstable, unmasterable space of writing and reading.

Montaigne appears to sense the futility of the effort to impose
one's authority in any absolute way, whether it be the authority that
the father would exercise over his offspring or, by extension, that the
writer would seek over his text or the reader. In "De l'affection des
peres aux enfans" (II, 8) he argues against those fathers who use
money and material wealth to control their families or who use the
legal force of wills and testaments to extend their domination into the
future. "Nous prenons un peu trop à coeur ces substitutions mas-
culines," he says, referring to the line of succession and inheritance
that could be specified in the will in case the heir died before the
testator, "et proposons une éternité ridicule à noz noms" (397c) ("We
take these male entails too much to heart. And we look to a ridiculous
eternity for our names" [289]). The father's proper role is to pass on
his goods in the present, to pass on a measure of his authority, because, as we saw earlier, it is in the natural order of things that the
father relinquish his place and allow the child to live. For the father
not to make way usurps the proper place of the child. Montaigne
criticizes those cruel, greedy, and tyrannical fathers who unnaturally
stifle the life that is rightfully the child's.

To emphasize how he has acted differently, Montaigne uses the
language of the more liberal and reasonable *donation entre vifs* as he
liberates the child of his mind, his writing: "Ce que je donne, je le
donne purement et irrevocablement, comme on donne aux enfans
corporels: ce peu de bien que je luy ay faict, il n'est plus en ma
disposition; il peut sçavoir assez de choses que je ne sçay plus, et tenir
de moy ce que je n'ay point retenu et qu'il faudroit que, tout ainsi
qu'un estranger, j'empruntasse de luy, si besoin m'en venoit" (401–

402c) ("What I give I give purely and irrevocably, as one gives to the children of one's body. The little good I have done for it is no longer at my disposal. It may know a good many things that I no longer know and hold from me what I have not retained and what, just like a stranger, I should have to borrow from it if I came to need it" [293]). The relation between the generations should be defined by affection, not the exercise of authority, and by the recognition of filial autonomy and paternal debt. The son should be allowed to make his own way in the world, whatever the risk to the father.[16]

In his own case Montaigne presents himself as a son who has both respected and challenged paternal authority, that of his biological father and of his intellectual fathers, the bookish tradition within which he writes. He recognizes the fundamental linking of generations and marvels at the resemblance of children to their fathers— that is, at the ability of the father to reproduce himself in the son, to carry himself over into the next generation so that the son carries (him) on. "Quel monstre est-ce," he asks, "que cette goutte de semence dequoy nous sommes produits, porte en soy les impressions, non de la forme corporelle seulement, mais des pensemens et des inclinations de nos peres?" (II, 37, 763a) ("What a prodigy it is that the drop of seed from which we are produced bears in itself the impressions not only of the bodily form but of the thoughts and inclinations of our fathers!" [578]).[17] At the same time, in the poignant relationship he evokes with his late father, the son explains and justifies not "carrying on" in the way the father had desired and intended. Montaigne describes how he has not carried out his father's wishes in the management of his household, and we also see that he has not produced a text that is entirely consistent with the historical precedent established by his intellectual fathers. The *Essais* announce and incorporate the authority of the classical (paternal) tradition, particularly of Socrates and Plutarch, at the same time as they critique a slavish adherence to it and insist on their own originality. And they do so in the still immature, filial language of the vernacular rather than the Latin of earlier generations, the Latin that his own father had him taught as his mother tongue.

The son is thus caught in the impossible position that requires him to be true to his father(s) while remaining true to himself. Montaigne finds that in order to bear witness to what *he* was, and to affirm his presence, his being, he was obliged to turn against the fathers to speak for himself. Not completely, as the *Essais* remind us, for neither the son nor the writer as intellectual child can entirely reject the past even when he claims for himself absolute originality. The past inhabits the present and the future just as the father inhabits the son, even in spite of what the son would hope, or claim. One might even argue that absolute rupture is never possible, that the presence of the father is indelibly inscribed in the child, that that is an aspect of what it means to be a child. The genetic link can never be broken, nor, it could be claimed, can the psychological one. Even neglecting the father, breaking with or revolting against him, is another affirmation of his presence and his authority, since the father still remains the source of motivation and desire, and even after his death. What is always written and read—whatever else is written or read—is the inexorable tension of the generations and the generation of tension itself: the tension between past and present/future generations; between the competing demands of imitation and originality that generate writing; between authorial control and the generation of the polysemous text; and tensions between intention and the multiple possibilities of interpretation that reading generates; and tensions among those readings themselves.

·   ·   ·   ·   ·   ·   ·

These tensions that lie at the heart of writing and reading are captured in (generated by?) the problematical relationship between the literal and the figurative that I have located at the center of my reading and that figures prominently in the *Essais* in the metaphor of the child of the mind. I have been attempting to elaborate on the implications of writing and textuality by drawing out two thematic and rhetorical elements that the *Essais* juxtapose and seek to associate: the father/child relationship and that of author and text. The structure of this association resembles the metaphoric form that Aristotle in the *Poetics* calls analogy or proportion, in which the second and fourth terms can be exchanged or substituted for each other. In Montaigne's case the substitution seeks to transfer to the relationship of author/text the natural and organic bond that exists between parent and offspring and is represented in the *Essais* through the biological transfer of the seed, the *semence*. Montaigne does not simply repeat the commonplace that the text is a child, he reinvents the metaphor and reinvests it with an energy intended to allow it to transcend the

limitations, the factitiousness, of its own rhetorical origin, to participate in the substantial link of father to son and to share the essential
characteristics of consubstantiality and resemblance. What I might
call the literalizing power of metaphor, or its naturalizing force, of
course represents the ultimate aspiration of the figure, and perhaps
the ultimate aspiration of all figures, to take on the properties of the
letter, to become its truth. The history of those readings of the *Essais*
that have taken the text literally as Montaigne's offspring, as a substance produced by him and identical to him, offers striking testimony to the persuasive force of the child of the mind.

The analogy between biological offspring and writing is obviously
meant to advantage textuality, to endow writing with animate qualities and to give it life. But a problem arises because the terms of
analogy and the making of metaphor allow the process to reverse.
The transfer by which the text accedes to the status of the son opens
up the play of substitution that allows the son to take on the properties of a text. This double movement reveals that the son, whose
desired, paradigmatic qualities motivated the transfer, was not (ever)
entirely what he was taken to be, that he was not a homogeneous
entity whose unified truth could be carried over in any simple way to
benefit writing, but that he was already complex, contradictory, and
different from himself. What the writer was seeking to overcome by
the creation of metaphor in the first place—the factitiousness of writing, its status as mere representation, its internal contradictions—
shows up as inhabiting the very agent that was meant to elevate or
redeem the writing. Here is how the reversal works.

Earlier I quoted the words that Montaigne speaks as he marvels at
the ability of the seed to transfer the qualities of the father to the son,
to ensure their resemblance. They bear repeating in this context because they suggest that the relationship between the family generations cannot be expressed without recourse to the language of textuality—impressions, signs, marks—and without recalling the process
of mimesis. "Quel monstre est-ce," he asks, "que cette goute de semence dequoy nous sommes produits, porte en soy les *impressions,*
non de la forme corporelle seulement, mais des pensemens et des
inclinations de nos peres [my emphasis]?" In a reversal of the transfer of natural properties to the artificial, the wondrous and unfathomable natural link is made familiar and explained by a figure borrowed from the artificial, mechanical process of printing or writing.

Ancient culture had already expressed such a conflation of the natural and artificial in the concept of "character" as a mark or impression on the soul. Montaigne's language implies that physical, mental, and emotional attributes are marked on the seed in the same way that letters are inscribed or printed in the text. The seed reproduces those attributes just as writing represents the sounds uttered by the voice in speech or as its content, its subject, functions to represent nature, or an action. The natural resemblance of children to their fathers is thus expressed as if it were the effect of another sort of mimesis; it is thus unavoidably contaminated by the arbitrary and contingent status of both mimesis and writing itself precisely at the point when it insists that resemblance is both natural and necessary.[18]

This reading has important consequences for Montaigne's desire that his text be taken as a natural child and for the metaphoric transfer he operates to accomplish that end. The natural, my discussion reveals, is not absolutely originary, nor can it wholly transform what is inorganic or factitious by transferring its own properties because those properties are never primordial, pure, and integral but are always already inscribed in a context of difference. When Montaigne asks the question, "Quel monstre est-ce," he asks not only what this "marvel" is. His language and the form of the rhetorical question exceed this figurative and commonplace meaning to affirm that the seed is also literally a "monstrous thing" and thus by definition mixed, multiple, and impure. In its monstrousness the seed betrays this complex nature: that which transfers resemblance between parent and offspring as a seed also transfers difference as a monster, for the name of monster applies precisely to the child whose shape does *not* conform to that of its parents.[19] The child and the text as child, the seed and the word: forms of resemblance and of difference, of fidelity and of betrayal.

2

Montaigne's Dutiful Daughter

J'étais sa fille, je suis son sépulcre, j'étais son second être, je suis ses cendres. Marie de Gournay

I was his daughter, I am his sepulchre. I was his second being, I am his ashes.

In the preceding analysis of the complex status of the child of the mind we encountered the gap between the father's intention and the way the child carries it out, and I concluded with the image of a textual offspring who is at the same time faithful and rebellious, who simultaneously represents its author and betrays him as well, both in spite of itself and because it is in its nature to do so. In this context we witnessed Montaigne's concern for what he himself identified as the intended meaning of La Boétie's writing and the role he took on to protect the integrity of his friend and his text. And we witnessed as well the essayist's misgivings about the future reading of his own text as he positioned himself, once again, beyond the grave. Who, I asked, would second Montaigne's offspring, the *Essais*, after the death of their father, who would speak to ensure his (their) intention as Montaigne had spoken to safeguard La Boétie's? Deprived of the guardianship of the father's friend, the textual progeny would be left entirely on its own to fend for itself, endlessly, insistently, and perhaps desperately to repeat the father's words to those who would challenge it or threaten to tear it, as they threatened to tear La Boétie, into a thousand different faces. Or we might also picture it uninhibited by guardianship, gleefully opening itself up to misreading, complicitous in the production of perverse meaning. Even the friend, of course, as surrogate father or guarantor, would not ultimately have the last word (any more than the text itself does), but at least he could speak from the shared experience of the relationship to assuage Montaigne's immediate concern, perhaps even his anxiety, at leaving the entire responsibility for protecting him to his child of the mind and at being misread and misrepresented in his absence.

The *Essais* thus appear not only to originate in the loss of the friend but in a sense to project that loss and its consequences into the future, beyond the writing, into the reading.[1] The plaintive cry, "O un amy!" which echoes in "De la vanité" (III, 9, 981b), sounds Montaigne's regret and his longing for companionship, and it anticipates as well the loneliness that will accompany his progeny: "Si à si bonnes enseignes je sçavois quelqu'un qui me fut propre, certes je l'irois trouver bien loing; car la douceur d'une sortable et agreable compaignie ne se peut assez acheter à mon gré. O un amy! Combien est vraye cette ancienne sentence, que l'usage en est plus necessaire et plus doux que des elemens de l'eau et du feu" ("If by such good signs I knew of a man who was suited to me, truly I would go very far to find him; for the sweetness of harmonious and agreeable company cannot be bought too dearly, in my opinion. Oh, a friend!" [750]). These are mediocre times, as the essayist informs us in "De la praesumption" (II, 17), when few have measured up to the standards of the past or to Montaigne's highest aspirations. La Boétie, of course, was the exception, "un' ame à la vieille marque" (659a), and he remains the model to which all other contemporaries are compared and found wanting. There have been some others worthy of note—military leaders, men of uncommon virtue, poets, and noble souls—but "de grand homme en general, et ayant tant de belles pieces ensemble, ou une en tel degré d'excellence, qu'on s'en doive estonner, ou le comparer à ceux que nous honorons du temps passé, ma fortune ne m'en a fait voir nul" (659a) ("as for an all-around great man having all these fine parts together, or one part in such excellent degree as to cause amazement or comparison with the men of the past whom we honor, I have not had the good fortune to find any" [500]). Ordinary friendship is a common thing and should not be confounded with its perfect form, Montaigne claims in "De l'amitié," where the paradoxical words of Aristotle serve to describe the essayist's condition, friendless in the midst of friends: "O mes amis, il n'y a nul amy" (190c) ("O my friends, there is no friend" [140]). If this is the legacy that the essayist will leave to his child of the mind, then the answer to my opening question is that no one will second that offspring, no one will protect it (and its author) from being misread and misrepresented.

Here history and literature converge, and the literal and the figurative confound, to produce an extraordinary sequel to the story of the orphaned text. In the space in the *Essais* that Montaigne clears of family and natural offspring so that the child of the mind can grow and prosper unencumbered, undisturbed by sibling rivalry that would vie for the attention of the father, another child surges forth unexpectedly as a figure of the writing at the end of "De la prae-sumption" (II, 17, 661–62c). This second child, after Montaigne's death, will materialize in history to play out literally the role of guar-antor that the text had assigned to the friend; but not as the son on whom patriarchal tradition bestowed this right and this responsibil-ity, not as the male offspring destined to carry on the father's name and to speak in his place. Instead, Montaigne names a daughter, Marie de Gournay le Jars, whom he calls "ma fille d'alliance"; he elevates her to a level equal to that of the greatest men of his time; and with unrestrained praise he confers a mantle of nobility that establishes her as a legitimate and worthy heir(ess). This startling substitution, which also bypasses Montaigne's natural daughter, designates a young woman whom contemporary readers will recog-nize primarily, if not exclusively, as the editor of the posthumous 1595 publication of the *Essais* they have in their hands. Let us begin to explore the implications of this designation for the father, for his text, and for the "daughter" herself by analyzing what Montaigne has to say about her as he presents her to the world.[2]

From the outset we encounter a major difficulty: we literally do not know if Montaigne says anything at all about Marie de Gournay in the *Essais*. The authenticity of the single passage in which she is named and praised has been questioned by numerous scholars, some even suggesting that its author might be Marie de Gournay herself. The Villey-Saulnier edition expresses the sentiments of Frame and others: "Cet éloge de Marie de Gournay ne figure pas dans l'exemplaire de Bordeaux, où pourtant la place n'aurait pas manqué pour l'inscrire. C'est ce qui a fait soupçonner parfois qu'il est de Marie de Gournay elle-même" (661 n) ("This praise of Marie de Gournay is not to be found in the 'exemplaire de Bordeaux,' where there was room to include it. This has occasionally led some to sus-pect that she wrote it herself"). Others have disagreed, however. Taking into account Montaigne's habit of writing on separate pieces of paper and the notational system for his textual additions, Maurice Rat, the editor of the Pléiade edition, remarks that, although the paragraph is not in the Bordeaux edition, "il y a des signes de renvoi sur la page, et le feuillet a dû se perdre" (1,595 n. 10) ("there are reference marks on the page, but the loose-leaf sheet must have been lost"). My own analysis of the rhetoric and thematics of children and friendship also suggests that Montaigne might have marked a place for Marie de Gournay in his text in anticipation of her future role. But rather than attempt to address the problem of attribution, I prefer to exploit the uncertainty of authorship and read the passage twice, as if it had been written by both Montaigne and Marie de Gournay. These readings, I am going to say, are mutually inclusive, and from their double perspective they cross generational lines and gender difference, they challenge the dominant father-son model of transmission and representation, and in the process they open up critical perspectives on issues of authority, of friendship and filial responsibility, and of textual integrity and meaning.

.   .   .   .

During the years up to 1588 the *Essais* expressed Montaigne's belief that his text would be left on its own after his death. In the passage in "De la vanité" where he threatens to return from beyond the grave to set his readers straight about himself, and where he speaks of his own defense of La Boétie, the essayist acknowledged his solitude and looked ahead to his own absence: "Je sçay bien que je ne lairray apres moy aucun respondant si affectionné bien loing et entendu en mon faict comme j'ay esté au sien. Il n'y a personne à qui je vousisse pleinement compromettre de ma peinture: luy seul jouyssoit de ma vraye image, et l'emporta. C'est pourquoy je me deschiffre moy-mesme, si curieusement" (983 n. 4) ("I know well that I will leave behind no sponsor anywhere near as affectionate and understanding about me as I was about him. There is no one to whom I would be willing to entrust myself fully for a portrait; he alone enjoyed my true image, and carried it away" [752]). Because there is no one pledged to him, ("aucun respondant," from the Latin *respondere*, to promise in return, to make a pledge), no one who has returned his promise of friendship and to whom he could entrust his portrait ("compromettre de ma peinture"), there will be no sponsor, no one who will respond on his behalf to those who would misinterpret and misunderstand him after he is gone. The text will be asked to carry a burden it will not be able to manage, to assume a responsibility it cannot fulfill by itself, whatever support Montaigne gives it—that is, however painstakingly and fully he succeeds in writing (and reading) himself and his intention into it. The child of the mind will, as we said, faithfully (and stupidly) repeat what it says to those who would interrogate it, but that will not be enough to forestall the fragmenting effects of commentary and the distortions of misreading. If not willfully, then inadvertently, the child betrays the father.

The 1595 edition contains two revisions that dramatically alter this picture of the friendless essayist and his soon-to-be-orphaned text. Montaigne had thought first to sharpen that picture. In the "exemplaire de Bordeaux"—the 1588 edition that he amended and revised in his own hand—after "peinture" in the passage we quoted above, he added, "Et si en y a que je recuse, pour les cognoistre trop excessivement proclives en ma faveur" ("And if there should be any, I repudiate them, for I know them to be excessively prejudiced in my favor"). He had already said with a certain bravado that he would return from the other world to give the lie to any man who portrayed him other than he was, even if it were to honor him, as if the writing did not need anyone else to defend it. Here Montaigne again affirms that there is no one to whom he would entrust himself fully, but even if there were, he continues, I repudiate this potential friend in advance. But this marginal addition that confirms the solitary status of the text never made it into print. Montaigne crossed it out, and, more significant, he did what he says he never does ("j'adjouste, mais je ne corrige pas"), he deleted its immediate context entirely from the body of his text—from "je sçay bien" to "si curieusement." What remains, then, is the expression of his desire not to be represented even by someone acting on his behalf, the statement of his own defense of La Boétie as the expression of his friendship, and the opening—which he had previously foreclosed—that indeed allows the sponsor, the "respondant," to emerge.

The second revision occurs several hundred pages earlier, at the end of "De la praesumption," where Marie de Gournay le Jars becomes a textual persona in the addition to the 1595 edition to which we have referred and that bears quoting in full:

> J'ay pris plaisir à publier en plusieurs lieux l'esperance que j'ay de Marie de Gournay le Jars, ma fille d'alliance: et certes aymée de moy beaucoup plus que paternellement, et enveloppée en ma retraitte et solitude, comme l'une des meilleures parties de mon propre estre. Je ne regarde plus qu'elle au monde. Si l'adolescence peut donner presage, cette ame sera quelque jour capable des plus belles choses, et en-

tre autres de la perfection de cette tres-saincte amitié où nous ne lisons point que son sexe ait peu monter encores: la sincerité et la solidité de ses moeurs y sont desjà bastantes, son affection vers moy plus que sur-abondante, et telle en somme qu'il n'y a rien à souhaiter, sinon que l'apprehension qu'elle a de ma fin, par les cinquante et cinq ans ausquels elle m'a rencontré, la travaillast moins cruellement. Le jugement qu'elle fit des premiers Essays, et femme, et en ce siecle, et si jeune, et seule en son quartier, et la vehemence fameuse dont elle m'ayma et me desira long temps sur la seule estime qu'elle en print de moy, avant m'avoir veu, c'est un accident de tres-digne consideration. (II, 17, 661–62)

I have taken pleasure in making public in several places the hopes I have for Marie de Gournay le Jars, my covenant daughter, whom I love indeed more than a daughter of my own, and cherish in my retirement and solitude as one of the best parts of my being. She is the only person I still think about in the world. If youthful promise means anything, her soul will some day be capable of the finest things, among others of perfection in that most sacred kind of friendship which, so we read, her sex has not yet been able to attain. The sincerity and firmness of her character are already sufficient, her affection for me more than superabundant, and such, in short, that it leaves nothing to be desired, unless that her apprehension about my end, in view of my fifty-five years when I met her, would not torment her so cruelly. The judgment she made of the first *Essays,* she a woman, and in this age, and so young, and alone in her district, and the remarkable eagerness with which she loved me and wanted my friendship for a long time, simply through the esteem she formed for me before she had seen me, is a phenomenon very worthy of consideration. (502)

I will begin by reading the passage as if it were Montaigne's own. Although nothing in these lines explicitly appoints Marie de Gournay as Montaigne's future guardian, she does assume a privileged position that bears upon the future. As the only person in the world the essayist claims still to think about, she displaces Montaigne's family and becomes a "fille d'alliance" who takes the place of wife and natural daughter, linked to the father through a personal alliance that has both the legal weight of a pact and the sacredness of a covenant. But Marie de Gournay is even more than a covenantal daughter. She is naturalized by Montaigne's language, made a part of him like the other parts of his being, physical or spiritual, including the part that is called the child. And as one of the best parts, we might imagine that she is rather like the metaphorical child of his mind, a product of his noble soul, an offspring of whom he is both father and mother and one who will represent him and bring him honor. This Marie de Gournay, the daughter of "De la praesumption," is literally a product of Montaigne's noble soul, in every sense a child of his creative imagination who is embodied in the writing. When Montaigne proclaims proudly that he has published her praises numerous times before, he confirms that the promising and perceptive young woman portrayed here as his daughter is in a real sense his textual progeny. Thus naturalized, sacralized, ennobled, this Marie de Gournay is more than "just" a daughter, and that is perhaps why Montaigne loves her "plus que paternellement."

The figure of this exceptional young woman, loving Montaigne through his writing, beloved of Montaigne as a part of his being, appears to be modeled on that of La Boétie and destined for the part that he can no longer play. The description of the privileged relationship in "De l'amitié" in which the two friends shared all, including being itself, reads as the subtext of Marie de Gournay's entrance into the *Essais*, and the youthful promise, both personal and intellectual, that was realized in the all-too-short life of the first friend bodes well for the future of the second and for the role she alone can now fulfill. Cast in the future tense, as an adolescent worthy of great expectations, as a soul that one day will be capable of the finest things, and among them the perfection of sacred friendship, Marie de Gournay represents the fulfillment of the bond broken by the death of La Boétie. In the passage in "De la praesumption" the essayist expresses his fatherly concern over the daughter's anxiety at his impending end, but this reference to the "end" also expresses the writer's own preoccupation with his death and with what will happen in his absence. By his projection of the model of the ideal daughter and his evocation of the perfect friend, Montaigne both anticipates and prepares the coming into being, or the return, of the one who will represent him and loyally defend his interests. Earlier the essayist had entrusted his portrait to La Boétie, to the friend who alone had enjoyed his true image, and the friend had carried it off in his death. Now after Montaigne himself has been "carried off" Marie de Gournay is meant to become the guardian of this textual self-portrait that he will leave behind, this other true image through which *she* has enjoyed him. Marie de Gournay enters the *Essais* for Montaigne's ultimate benefit, he inscribes her as the textual figures of both daughter and friend in the hope that life will imitate art. In this way he can be less troubled by his mortality and less concerned by what he cannot do in any real sense—that is, return from the other world to protect himself.

But what does it mean to place his fate in this way in the hands of a daughter? A son, our reading has indicated, would have spoken for the father, responded in his name, but could not have done so without also betraying the father, substituting for him and speaking in *his* own name. That is what it means to be a son. The daughter, at least in Freudian terms, does not rival the father and seek to take his place, and thus she would appear capable of expressing the father's will in the world without betraying herself. She can be dutiful without reservation and without compromising either the father or herself. One could argue, of course, that the issue of whether a son or daughter defends Montaigne is moot since it was already resolved by the historical role played by Marie de Gournay. But it is also true, as I have suggested, that Marie de Gournay is in a real sense Montaigne's textual creation and that, without what is written about her in "De la praesumption" and in Montaigne's public praise, this "Marie de Gournay" could not have been. Life does imitate art, and in the dynamics of what I have called sponsorship, gender does matter. The dutiful daughter is meant to compensate for the unavoidable perversity of the son.

At least this would be the ideal, and it would explain why Montaigne designates the daughter (as gendered child) to be his spokesperson. But the status of the dutiful daughter and the role she is meant to play are fraught with paradox. Can she be child, woman, friend, and respondant? In "De l'amitié" Montaigne had ruled out the possibility of a perfect friendship with one's children, and, moreover, the slippage in that section of the essay from talk of "enfans" to "fils" to his relation to his own father confirmed the exclusion of the daughter. Women too were banned from the sacred bond, although they are acknowledged before being set aside: "D'y comparer l'affection envers les femmes, quoy qu'elle naisse de nostre choix, on ne peut, ny la loger en ce rolle" (185a) ("To compare this brotherly affection with affection for women, even though it is the result of our choice—it cannot be done; nor can we put the love of women in the same category" [137]). But Marie de Gournay escapes the bland indifference with which daughters—and Montaigne's natural daughter, in particular—were traditionally treated, and she escapes the restrictions put on friendship as well. But at a price, I would claim. Montaigne reminds the reader twice in "De la praesumption" that Marie de Gournay is a young woman, but in each case his comments suggest that his "fille d'alliance" is more (or less) than a woman. When Montaigne insists that it is remarkable that a woman has understood the *Essais* so well, the implication is that Marie de Gournay has indeed read like a man: "Le jugement qu'elle fit des premiers Essays, et femme, et en ce siecle, et si jeune, et seule en son quartier. . . ." And when he praises her nobility, her virtue, and the quality of her judgment, he honors her with traditional masculine traits that entitle her to the privilege of male friendship that obviously no woman could have enjoyed before: "la perfection de cette tres-saincte amitié où nous ne lisons point que son sexe ait peu monter encores." In the oxymoronic conjunction of daughter / woman and friend, in this "foolish" figure that implies that a woman can also be a man, Marie de Gournay acquires the "masculine" credentials that qualify her to speak in Montaigne's absence.

Is there a place for the feminine that does not disappear in masculine appropriation? Can the woman be a friend without also being a man? Can the daughter fulfill her duty to the father without also becoming a son, without becoming an active voice who also speaks for herself, promotes herself in her own name, and thus in some way betrays the father? The story of Marie de Gournay provides an occasion for examining these complex questions of gender. Here, as I begin that story in my reading of Montaigne's presentation of his "fille d'alliance," we meet Marie de Gournay in her adolescence at a time when she is not yet the person she is destined by the writing to become. At this point Marie de Gournay remains silent. Montaigne speaks for her and about her ("J'ay pris plaisir à publier en plusieurs lieux l'esperance que j'ay de Marie de Gournay le Jars"), inscribing her in his text as his "fille d'alliance," bound to him by their covenant and a part of his being. But my reading reveals that the covenant is formed in anticipation of the voice she will assume when the promise of her youth is realized. Or perhaps I might say that the covenant is formed in order to allow Marie de Gournay to speak, and to speak in a certain way, when that promise is realized, after Montaigne is dead. When Montaigne deletes the passage cited earlier from the 1588 version of "De la vanité" he stifles *his* own voice on the subject of his "respondant" and provides the silent space within which Marie de Gournay will be able to speak in *her* own voice.

I should continue to emphasize, however, that "speaking in her own voice" in the context of the *Essais* means that Marie de Gournay will speak for Montaigne. In the absence of the son and the (male) friend, where the writer and his text stand alone together, and where the text as child of the mind will soon stand all alone, Marie de Gournay comes from the outside, and as Montaigne narrates it she is drawn to him in a way that the writing makes necessary and natural: virtue recognizes itself in virtue, judgment in judgment, the aspiring intellectual finds the famous author, the promise of youth responds to the fulfillment of maturity. This is an affirmation of Montaigne, of who and what he is, and what he is here, among the other things I mentioned, is the father (figure) sought by the adolescent girl, the friend of she who one day will be capable of that sacred friendship. Thus, a solemn alliance is formed and inscribed, doubly bonded in family and friendship, a covenant that is also an exchange. Montaigne gives Marie de Gournay his name as father and his protection; he gives voice to her promise and accords her status by his praise; and he admits her—in the future—to the sacred bonds of friendship, allowing her to achieve what no woman has yet achieved. In return, as the gesture of deletion allows—and as subsequent history has revealed—Marie de Gournay will become more than a figure in Montaigne's text; she will become the literal "respondant," the friend who in her turn gives voice to protect the father, the writer, and his text, who returns the pledge of friendship and fulfills the promise of the covenant. In the complex and paradoxical rhetoric of Montaigne's praise of Marie de Gournay, the most faithful friend is a woman, the most dutiful son a daughter.

·   ·   ·   ·   ·   ·   ·

One could argue, persuasively at this point, I believe, that in spite of this elevation or "liberation" of Marie de Gournay, Montaigne has dominated his "daughter" and forced her to do his bidding, and that even the voice she will attain, and that I have called her own historical voice, derives exclusively from him and is in a certain sense an extension of him. As if the essayist were going to practice a kind of ventriloquy from beyond the grave, where Marie de Gournay would merely mouth the words the father intended, like a kind of alter ego well ensconced within a traditional patriarchal order. Or one might say, with more or less the same result but from the perspective of the textual dimension of the problem, that Marie de Gournay derives from the dominant rhetorical and thematic dynamic of the text, that she is a figure who serves the norms and values expressed in and as Montaigne's text, an element in the discursive network of children and friends meant to carry on in the absence of the father/friend. Marie de Gournay thus fulfills her role in the *Essais* as "fille d'alliance," one might add, just as all the other historical and literary personages (or offspring) play theirs, even Socrates and La Boétie himself. In either case the autonomy and integrity of the feminine voice is compromised, subordinated as it has been historically to (and within) the dominant masculine discourse.

But only if the discussion ends here. This picture changes radically when I assume that the passage at the end of "De la praesumption" was written by Marie de Gournay herself and inserted in the 1595 edition after Montaigne's death. In this reading she is no longer Montaigne's creation, or his creature, but her own, no longer a daughter to whom the father (alone) has given birth but a writer who has engendered herself as daughter, who has projected her own image and inscribed her own being in the text of the father. The essayist does not speak for and about the passive, silent daughter; rather, the active feminine voice usurps that of the father to speak in his name and writes herself into the family, the father's being, the book.

One might claim that only the father's death allows this bold, unauthorized action, that Marie de Gournay would not have dared to threaten the father and to displace him in his presence. But paternal authority extends beyond the grave; one always runs the risk of being an insurgent, of contravening the father's will, even when one is only confronting his memory. Moreover, in this case authority maintains a concrete presence, embodied in the (male) child/text of the mind that transmits the paternal indefinitely into the future. Marie's intrusion into the *Essais* challenges the place of the father and of the son as well; she breaches the order of masculine succession by inserting herself as the legitimate heir and friend and by anticipating her future role as defender of paternal intention and meaning.

I have expressly chosen the active metaphors of breaching and intruding to characterize the force and willfulness of Marie de Gournay's gesture and to represent her seizure of a traditional male prerogative. Here again, one might say, the daughter also seems to be a son. She herself will articulate this same strength of purpose and design in the intensity of her accounts of her first contact with the *Essais* and of her desire to meet and to know Montaigne. At the same time we recognize that the challenge takes place indirectly, that she writes herself into the role of dutiful daughter and speaks in the guise of the father's own voice and consistent with his style, both textual and personal. We might want to say that at this stage Marie de Gournay is a ghost writer, one who writes for and in the name of another and that she is not yet what can be called an autonomous speaking or writing subject. She enacts here the appropriation of masculine discourse that Hélène Cixous has expressed by the verb *voler* (to steal the discourse, to fly beyond it) and that represents for her the first stage of feminine writing.[3] The passage in "De la praesumption' is a presumptuous theft of Montaigne's voice and counterfeit of his writing, but it is also a subterfuge. Reacting to the muffling and marginalizing of the feminine voice in the sixteenth century, and in the *Essais*, the voice of indirection attains a covert, muted, and masked presence. This then is a "ghostly" presence, transparent yet palpable, seen yet absent. And Marie de Gournay's gesture is presumptuous in yet another way, for to presume is to take in advance, to speak or to act in anticipation of the future. Although not yet willing (or able) because of personal, social, or political reasons to write in her own name, Marie de Gournay opens the way for herself to *become* a writer by positioning herself to fulfill (usurp) the traditional roles of the son and of the friend.

In this second reading, "Montaigne's" textual praise of Marie de Gournay in "De la praesumption" and the privileged status it accords her as "fille d'alliance" becomes an aegis, a historical shield, under which she can begin her long career as writer and as editor, novelist, poet, translator, literary critic, autobiographer, and feminist. The fact that these words inscribed in the essay authorize her to speak in her own name and lend authority to her writing might be reason enough to suppose that Marie de Gournay added the passage to Montaigne's essay, precisely at a time when she was about to publish, or had just published, her first work, "Le proumenoir de Monsieur de Montaigne par sa fille d'alliance" (1594), and while she was preparing the edition of the *Essais* that would appear in 1595 and the preface that introduced it. A young, unknown writer and a woman would benefit immeasurably from the association, as she reveals by repeating Montaigne's name in her titles and by identifying herself as his covenant daughter. The question of intention, though, is essentially a moot one. What interests me is rather the way in which Marie de Gournay attempts to protect the father's word and image, the *Essais*, and how that effort signals the emergence of her own word and her own emergence through her words. The "Preface sur les *Essais* de Michel Seigneur de Montaigne, par sa Fille d'Alliance" gives voice to Marie de Gournay and to the "respondant" that Montaigne feared he had lost.[4]

.   .   .   .

At the time that Madame de Montaigne sent a copy of the annotated text of the *Essais* to Marie de Gournay in 1594, contemporaries both great and small were debating the merits of the work. Scaliger scoffed at the treatment of Sebond, Lipsius lauded the essayist's practical judgment, Badius his psychological insight, and Pasquier praised Montaigne as "un autre Seneque en notre langue" while pointing to shortcomings of language and of clarity. Various lesser luminaries were shocked by Montaigne's Gasconisms, annoyed by what they considered the triviality of his self-portrait, scandalized by his sexual license and by what was read as his religious indifference.[5] The essayist had responded to the charges of obscurantism and linguistic abuse in "Sur des vers de Virgile" in his 1588 edition (III, 5, 875b), alleging that his faults were what made him himself, and he had expressed there his confidence in the integrity of his portrait, "tout le monde me reconnoit en mon livre, et mon livre en moy" ("everyone recognizes me in my book, and my book in me" [667]). But controversy about his "vraye image" persisted. Marie writes her "Preface" to respond to what she calls the "censeurs" and "mépriseurs," the misreaders and the misrepresenters, and she responds as well to the call for a friend, "O un amy," the call to s/he who will respond.[6]

Filial duty and friendship (can the two be separated out in this case?) motivate the daughter's desire to defend the father, but what right does she have to speak, either to speak for the father or to speak on her own? Marie de Gournay is a daughter who is not even a daughter, a daughter whose honorific status as "daughter" is as much a Renaissance commonplace as it is a sacred covenant; she is a woman friend who cannot be a friend, a woman who aspires to a friendship that Montaigne himself admits cannot admit of women. And now she desires to be a writer and a reader in a world in which men alone count as writers and readers. To write a preface to the *Essais*, to introduce the edition and its author to their readership, to justify and explain what Montaigne has said, this demands that Marie de Gournay introduce herself, that she justify not only *what* she writes but *that* she writes. A son, a male friend, would have taken on the mantle of authorship as a legitimate, natural right of inheritance in the transmission of authority from male to male. Montaigne did not have to justify writing about his natural or intellectual fathers or about La Boétie. Marie de Gournay must claim authorship, she must appropriate it, guard and defend it.

In the preface to the posthumous edition of the *Essais*, the complex relation between daughter/friend and father that I have been describing and the tensions that inhere in it both structure the writing and constitute its content. Because Marie de Gournay cannot defend Montaigne without defending herself, her discourse must constantly reflect upon itself, it must double back to speak up for the right to speak.[7] In this sometimes dizzying play of mirrors, discourse and metadiscourse generate and reflect each other just as the father engenders the covenant daughter and the daughter as writer and the daughter in her turn originates the father's true image and meaning and her own as well. The form is unorthodox, unclassical. The nascent voice of the feminine, and, I should say, the insurgent voice proclaiming its right to be heard, articulates itself as the complex subject matters and multiple discursive voices, the abrupt shifts in perspective and sharp transitions, the unapologetic tone. All these elements constitute what has long been regarded as a perverse, or false, rhetoric, as if this illegitimate and unsanctioned mode of expression posed a threat to order—social and political as well as aesthetic and rhetorical—that needed to be stifled. We should not be surprised that contemporary writers mocked Marie de Gournay and that even Montaigne's elevating praise could not place her above ridicule. Where gender alone could determine what she would call "le crédit d'en estre creu, ou pour le moins escouté" ("the credit one has to be believed, or at least heard"), a determined woman writer directly confronted the reproach, and the sarcasm, of the dismissive "c'est une femme qui parle" (27).[8]

Marie de Gournay's design is, in part, to set Montaigne beyond reproach, to situate him outside the critical grasp of a public unequal to his genius, or to his virtue, and to authorize her own voice through strategies of association and resemblance. Whether the vulgar readers criticize or praise the *Essais* is moot: "qu'est-ce donc que le dire de la commune?" ("Of what value is the opinion of the common herd?"). Montaigne's text is inherently worthy, and its value is underscored by the positive judgment of a man of learning like Justus Lipsius. And the appraisal of this great scholar corroborates Marie de Gournay's own reaction, it authenticates her natural, spontaneous response to her first reading of the *Essais*—"ils me transsissoient d'admiration" (24) ("I was transfixed with admiration")—and it provides the cover for her defense of the text on intellectual grounds. By the complex logic of mutually reflecting worth (Justus Lipsius is a worthy man who recognizes the intrinsic worth of the essays; he is also worthy *because* he recognizes their worth; Marie de Gournay recognizes their worth as well; she is thus doubly a woman of worth), Marie de Gournay attempts to situate herself in the charmed circle of authentic readers and to participate in their privileged insight and authority. "C'est de telles ames," she says, "qu'il fault souhaitter la ressemblance et la bonne opinion" (25) ("We must seek to resemble such minds and desire their good opinion").

Genealogy also bestows privilege in the "Preface." The title of the introduction identifies its author not by name but as Montaigne's "fille d'alliance," and on at least nine occasions she refers to the essayist not by his name but as "mon père." These honorific titles may be Renaissance commonplaces, but they acquire uncommon significance in this case where Marie de Gournay derives her identity, her being, her self from them: "Je ne suis moy-mesme que par où je suis sa fille" (25) ("I am only myself insofar as I am his daughter"). I will have to come back to this extraordinary self-subordination on the part of a woman insisting on the right to speak in her own voice. For the moment I want to emphasize the rhetorical advantage of this filiation that assures both intimacy and empathy. Marie de Gournay's ecstatic reaction to her discovery of the *Essais* and her intense desire to meet Montaigne ("apres qu'ils [les *Essais*] m'eurent fait souhaitter deux ans cette sienne rencontre, avec la vehemente solicitude que plusieurs ont cognue" [24]; ["after having made me want to meet him for two years, with the intense desire many knew of"]) compose a story told in Montaigne's pages and retold numerous times. Here in the "Preface" they are inscribed as the history that foretells the forging of the family link and the ultimate fulfillment of filial obligation in the defense of the father.

From within the family, in the name of the father, the daughter presumes to speak, to interpret his intention ("je te dirois qu'il a pensé" [23]), and to express his meaning ("Je te diray que la faveur dont il parle n'est pas celle" [24]), even and especially about his most personal religious attitude, which the writing may not entirely clarify: "C'est à moy d'en parler; car moy seulle avois la parfaicte cognoissance de cette grande ame, et c'est à moy d'en estre creue de bonne foy, quand ce livre ne l'esclairciroit pas. . . . Je dis donc avec verité certaine que . . . " (34) ("It is my place to speak of it: I alone had perfect knowledge of that great mind and I alone can be believed in good faith, when this book does not clarify it . . . I say then in absolute truth that . . . "). In the juxtaposition of the "I" that speaks and the "he" that is spoken for, the daughter's voice repeats and supplements that of the absent father, because their thoughts and their souls were one. Reading Montaigne, and rereading him as she prepares her edition, Marie de Gournay finds herself in him and finds him in herself:

Et parce que mon ame n'a de sa part autre maniement que celuy de juger et raisonner de ceste sorte [like Montaigne], la nature m'ayant faict tant d'honneur que, sauf le plus et le moings, j'estois toute semblable à mon Pere, je ne puis faire un pas, soit escrivant ou parlant, que je ne me trouve sur ses traces; et croy qu'on cuide souvent que je l'usurpe. Et le seule contentement que j'euz oncques de moy-mesme, c'est d'avoir rencontré plusieurs choses parmy les dernieres additions que tu verras en ce volume, lesquelles j'avois imaginées toute pareilles, avant que les avoir veues. (45–46)

"And because my mind, for its part, has no other way of working than to judge and to reason in that way (i.e., like Montaigne), nature having bestowed such honor on me that, except in the smallest and greatest things, I completely resemble my Father, I cannot take a step, either in writing or speaking, where I do not find myself following in his footsteps; and I think that people often believe that I am usurping his place. And the only satisfaction that I have ever had has been to find among these last additions that you will see in the present volume several things that I had thought myself, before having seen them there."

Marie de Gournay naturalizes the resemblance ("nature m'ayant faict tant d'honneur") as if to lend to her covenantal relation with her "father" the profound and mysterious identity that nature passes to future generations in the seed that the essayist evokes in "De la ressemblance des enfans aux peres." There Montaigne's legacy of resemblance was bequeathed to the son, although not unequivocally so, as my discussion revealed; here the daughter appropriates it and inscribes it as her own.

The echoes of that other "he" and "I," Montaigne and La Boétie, and of the perfect knowledge each had of the other, reverberate through this presentation of unity and resemblance, sounding another aspect of Marie de Gournay's genealogy. My discussion of that passage of disputed authorship in "De la praesumption" indicated that in a real sense Marie de Gournay is as much the descendant of La Boétie as she is Montaigne's offspring. Here in the "Preface," with barely a mention of the name of the revered friend (and perhaps in this way making him all the more present), she takes the place of this other "father." La Boétie survives in the person of the daughter as the perfect friend; this time he could be said to survive Montaigne and to keep him, in his turn, from being torn into a thousand faces: "Il ne m'a duré que quatre ans," she writes, "non plus qu'à luy la Boetie" (51).

In a sense Marie de Gournay rewrites Montaigne's essay "De l'amitié" as her "Preface," she writes herself into that long tradition of essays on friendship that reaches back to Aristotle and to Cicero, appropriating the father's voice, and his role, and making them her own. Drawing from Montaigne's paean to male friendship, she turns its conceptual framework to her own ends so that it serves the writer of genius maligned by his public, and the daughter who would speak on his behalf. The force of resemblance that bound Montaigne and La Boétie—expressed in "De l'amitié" by such terms as *correspondance, communication, concorde, convenance, conference, couture*—here becomes the agency that draws the "grand esprit" toward "un pareil," "un semblable." Marie de Gournay is, of course, talking about the ideal relationship between writer and reader, between Montaigne and his public, and, most central, between the essayist and herself as reader, and her goals are to protect the "grand esprit" from the judgment of those unequal to him and, by extension, to authenticate the judgment of those like herself who recognize greatness. We saw this strategy operating earlier in what I referred to as the logic of mutual worth. But even more is at stake here. When Marie de Gournay defines friendship as movement toward a kindred soul, and movement as the source of being (recalling Montaigne's words in "De l'affection des peres aux enfans": "estre consiste en mouvement et action" [II, 8, 386c]), she locates the sense of self in the impulse toward union with the other. "Les grands esprits," she claims, "sont desireux, amoureux, et affolez des grands esprits: comme tenans leur estre du mouvement, et leur prime mouvement de la rencontre d'un pareil" (47) ("Great minds desire, are in love with, are mad about other great minds; as if their being derives from movement, and their primary movement from meeting an equal"). This is, of course, the paradoxical other of friendship, the other who is not other but another oneself, in whom the self both loses and finds itself.

The fulfillment of the writing act, like the realization of friendship, is a merging of understanding, a life-giving union that is predisposed, predetermined, waiting to happen. The "grands esprits . . . desireux, amoureux, et affolez des grands esprits" move toward the object of desire, open themselves up in order to make themselves known, seek to couple in that fusion of self and other from which the sense of being derives. In the self-reflecting grammar of the "grands esprits" as both subject and object, where the disparity of self and other is already overcome, writer and reader, friend and friend (the two pairs are purposely interchangeable in the "Preface") meet in this markedly narcissistic act whose sexual undertones are unmistakable, as if the spiritual union must be concretized, materialized, eroticized (as it so often is in religious and especially mystical discourse) in order to be expressed, communicated. On its own the self clearly cannot know itself in any absolute way, nor can it be the sole source of its being; if it could, it would not have to write or yearn after a friend. But the self can desire and seek that which is most like itself; it must, if it is to be a "self," look to meet another itself, in order to complete itself and to experience the ecstasy of being.

Paradoxically, friendship and reading—as they are constituted both by Montaigne and Marie de Gournay—are not the present participation in this union or in the fullness of being but are their aftermath, the experience of separation and of absence, of rupture and of deprivation. In effect, to be a friend or a reader in the context of the *Essais* and of the "Preface" is to function in the void of loss and of nonpresence, to confront traces inscribed in memory or the signs marked as textuality (is there a fundamental difference?), in a word, to be forced to remember, to reconstitute, to resurrect what has been lost. And what has been lost is not only the missing other for whom one has become the "respondant," the dead friend / author who can no longer speak for himself, but one's own self that is now also missing. Like the isolation and anonymity that precedes "la rencontre d'un pareil," the desolation that follows the death of the kindred soul is provoked by being only half of what one is. Montaigne had written in "De l'amitié," "J'estois desjà si fait et accoustumé à estre deuxiesme par tout, qu'il me semble n'estre plus qu'à demy" (I, 28, 193a) ("I was already so formed and accustomed to being a second self everywhere that only half of me seems to be alive now" [143]). Marie de Gournay rewrites this experience of cleavage in the "Preface": "Estre seul, c'est n'estre que demy. Mais combien est encore plus miserable celuy qui demeure demy soy-mesme, pour avoir perdu l'autre part, qu'à faute de l'avoir rencontré!" (47) ("To be alone is to be only half alive. But how more miserable is s / he who remains only half alive for having lost the other half than for never having met it").

And yet the writing that articulates the experience of rupture and of fragmentation is also meant to overcome it, to be the means by which the self recovers itself, by which it comes to know itself (as in the case of Montaigne) or to assert and be itself (as in the case of Marie de Gournay). The desire to recuperate the self in this way derives from the convictions that writing incorporates the self into the text ("tout mouvement nous descouvre," Montaigne says [I, 50, 302]) and that reading can derive it there. In Marie de Gournay's (feminine) version of "De l'amitié" she inscribes friendship as the origin, the mother of being, that friendship that she experiences as ideal reading and that is also the mother of both writer and reader. The sense of her own selfhood that she earlier ascribed to her privileged status as Montaigne's daughter can now be named an effect of her friendship with the essayist, the paradoxical consequence of its loss, and, most profound, the effect and consequence of Marie de Gournay's own textual formulation and expression.

In her account of the movement that propels writer and reader toward each other, in the *communication, concorde, convenance,* and *correspondance* (to repeat Montaigne's lexicon of friendship) that results from their conjunction, Marie de Gournay discovers herself as *un semblable, un pareil,* and she discovers as well her role, and the role of all serious readers, in the regeneration of the writer. Writing must be a public act through which the writer makes him/herself known, through which s/he bears witness to what s/he is to a worthy reader, a reader who is him/herself "capable de le gouster," "un homme de bien" (48), "un grand tesmoing" (49). For Marie de Gournay, as for Montaigne before her, to be wholly private, or to be unknown, or to be known by those incapable of truly knowing is not to be at all. In a sense, it is to be dead: "Estre incogneu c'est aucunement n'estre pas; car estre se refere à l'agir; et n'est point, ce semble, d'agir parfaict, vers qui n'est pas capable de le gouster" (48) ("To be unknown is essentially not to exist; for being refers to acting, and it seems as if action cannot be perfect if it inclines toward one who is incapable of savoring it"). After the death of the writer/friend, Marie de Gournay, again like Montaigne, having been a reader comes to her own vocation as writer. Or perhaps we should say that it is through the writing that she both seeks and enacts her vocation, that writing in her own voice is both the call (Latin *vocare*) to selfhood and its response. Having been a witness to the other, having allowed that other "to be," Marie now bears witness to herself, she acknowledges and realizes herself.

．　　．　　．　　．　　．　　．　　．

Marie de Gournay thus writes to perform her coming into being as a reader/writer, her "coming out" of anonymity by making herself known. This is the story that she narrates as the subject matter of her text, the story that tells of her active role in the desiring, loving, infatuated pursuit of Montaigne (where she embodies the "grand esprit" pursuing what in the equation of resemblance is *her* "pareil"), the story that recounts and announces the emergence on the public stage of Marie de Gournay the editor of the *Essais,* the writer of this "Preface," the daughter, the friend, the "semblable" of Montaigne. A story to be read, a persona, a self, to be witnessed, acknowledged, known, and brought to life in its turn by a kindred spirit. But there is a disconcerting aporia within this narrative of the self-assured public presentation of self. Speaking of the "sage" who languishes (dies?) if a worthy man does not witness the purity of his conscience, Marie de Gournay adds, "La cognoissance de cette chetifve condition humaine, ne luy permettant pas aussi de s'asseurer ny qu'il face ny qu'il juge bien sans l'approbation d'un grand tesmoing, l'oblige à desirer un surveillant" (49) ("The knowledge of this pitiful human condition, which does not allow him the assurance that he does well or judges well without the approval of an illustrious witness, obliges him to desire that someone observe him"). The disturbing element is the need for the "approbation" of the other, the praise or approval that reassures the self that it is what it takes itself to be or what it has made itself out to be. Going public may initiate the experience of being, as we saw above; it must also confirm one's own self-image. But can it be that virtue does not recognize itself, does not or cannot authenticate itself? Or that moral action or judgment is not sufficient in itself, or does not announce itself for what it is? Marie de Gournay blames the weak and pitiful state of the human condition for what appears to be the impossibility of self-knowledge, even the knowledge that one is virtuous or engaged in moral action. All knowledge, it would appear, must be mediated by the other, all sense of oneself, moral as well as psychological (and, I should add, ontological), is determined by the sanction of the other and must be read in his words, his gaze.

But can one be confident of the meaning of those words or the significance of the gaze? Why should "reading" the other be any less problematical than knowing one's own action or judgment? Can "cette chetifve condition humaine" avoid contaminating the relation between self and other? And what does it mean to make *approval* (for "approbation" is approval as well as confirmation, sanction) from the other the basis of one's sense of self? Marie de Gournay does not explore the disquieting implications of her own discourse. For rhetorical and individual ends she treats friendship and the community of worthy souls as if they were immune from any undermining uncertainty or instability.

Montaigne too had privileged true friendship as the source of being and of self-knowledge, but while Marie de Gournay's formulation draws from a common lexicon it appears to engage a different personal, social, and historical dynamic. Where Montaigne the father depicted a unique and irreplaceable relationship, "si entiere et si parfaite que certainement il ne s'en lit guiere de pareilles, et, entre nos hommes, il ne s'en voit aucune trace en usage" (I, 28, 184a) ("so entire and so perfect that certainly you will hardly read of the like, and among men of today you see no trace of it in practice" [136]), the daughter extends the possibility and the hope to every meeting of great and worthy minds. Under the right conditions every reading encounter might perform the functions of friendship. While the plaintive cry for a friend, "O un amy," reverberates in the *Essais*, the writing becomes Montaigne's response to the absence of both other and self. The text enacts both an opening out and a turning back upon itself, both the desire for friendship and the statement of its impossibility (we recall the paradoxical "O mes amis, il n'y a nul amy"), and it provides the compensatory means by which the self becomes its own friend ("son plus proche et plus amy, sçavoir est soy mesme" [II, 3, 353c]). In Marie de Gournay's preface, by contrast, the writing both expresses and performs the insistent and unending desire for the other in friendship, and it is meant to be its active mediator. The intensity of need that originally impelled her toward the essayist now expresses itself after his death in the broad, thinly veiled appeal to her own readers. The irreparable loss of the friend left Montaigne in epistemological and ontological uncertainty, with needs that might be called broadly psychic, intellectual, and spiritual. The daughter experiences similar needs, but her references to reassurance and to approbation betray above all an uncertainty and an insecurity that are both deeply personal and social.

Marie de Gournay's program in the "Preface" and her posture appear to respond to her own experience as a woman. What we read there is the dynamic interaction of textuality and history, the complex expression of an active feminine self emerging to assert itself and its right to speak at the same time as it expresses its desire for the reassurance of male authority. The daughter who has boldly transgressed traditional patterns of female behavior, who has educated herself, ventured out into public as a professional writer, and dared to challenge male intellectuals on equal footing, this daughter who gives voice to her own aspirations also looks to others, to her "father" and even to other father figures for confirmation. Marie de Gournay performs the tenuous, and double-edged, sociointellectual status of women in late Renaissance France. There was much in her personal and public experience that could have undermined her confidence; throughout her life attacks in satires and caricatures of her person and her writings that could have made her long for the support and reassurance of the "grands esprits." In her private relationship with

Montaigne (or in the relationship she *inscribed* with Montaigne), she sought and discovered the generous father figure who sanctioned the activity she claimed for her own. In her public expression she in turn posited a generous, open, and accessible friendship based on equality and resemblance, a friendship that invited her readers into a mutually supporting union. But we recognize as well, in the need for this friendship and the approval it confers, the residue of dependence and subordination and the traces (or scars) of the paternal hierarchy it seeks to escape.

.   .   .   .

The "Preface" thus reaches out to the worthy reader in the intense desire and uncertain anticipation of friendship while boldly asserting its defense of Montaigne and the vigorous fulfillment of that originary friendship. The dutiful daughter who needs reassurance from others now that the legitimizing father is dead speaks forcefully in her own name to protect him. Even the preparation of manuscript copy, Montaigne's literal word, requires the guardian's watchful eye. In the closing pages of her "Preface" Marie de Gournay addresses the editorial work that must be carried out if the text is to represent its author faithfully. The task is not an easy one, especially in the case of posthumous editions, and particularly in the case of the *Essais:* "outre la naturelle difficulté de correction qui se void aux *Essays,* ceste copie en avoit tant d'autres que ce n'estoit pas legere entreprise que la bien lire, et garder que telle difficulté n'apportast ou quelque entente fauce, ou transposition, ou des obmissions" (53) ("besides the natural difficulty of correction in the *Essays,* this edition had so many others that it was not a simple task to read it properly, and to be sure that any given difficulty not bring about misunderstanding, or cause transpositions, or omissions"). Whether she is referring to the vagaries of sixteenth-century French grammatical practice evident in Montaigne's text—varied spelling, the inconsistent use of subject pronouns, unevenness of verb forms, syntactical variety—or alluding to the essayist's corrections, emendations, and additions in the margins and on separate slips of paper, or to his sometimes dense and complex style, the issue is the same: textual integrity and the author's meaning are always open to misreading and misrepresentation. Before the book ever makes its way out in public, and exposes itself brazenly and knowingly to a readership anonymous and removed, it runs the risk of distortion at the hand of its editors, even when they are diligent and sympathetic: "non pas seulement la vigilance des Imprimeurs, . . . mais encore le plus esveillé soing que les amys ayent accoustumé d'y rendre, n'y pouvoit suffire" (52) ("Not only the vigilance of the printers . . . but also the most careful attention that friends were accustomed to pay to it, could not suffice").

No common professional concern of the printer / publisher, and no concern of the common friend, will suffice. To explain the unusual soundness of Montaigne's text, and its public success in the past, Marie de Gournay evokes the presence of a guardian angel: "quelque bon Ange a monstré qu'il l'estimoit digne de particuliere faveur" (52) ("a friendly angel has shown that it deems him worthy of special favor"). The reference is not entirely playful, or metaphorical, for the dangers of what she calls "la miserable incorrection," the risk that the printing will betray the text of the manuscript, are real. This time she herself will be the uncommon guarantor, the "tuteur" (from *tutus,* past participle of *tueri,* to watch, protect, guard): "Somme, apres que j'ay dict qu'il luy falloit un bon tuteur, j'ose me vanter qu'il ne luy en falloit, pour son bien, nul autre que moy, mon affection suppleant à mon incapacité" (53) ("In all, after having said that he needed a good tutor, I dare boast that, for his welfare he needed only me; my affection makes up for my shortcomings"). "Nul autre que moy": no one else is needed to protect Montaigne, but Marie de Gournay's preface also implies that she alone can protect him. In the mysterious bond of perfect friendship that transcends rupture and absence, and in the affection that this "enfant" expresses for her "père," (a love that responds to and requites the paternal affection of Montaigne's "De l'affection des peres aux enfans" [II, 8]), the will of the father and his word survive intact. Even where Montaigne's writing might have left itself open to editorial revision, even where it was in Marie de Gournay's words, "corrigeable," she has bowed to both will and word, to the weight of paternal authority, as it was accessible to the privileged friend and daughter: "soubs ceste seulle consideration que celuy qui le voulut ainsin estoit Pere, et qu'il estoit Montaigne" (53) ("only because the one who wished it so was the Father, and he was Montaigne").

"Il ne luy en falloit, pour son bien, nul autre que moy" ("For his welfare he needed only me"); yet Marie de Gournay is not entirely alone, either in her defense of the *Essais* or in the preparation of the

1595 edition. From the pages of the "Preface" emerges a small band of supporters who admire and sustain Montaigne and Marie de Gournay herself and whom she generously acknowledges: Lipsius, equal to the task, who has opened "les portes de louange aux *Essais*" ("the gates of praise"); Pierre de Brach, whose editorial concern earns him the name of "bon amy"; and, most significant, Mme de Montaigne. The *Essais,* as we know, relegate Mme de Montaigne to the outermost margins of the writing, a "woman's" place, but also the place created by Montaigne's introspective turn toward the self, as he explains in "De la solitude": "Il se faut reserver une arriere-boutique toute nostre, . . . en cette-cy faut-il prendre nostre ordinaire entretien de nous à nous mesmes, et si privé que nulle acointance ou communication estrangiere y trouve place; discourir et y rire comme sans femme, sans enfans et sans biens" (I, 38, 241a) ("We must re-serve a back shop all our own, entirely free, in which to establish our real liberty and our principal retreat and solitude. Here our ordinary conversation must be between us and ourselves, and so private that no outside association or communication can find a place; here we must talk and laugh as if without wife, children, without posses-sions, without retinue and servants" [177]). Only four times in his text does the essayist mention "ma femme," each a passing reference, and once to comment that he might have preferred to produce a perfectly formed child by intercourse with the muses rather than by intercourse with his wife (II, 8, 401b). For her part, Marie de Gournay recuperates Mme de Montaigne from the oblivion to which the *Essais* (and traditional, male-dominated history) had consigned her: she inscribes her in the "Preface" and restores to her a central place as Montaigne's wife and as a figure in Marie de Gournay's own geneal-ogy and in that of the edition itself.

In a very real sense, Michel de Montaigne and his wife, Françoise de la Chassaigne, are more than the spiritual parents of Marie de Gournay. Her natural father died when she was nine or ten years old, and her mother, as she recounts the story in her various autobio-graphical writings, opposed her efforts to acquire an education and intended either that she marry or enter a convent. Montaigne re-places the absent father, and, in terms that are perhaps more than metaphorical, one might say that the essayist fathers Marie de Gour-nay as a writer. She repeatedly indicates that the experience of first reading the *Essais* and her early meetings with Montaigne signal her coming of age and the discovery of her vocation. And after the death of the covenant father, Mme de Montaigne in her turn becomes a substitute parent and "mothers" Marie de Gournay, conceiving her as editor of the annotated manuscript of the *Essais* and inaugurating her lifework as "tuteur" for Montaigne. While the choices offered by her natural mother (as Marie de Gournay tells the story) are bound by the traditionally female world of the body and physical reproduction—its exclusion in the convent and its exclusivity in marriage—her substitute mother opens the way to the traditionally male world of the mind and to cultural production.

Marie de Gournay, for her part, restores Montaigne to life as father (both as her father and as the father of his text), and she can be said to generate Mme de Montaigne as well, or, perhaps more correctly, to regenerate her, to bring her back through her story out of silence into history. In the narrative of the publication that the "Preface" recounts, Montaigne's wife fulfills what is called "les offices d'une tres ardente amour conjugale" (25), she ensures the integrity of her husband's text and his reputation by dutifully collecting and noting the corrections and additions to the "exemplaire de Bordeaux" and by ushering the text toward its appearance in print. As Marie de Gournay tells it, Mme de Montaigne cannot be simply forgotten or dismissed, for the whole region has witnessed her devotion: "Elle a tout son pays pour tesmoing." And the daughter herself testifies as witness, here in print and in public, to Mme de Montaigne's presence as dutiful wife: "Je puis tesmoigner en verité, pour le particulier de ce livre, que son maistre mesme n'en eust jamais eu tant de soing, et plus considerable, de ce qu'il r'encontroit en saison, en laquelle la langueur, où les pleurs et les douleurs de sa perte l'avoient precipitée, l'en eust peu justement et decemment dispenser" (25) ("I can truthfully testify, in the particular case of this book, that even her master could not have brought to it as much care, and the most considerable care, as it received at a time when her languor, into which her tears and the pain of her loss had precipitated her, could justly and decently have exempted her"). In a sense, the dutiful wife reclaims *her* rightful place as her husband's guarantor and thus allows the daughter (*her* right) to be dutiful. Mme de Montaigne's presence also guarantees that the daughter remains a daughter, that her charged expressions of passion and desire, her talk of being one with Montaigne, are not misconstrued, that Marie de Gournay herself is not mistaken for the wife.

The return to history of Mme de Montaigne is thus not without paradox, for it could be said that she returns not in her own right and not to her own history. Mme de Montaigne returns as wife to Montaigne's history (and thus does not escape the domination of the husband), and she returns as well to Marie de Gournay's history (and thus does not escape the domination of the daughter). In fact, in Marie de Gournay's paean to her benefactress, in the text through which "this" Mme de Montaigne comes into the world, she praises the essayist's wife not for being what she is but for becoming what her husband was:

> Chaqu'un luy doibt, sinon autant de graces, au moins autant de louanges que je faiz: d'avoir voulu r'embrasser et r'échauffer en moy les cendres de son mary, et non pas l'espouser mais se rendre une autre luy-mesme, ressuscitant en elle à son trespas une affection où jamais elle n'avoit participé que par les oreilles, voire luy restituer un nouvel image de vie par la continuation de l'amitié qu'il me portait. (26)

> Everyone owes her, if not as much gratitude, at least as much praise as I: to have wanted to embrace again and to rekindle in [through] me the ashes of her husband, and not to espouse him but to make herself into another him, reviving in herself at his death an affection in which she had only participated through hearsay, in truth, to restore to him a new image of life by continuing the friendship he had borne for me.

In this long and complex sentence, Mme de Montaigne takes Montaigne's place for her own but does not displace him. She is there as a forceful subject (expressed in the active verbs *r'embrasser, r'échauffer, se rendre, ressusciter, restituer*), the agent of transitive actions that affect both her late husband and Marie de Gournay as objects, but it could also be said that she loses herself in transit. Mme de Montaigne revives Montaigne's presence for (in) Marie de Gournay so that it burns brightly once again. The essayist's ashes and the daughter who herself had become his ashes are both revived and glow anew. Mme de Montaigne reawakens in herself the friendship that had existed between father and daughter and from which she herself had been excluded; she restores to it ("luy restituer") and to each of its constituents a new vitality. But we might also want to exploit the dense prose of the sentence and "misread" Montaigne himself, "son mary," as the antecedent of "luy," for it is he who comes most prominently back to life in a new image. Montaigne comes back, we could say, in the image of Mme de Montaigne herself, who has made herself, or been transformed, into "une autre luy-mesme." The friendship is renewed but not for its own sake, just as Mme de Montaigne does not return for her own sake. Both serve to mediate Montaigne's unhoped-for resurrection.

·   ·   ·   ·   ·   ·   ·

In my discussion of textual progeny, I spoke of the author/father's desire to write himself down, to represent and thereby perpetuate himself, and of the dangers to which he exposed himself, dangers of disfigurement and misrepresentation by others, and, paradoxically, of displacement by the very offspring meant to embody him. My reading disclosed that the child (the son) has its own life, and when it begins to speak, even in support or in defense of the father, paternal authority and prominence are challenged and the father's voice displaced, muffled, even muted. This is the natural order of things, Montaigne implied in "De l'affection des peres aux enfans," in which he recognizes that the very existence of the child both demands and effects the withdrawal and the absence of the father. But the death of the father and his irresistible displacement do not alone guarantee either the autonomy of the child or the authenticity of its voice. One of the questions I have raised in this chapter is whether the situation of the child is different when she is a daughter. Does the "affiliative" status that exempts her in Freudian terms, for example, from competing with the father, or in social and legal terms from inheriting his name or his property, also exempt her from displacing him or being displaced by him? What happens to the daughter when she begins to speak for the father? When Marie de Gournay attempts to speak for Montaigne, her task is fraught with perils that are social, intellectual, personal, and textual, but none is so great as the risk to her own selfhood posed by the very act of speaking for the other.

The genealogy by which Marie de Gournay claims her identity is paradoxically the genealogy by which she risks losing it. Earlier I evoked the image of the father as ventriloquist, providing the language spoken by the offspring, even from beyond the grave, and I recalled the figure of Socrates in the *Phaedrus* condemning the textual offspring for stupidly, if faithfully, repeating the father's words in his absence. But how could the child speak otherwise and still remain a loyal surrogate for the father? At the same time, if the child is to become someone in itself, the father's wishes must be exceeded and his intentions surpassed; in a word, the child must betray the father to speak in its own name, even if the child is a daughter. This is precisely the double bind within which Marie de Gournay's 1595 "Preface" speaks for the father Montaigne and that solicits the revised prefaces that accompany her later editions of the *Essais*.

Dutifully, the daughter proceeds to defend the father, but there is something so troubling in this defense that she seeks almost immediately to disavow it. Scarcely a year after the publication of the 1595 edition, Marie de Gournay confesses her regret at having written the preface in a letter to Justus Lipsius at Louvain:

> J'ai fait une preface sur ce livre-là dont je me repens, tant à cause de ma foiblesse, mon enfantillage et l'incuriosité d'un esprit malade, que par ce aussi que ces tenebres de douleur qui m'enveloppent l'âme, on semble prendre plaisir à rendre à l'envi cette sienne conception si ténébreuse et obscure qu'on n'y peut rien entendre.[9]

> I wrote a preface for that book, of which I repent, as much because of my weakness, my childishness, and the incuriousness of a sick mind as of the darkness of that pain that enveloped my soul; people seem to take pleasure in making, to their heart's content, his own ideas so shadowy and obscure as to be totally incomprehensible.

Moreover, she entreats Lipsius to make certain that the "Preface" is not included in any publication of the *Essais* in Louvain, at least before it is "corrected."

Six months later, Marie informs Justus Lipsius that he will find eight or ten pages cut from the beginning of each of the three copies of the *Essais* that she has sent him: she has removed the preface "que je lui laissois couler en saison où ma douleur ne me permettoit ni de bien faire ni de sentir que je faisois mal" (that I allowed to slip at a time when my pain did not permit me either to do well or to sense that I was doing poorly").[10] In its place, she adds, he will find a ten-line introduction:

> LECTEUR, si je ne suis assez forte pour escrire sur les *Essais,* aumoins suis-je bien genereuse pour advouër ma foiblesse, et te confesse que je me retracte de cette Preface que l'aveuglement de mon aage et d'une violente fievre d'ame me laissa n'aguere eschaper des mains: lors qu'après le deceds de l'Autheur, Madame de Montaigne, sa femme, me les feit apporter, pour estre mis au jour enrichis des traicts de sa derniere main. Si je me renforce à l'advenir, je t'en dirai, sinon ce qu'il faudroit, aumoins ce que je pense et ce que je sçay: ou si je ne sçay rien, encore prendray-je la plume pour te prier de m'apprendre ce que

tu sçauras. Pour cette heure, dis-je, ne te donneray rien que mes
oreilles afin d'ouyr quel sera ton advis sur ce livre. Que t'en semble
donc Lecteur?

READER, if I am not strong enough to write on the *Essays,* at least I am
generous enough to admit my weakness, and I confess that I disavow
that Preface that the blindness of youth and a violent mental fever
caused me to let slip out of my hands; when, after the death of the Author, Madame de Montaigne, his wife, had them (Montaigne's MSS)
brought to me so that they could be published, enriched by the latest
additions in his hand. If I gain strength in the future, I will speak of it
(the MS), if not all that need be said, at least what I think and what I
know of it: or if I do not know anything, I will still take up the pen to
entreat you to teach me what you know. For the moment, I will only
lend you my ears so that I can hear your opinion of this book. What
do you think of this, Reader?

Just to complete the story, this preface first appeared in print in the
1598 edition and remained in successive editions until 1617 when
it was replaced with a reworked version of the original 1595 text.
Forms of that first preface accompanied the editions of 1625 and
1635; Marie de Gournay also republished it in its original state in the
third edition of her *Proumenoir de M. de Montaigne* in 1599.[11]

What explains the curious genealogy of the 1595 "Preface," its
public disavowal and removal, and its diverse reappearances? François Rigolot has suggested several possibilities: that Marie de Gournay might have realized that its naïve enthusiasm was offensive; or
she may have felt that its response to Montaigne's critics was too
strong; perhaps she sensed that her occasional "feminist" remarks
were out of place here and would be more persuasive in another
form; or finally, that by withdrawing the text and taking up its arguments elsewhere she was creating the occasion to speak in her own
name and her own voice. Marie de Gournay's own words provide a
somewhat different perspective on her vagabond preface. Without
alluding to any specific failings of her text, they condemn it in her
letter to Lipsius as the product of her weakness, her childishness, and
her grief. And, most profound, her words condemn *her,* for having
been weak and childish and for having allowed her sorrow to obscure her thoughts and make her careless. Marie de Gournay publicly confesses her fault and her guilt; she repents of her action and
attempts to redeem herself by taking back her words. This extraordinary gesture may be occasioned by the shame she feels at the effu-
siveness of her prose or the boldness of her criticism, but much more

appears to be at stake here. We might insist on asking, "Of what is Marie de Gournay guilty"?

I would argue that Marie de Gournay is guilty of having misspoken and, more serious, that she is guilty of having spoken at all. Traditionally, as the daughter she has no right to speak, even if, as in this case, the father seems to have authorized her voice in his text and again from his deathbed when he bequeaths the editorship of the *Essais* to her. The fact that as the offspring she has the obligation to speak in the name of the father, that she is destined to speak in this way, underscores the problematical situation of the child per se, but it sets in particularly bold relief the impossible position of the child as *daughter*. Marie de Gournay cannot speak, but since she must speak she can only do so as the daughter; she must draw attention to her voice and to the voice that is always identified as a woman's—because she is forced to defend it—and demand *her* right to speak as herself, as Montaigne's (intellectual) heiress. Thus, as we have seen, her discourse is always excessive, always in excess of a direct defense of the father and always "overstated" in order to make her voice heard and to give it authority. Unlike the son who does not have to justify himself, the daughter must always speak of herself as daughter when she speaks of the father, she must always center herself in her discourse merely to speak, she must make herself the subject of her discourse, even as she seeks, and speaks, only to protect the father. But like all children who speak, and even or especially those who speak to remain faithful to the father, Marie de Gournay, the woman, the daughter, irresistibly displaces the father, competes for textual space (and social and psychological space as well), rivals and betrays him.

Unless she speaks in another way, in a way that uses discourse paradoxically to deny her own right to speak. In her new preface, Marie de Gournay's confessional mea culpa and her public retraction relinquish her claim to represent the father and herself; they enact a withdrawal to the traditional role of dutiful daughter. Her language of self-condemnation, which reflects the historic condemnation of the feminine as weak, childlike, and emotional, accepts *that* feminine as her own and puts her back in her "place," the place contemporary critics reserved for her and for all women when they said that her proper role was spinning ("la quenouille").[12] A domestic rather than a public life, handiwork rather than intellectual activity, silence instead of discourse. Marie disavows the presumptuous speech of the past and attributes it to that vulnerability that is taken for woman: "I was weak, I was blinded by youth and feverish emotion, I was passive, and the preface escaped from me." She confesses in the contrite speech of the present that she spoke *when* she should not have spoken, or *what* she should not have spoken, but speaking *this* way now makes her a woman who still has no right to speak. If I grow stronger in the future, she now says to her reader, I will (have the right to) speak of what I know, or I will admit what I do not know and solicit your teaching. For now, Marie de Gournay is all ears ("ne te donneray rien que mes oreilles"), the silent and submissive (feminine) listener, passively deferring to the reader's will and to his words. Montaigne will have to speak for himself, his textual offspring, his book, will be obliged to speak for itself in the name of the father, and the reader will have the last word, speaking undeterred, unchallenged, unopposed, in the empty space of Marie de Gournay's suppressed voice and of her silence. "Que t'en semble donc Lecteur"?

This extraordinary act of self-abnegation thus redeems the dutiful daughter who would remain silent and condemns the dutiful daughter who would speak for the father. But if filial deference ensures faithfulness to the father, the reluctance to speak in his name betrays him. How can the daughter be dutiful? Only by speaking and not speaking at the same time, only by denying herself and simultaneously asserting herself as herself. Perhaps Marie de Gournay escaped some of the impossible burden of this schizophrenic bind by finding another self already split off from her in the person of Montaigne's natural daughter, Léonor, who, she says, "la chérissait plus que fraternellement."[13] Here was the daughter who remained dutifully silent, who did not challenge the father by her presence during his lifetime but was not present either to defend him after his death. In a sense then, Marie de Gournay did not have to be *that* dutiful daughter; she could be the daughter who spoke up for the father and for herself, who protected him by displacing him, and who found her proper place herself. If in the preface of 1598 she temporarily abdicates that role to become (like) Léonor, the return of the original text of the "Preface" and the history of its successive versions enact her desire, and her courageous resolve, to speak the complex discourse of the dutiful, and wilful, daughter.

3

The Imposing Text and the
Obtrusive Reader

Il n'est aucun sens ny visage . . . que l'esprit humain ne trouve aux
escrits qu'il entreprend de fouiller.

(III, 12, 585)

There is no sense or aspect . . . that the human mind does not
find in the writings it undertakes to search.

My discussion of textual children—of the text as child of the mind and
of Marie de Gournay as the child of Montaigne's text—has produced
the figure of the errant text, the work that wanders or risks wandering
off the "proper" path to fall into the error of misinterpretation. No
matter what the father says or does, no matter how strongly he in-
vokes his authorial (paternal) authority, these offspring, both the
rhetorical and the historical figures, cannot forestall the ultimate
"misreading" of the father and his intentions. Perhaps Montaigne
sought a hedge against this inevitability by restricting the readers of
his book in the prefatory "Au lecteur" to the circle of his immediate
family and friends. "Je l'ay voué à la commodité particuliere de mes
parens et amis," he says, "à ce que m'ayant perdu (ce qu'ils ont à faire
bien tost) ils y puissent retrouver aucuns traits de mes conditions et
humeurs, et que par ce moyen ils nourrissent plus entiere et plus
vifve, la connoissance qu'ils ont eu de moy" (3a) ("I have dedicated it
to the private convenience of my relatives and friends, so that when
they have lost me [as soon they must], they may recover here some
features of my habits and temperaments, and by this means keep the
knowledge they have had of me more complete and alive" [2]). The
essayist presents his portrait to those closest to him so that his memory will live on with them, but much more is at stake here. After his
death, when he will no longer be around to ensure that he is understood, only these faithful intimates who knew him best will be able to
understand him. Only because they already knew him will they be

able to recognize in his book what they already know, and this will preserve him. The book in which Montaigne speaks will speak of him, and for him, and his friends and family will not misread him. With the familiar portrait of Montaigne in their hands, this informed and faithful readership will ensure that after his death he will remain complete and, as it were, alive.

Over the past two decades interpretations of the *Essais* as Montaigne's effort to found and form a self in language have challenged the more traditional reading of the text as self-portrait. The dynamic, open-ended process of self-fashioning through writing appears incompatible with the apparently static and closed medium of portraiture. But I would argue that each of the two readings must be given its due because each represents an equally powerful *and* competing inclination operating within both reading and textuality itself. On the one hand, the notion of self-portraiture maintains a relation with what might be considered the "outside" of the text, what exists "before" writing. Whether it is called authorial intention or referentiality (the two cannot be completely disassociated), the "hors texte" could be said to give the work both its content and its form. In the self-reflexive gesture of the self-portraitist, the essayist represents himself as present to himself in his work, he poses "as himself" to impose himself as the meaning of the text. This is representation as symbol, where sign and referent are meant to be indistinguishable from each other and where the sign is invested with all the truth value of the thing itself. "Ainsi lecteur," Montaigne says in the "Au lecteur," "je suis moy-mesme la matiere de mon livre" (3) ("Thus, reader, I am myself the matter of my book" [2]). His insistence on his sincerity and on the truthfulness of his portrait are intended to guarantee that the text will be transparent, guileless, worthy of the reader's trust. This is the author's text, backed by his authority. Montaigne both signs his text and situates his writing in his farewell to the reader, "de Montaigne," and he dates it "ce premier de Mars mille cinq cens quatre vingts." At the moment of stasis, at the intersection of the axes of time and space, subjectivity imposes itself; the day after his birthday on February 28, the essayist is reborn as the subject of the text. When Montaigne affixes his name to the preface his signature fixes his identity and it identifies the work as his property, thus mirroring the act by which the property named Montaigne provided him his identity. The book will be his gift and his memorial, an icon for those close to him who will find in it the confirmation of what had already existed outside it.

On the other hand, the second reading presumes a different kind of author, a different kind of text, and a different kind of reader. The author who writes himself as the text cannot guarantee its stability, or his own, since he and his writing are always in process, under revision, continually being looked at again and recast. Rather than standing outside the text and prior to it, "Montaigne" becomes a function of the writing, his name "bracketed" to underscore its complex and problematical status as both motivator of the writing and the subject generated by it. What can be said in this context about the author's authority, intention, and meaning when the expression of this particular "self" is predicated on stripping away the delusions of authority, intention, and the dependability of meaning itself? And what can be said about form—of the writer or his text—when in structural and epistemological terms the *Essais* characterize the openness and indeterminacy of form itself. When Montaigne himself reads, his reading becomes the material within which, against which, he assays himself; he reads to rewrite the texts of others, to write himself into them, and to distinguish himself from them. The authority and intent of others must be bent to his own ends, *their* meaning transformed and their "portraits" disfigured, defaced, if they are to serve him. The violent uprooting that characterizes Montaigne's practice of quotation, its fragmenting effect, and its distortion of context and "meaning" emblematize this type of reading / writing.[1] Such a practice can only serve as an open invitation to *his* readers to rewrite the *Essais* as *their* own texts, to read and write against Montaigne's portrait.

Insofar as the "Au lecteur" inscribes a sympathetic and acquiescent reader, a family member or friend, Montaigne says, for whose private use the book / portrait is intended, the liminary statement would appear to exclude the active, self-serving, and, one might say, dangerously disruptive reader. But of course the point is that this reader who is excluded from the intimate circle of family and friends, this reader who is advised not to waste his time with this book, who is apparently the object of Montaigne's farewell—or dismissal—this is precisely the reader to whom Montaigne speaks, who is also inscribed in the text and thus included in the readership. The preface paradoxically asserts that the book that follows has been written exclusively for the familiar reader at the same time as it performs an address that has been written exclusively for the "unfamiliar" reader, the reader for whom the book has apparently *not* been written. One way to reduce the apparent contradiction is to take the comment about writing for family and friends, and like it the essayist's advice that the reader not spend his leisure on so frivolous and vain a subject, merely to express the traditional topos of the modest author. Montaigne would then be using this commonplace to differentiate his book from conventional philosophical or pedagogical writing with which it might seem to have something in common or to ensure that he not be taken for a professional writer.[2]

Rather than empty the topos of its literal content, I intend to give it its due and to read the "Au lecteur" as the problematic and open-ended address to two different types of readers. The rhetorical strategy of the "Au lecteur" might be to disarm the potentially independent reader by its frankness and sincerity and to create a sense of intimacy so the reading resembles that of a friend. But there is no guarantee that this reader will be persuaded (seduced?), and the danger of an intrusive or unfaithful reading always exists. Montaigne includes the lecteur in the preface because the lecteur *must* be included in the reading; no writing, and no reading, is possible without the reader, whatever the author's intent or wishes. As we have already seen from our previous discussion, the essayist needs this reader, and he cannot prevent him from reading on his own. If the traditional purpose of a liminary notice is to introduce the writing subject, to prepare the reading that follows, and to inscribe the intended reader (that is, the reader of the text's intentions), then Montaigne's preface exceeds these functions to raise the issue of readership and of reading itself.

The question at the heart of this discussion thus appears to ask, "Whose text is it, the author's or the reader's?" I have also put the issue another way, in the specific terms of Montaigne's *Essais*, by suggesting that the text is either a self-portrait or a fashioning in process. But these are false questions if they are phrased as either / or propositions since the answer in all cases must be "both." While what I earlier referred to as the two tendencies within textuality and reading are competing and irreconcilable, they do not stand independent and exclusive of each other but rather inhabit the same space, invade and overlap each other, and, in the most profound sense, they coexist. The "Au lecteur" makes this clear. It posits a set of norms—modesty, naturalness, truthfulness, sincerity, presence, completeness—that gives form to the reading, and it inscribes a readership that will read accordingly. The subject of the self-portrait authors himself and his meaning in the pages of his text, just as he authors the reader in whose memory he is "reborn." The writing and this reader are intended to function exclusively to affirm the coincidence of the textual and the historical (or existential) and to sustain and support subjectivity.

At the same time, the "Au lecteur" also inscribes, and thus includes, a reader it ostensibly seeks to dissuade from reading, a reader who has no memory of Montaigne, no referential ground upon which to fix the signs of the writing and confirm their meaning. This reader has no obligation to the author to respect his person or his word, no necessary sympathy for either. For him the "author" is a textual "subject," a pronominal "I" that he knows is an unstable shifter and can serve only to undermine confidence in subjectivity and selfhood. And this reader understands his own questionable status as well, anonymous, unnamed except as the second person singular "you," which cannot by itself admit him to intimacy. Thus, he can read the "Au lecteur" not as a set of imposing norms (or truths) but as the first figuring of a textual persona who will inhabit the book that follows, as the "representation" of a modest, humble figure, the product of a rhetoric of sincerity and truthfulness, a figure through whom the essayist's thought and judgment will be mediated and a "self" sounded and reformed. This is not an intimate portrait but a sometimes illusory and always problematic effect of textuality, and it is a perspective to be assayed and through which to produce essays.

These then are the terms in which the *Essais* pose the question of textuality and of the reading that inheres in it. Texts are complex, double in nature, and must be read as such, as the portrait that we can consider metaphoric to stress its necessary, essential character *and* as the essay that we can call metonymic to underscore its contingent, accidental, or contextual quality. In each case there is an appropriate reader, the intimate reader of the portrait and the impersonal reader of the essay, but here again the *Essais* remind us that the two readers are like the Siamese brothers of "D'un enfant monstrueux," separate yet bound to each other. In a sense we are dealing with the difference between the "intended" reader and what might be called the "obtrusive" reader, between the reader for whom the meaning of the text is intended and intentional, and who tries faithfully to read authorial meaning, and the reader who intrudes, or perhaps more precisely, obtrudes, who thrusts himself and his ideas with undue insistence and without invitation upon the text, or even against it and without its consent. But the obtrusion is not wholly uncalled for, not entirely without invitation, because this reader, like the intimate and compliant one, is already written into the writing, in the address "Au lecteur," which is also the punned apostrophe "O lecteur" that calls him (them) into being. This second reader is as much a creation of the writing as the first, even though the writing attempts to dismiss him and to dissuade him from reading.

In this sense we might say that writing can never be seen as entirely errant—that is, it never quite wanders off the proper way and falls into the wrong hands because there are no "hands" that are absolutely "wrong" and there is no exclusively "proper way" to read. While it might be tempting to see the faithful reader as the "author's" reader and the obtrusive reader as originating "outside" or elsewhere, Montaigne's "Au lecteur" reminds us that this second reader, and second readings, are already written "into" the writing and are also the "author's," however much the text might attempt to reject or co-opt them. The two readings and readers we have described are not different options between which we can choose but readings and readers that must accompany each other and that are always implicit in each other, no matter how incompatible and conflicted they might seem. Reading takes place in the space of inescapable difference and tension between the authority of the author / text to impose meaning and the freedom of the obtrusive reader to make meaning. If we recognize the complexities of textuality, it cannot be any other way.[3]

·   ·   ·   ·   ·   ·   ·

The model of an ideal reading in which author, text, and reader participate in a unified meaning, without difference and without tension, serves as Montaigne's undeclared point of departure for the "Apologie de Raimond Sebond" (II, 12). In the opening pages the essayist is concerned with the question of proper reading and interpretation, not only of Sebond's book the *Theologia naturalis sive liber creaturarum* (1487), which he had translated into French in 1569, but of the book Sebond himself undertook to interpret, the metaphorical book of nature. The misreadings that burden Sebond's text now occasion Montaigne's writing, and he seeks to respond in order to aid those who need additional help, and, as he says, especially the women. Having undertaken what he calls "une occupation bien estrange et nouvelle pour moy" (440a) ("a very strange and new occupation for me" [320])—that is, having taken on Sebond's voice and spoken it as his own through the translation (having essayed it, in fact, as if in anticipation of the way he will take on other voices in the *Essais* as the means to discover and formulate his own)—Montaigne now speaks, as it were, in Sebond's name to defend his text from obtrusive readings.

Sebond began from the traditional premise that the world, like the Bible, was a book in which God had written his truth for all to see and to read. Just as the letters and the words of scripture combined to express divine meaning, the elements and creatures of the physical world formed a lexicon and a syntax readable as the natural expression of that truth. In his desire to offer the book of nature as an open as well as an infallible text, Sebond even claimed that it was more accessible to human reason than scripture itself and incapable of being misunderstood (and for this he was placed on the Index). Like the first language given by God to man, this book, he insisted, could not be falsified or misread, even by heretics, so clear and certain were its signs. By viewing nature as a language, and language as a part of nature rather than as a signifying system separate from and secondary to it, Sebond could maintain that reading did not speak "about" nature but was identical with it. Therefore no learning, he would say, was a prerequisite for reading the book of nature since it was in every way a "primary" text; no commentary, no interpretation, needed to follow since its meaning was immediately apprehensible.[4] All of the conditions for the ideal reading were in place: the authority of the author immanent in his text, the integrity and transparency of the textual signs and the wholeness of language itself, the insight and good "faith" of the reader.

Sebond undertakes to provide just such a reading of the "liber creaturarum," to demonstrate (reveal) reason's direct access to the links between God and the world, to that immanence, and to the truths of creation contained in its signs. Paradoxically, then, he does just what he says does not have to be done: he reads for those who do

not need anyone to read to (for) them, and he reads to forestall misreading of a text that cannot be misread. But what Sebond's reading
reveals in spite of itself is that no ideal or unequivocal reading is
possible, no absolute reading that ends all further reading (or misreading), no matter what guarantees of authority or intentionality
are offered (even God's), no matter what guarantees of textual transparency or of the reader's competency. Sebond had intended that the
book of nature serve as a complement to scripture since in it could be
read unerringly all that is contained in the holy book while that book
itself allowed conflicting interpretations and even heretical readings.
And perhaps if he had read silently—that is, if he had "read" exclusively for himself and to himself, or, as Augustine says of Ambrose,
with his heart instead of his voice or his tongue—he might have
realized his intention, at least for himself.[5] But once Sebond begins to
read with his "voice" and as a form of writing, as a form of representation that is read in its turn, his reading / text betrays its intentions
and proves itself susceptible to interpretation and to dispute, to the
misreadings of his critics, whose misreadings characterize postlapsarian man and language after Babel and oblige Montaigne to speak
on Sebond's behalf.

Only in the opening pages of the essay does Montaigne articulate
an "apologie" for Raimond Sebond. Two issues are at stake: the truth
of the text that the theologian reads and the integrity of his reading.
Montaigne addresses the first question by reasserting the primacy of
nature as a work bearing the indelible imprint of its maker. Drawing
upon a familiar set of topoi to describe the world as God's work of
art, the essayist evokes the image of divinity as *architecte, ouvrier,
facteur,* and sculptor: "Aussi n'est-il pas croyable que toute cette machine n'ait quelques marques empreintes de la main de ce grand
architecte, et qu'il n'y ait quelque image és choses du monde, rapor-
tant aucunement à l'ouvrier qui les a basties et formées" (446a)
("And it is not credible that this whole machine should not have on it
some marks imprinted by the hand of this great architect, and that
there should not be some picture in the things of this world that
somewhat represents the workman who has built and formed them"
[326]). Nature contains God's "hauts ouvrages" in which he has
marked "le caractere de sa divinité" (447a); it is a most holy temple
into which man is introduced "pour y contempler des statues, non
ouvrées de mortelle main, mais celles que la divine pensée a faict

sensibles" (447b) ("To contemplate statues, not statues wrought by mortal hand, but those which the divine thought has made perceptible" [327]). Creation is the materialization of the divine spirit, the way that it is made visible and accessible to man, and Sebond, Montaigne tells his reader, labored at this worthy study ("ce digne estude") to show that there is no part of the world that belies its maker. That the universe sustains and affirms man's faith by its accessibility, by what I have suggested is its readability, is itself a sign of God's goodness and plenitude: "Ce seroit faire tort à la bonté divine, si l'univers ne consentoit à nostre creance" (447a) ("It would be doing a wrong to divine goodness if the universe did not assent to our belief" [326]). And here I want to note that although Montaigne does not specifically refer to nature as a book in these pages of the "Apologie," the inescapable resonance of Sebond's reading of the liber creaturarum as subtext, the passionate effort to rebut its critical misreading, the aestheticizing power of the topoi that transform creation into an artifact, and the lexicon of marks imprinted on creation as if on a page ("marques empreintes," "images," "caractere") all allow us to take his words as metaphors for texts and reading.

Montaigne must also defend the integrity of Sebond's rationalist reading of this liber creaturarum. He accomplishes this paradoxically by saving Sebond from himself and insisting that while the *Theologia naturalis* may represent the working of natural reason it does not represent it working on its own. In his own preface Sebond reiterates the accessibility of God's book, but he also adds, as if to acknowledge God's omnipotence and his own dependency, that divine grace has to accompany its reading: "nul ne peut veoir de soy, ny lire en ce grand livre (bien que tousjours ouvert et present à nos yeux) s'il n'est esclairé de Dieu et purgé de sa macule originelle" ("No one can see on his own, nor read in this great book—although it is always present and open before our eyes—if he has not been enlightened by God and purified of original sin").[6] Montaigne turns this caveat into the basis for his defense of Sebond and represents him as an inspired reader. Man's reason, he maintains, is like brute matter, unmolded clay or perhaps unassembled letters, and only when the divine artist gives it form by the infusion of grace can it attain to truth. "Or nos raisons et nos discours humains, c'est comme la matiere lourde et sterile: la grace de Dieu en est la forme," the essayist says, and our ideas and reasonings, he adds, "ils ont quelque corps, mais c'est une masse informe, sans façon et sans jour, si la foy et grace de Dieu n'y sont joinctes" (447a) ("Now our human reasons and arguments are as it were the heavy and barren matter; the grace of God is their form; . . . they have a certain body, but it is a shapeless mass, without form or light, if faith and divine grace are not added to it" [327]). In spite of his own emphasis on reason alone, the substance of Sebond's reading gained shape through faith. In the light of divine inspiration, each element in the author / text / reader triad can fulfill its ideal function: God's authority sustains the truth of his work; the text signifies the indelible presence of its maker; the reader, graced with what we might call "reading proficiency," unerringly reads that presence and its intention.

By approaching the question of reading through the opening pages of the "Apologie" I might appear to have made it unnecessarily complex, given the metaphysical perspective that is thus required and seems so uncharacteristic of Montaigne. At the same time my discussion of Sebond's reading of the book of nature, and of Montaigne's defense, allows a sharp perspective on reading and sets its implications in bold relief. Authorial authority and immanence are predetermined in Montaigne's idealized account, textual integrity and the substantiality of its signs are presumed, and man still cannot read without the intervention of divine grace, so problematic is the act of reading itself. As long as the reading is the author's reading—that is, as long as God deigns to reveal to the inspired reader his presence and his meaning—the reader reads correctly. But any effort on the reader's part to do his own reading, to be active and independent, to rely on his own resources and reason, leads him invariably to misread and misconstrue. This is the fate of Sebond's critics, but the skeptical perspective of the "Apologie" suggests that it is the fate of all readers operating on their own. Readers who obtrude upon a text with total disregard for its "truth" and who impose their own "uninspired" meanings only expose their own arrogance and their own weakness. But how can man do otherwise?

Among its innumerable examples of man's inanity and of the incompetence of reason, the "Apologie" cites the experience of reading and man's propensity to read anything anywhere, regardless of what is actually "there": "il n'est aucun sens ny visage, ou droict, ou amer, ou doux, ou courbe, que l'esprit humain ne trouve aux escrits qu'il entreprend de fouiller" (585a) ("There is not sense or aspect, either straight or bitter, or sweet, or crooked, that the human mind does not find in the writings it undertakes to search" [442]). Whether interpreting sacred or profane texts, Montaigne implies, human ingenuity will always find a way to turn the writing to its own advantage, like those who twist the words of the interpreters of prophetic myths: "il y a tant de moyens d'interpretation qu'il est malaisé que, de biais ou de droit fil, un esprit ingenieux ne rencontre en tout sujet quelque air qui luy serve à son poinct" (586a) ("There are so many means of interpretation that, obliquely or directly, an ingenious mind can hardly fail to come across in any subject some sense that will serve his point" [442]).

In the maelstrom of the essay's unrelenting assault against reason, man reading on his own is thus swept up and entirely confounded. Montaigne contends ironically that authors need not worry about posterity; all they have to do is to write obscurely and paradoxically and the readers will squeeze out their own meanings, "ou selon, ou à costé, ou au contraire de la sienne, qui lui feront toutes honneur" (586c) ("either like his own, or beside it, or contrary to it, which will all do him honor" [442]). "Est-il possible qu'Homere aye voulu dire tout ce qu'on luy faict dire" (ibid.), the essayist asks, in terms that recall Alcofribas's question about allegorical reading in the "Prologue" to *Gargantua:* "Croiez vous en vostre foy qu'oncques Homere escrivent l'*Iliade* et *Odyssée*, pensast es allegories lesquelles de luy on calfreté Plutarche, Heraclides Ponticq, Eustatie, Phornute, et ce que d'iceulx Politian a desrobé?" ("Do you believe in all good faith that Homer, writing the *Illiad* and the *Odyssey*, ever thought of all the allegories with which he had been calked by Plutarch, Heraclides, Ponticus, Eustathius, Cornutus, and what Poliziano stole from them?").[7] The echo of the wildly unreliable Alcofribas's inconsistent musings on reading reverberates in Montaigne's own highly rational discourse and serves to undermine further any confidence in reading and to underscore its problematical nature. Plato too has been twisted and turned, and made to differ from himself, vigorously and powerfully, Montaigne says, "autant qu'est puissant et vif l'esprit de l'interprete" (587c) ("in so far as the mind of the interpreter is powerful and vigorous" [443]). And Montaigne complicates the issue even more by evoking the conflicting thoughts of Heraclitus and Democritus: the first holds that things actually do contain all the aspects found in them, the second that they have nothing at all of what is found in them. In a prior remark Montaigne had implied that it is always possible for texts themselves to be nothing at all and, in another reminiscence of Rabelais, had inverted the notion of the *sustantificque moelle* to depict the readers of certain philosophical writings chewing on a hollow bone, without marrow or substance: "(un) os creux et descharné" (508b).

Sebond's inspired reading of the book of nature thus stands as a privileged instance, although it too falls victim to what emerges from the "Apologie" as man's inevitable proclivity for misreading. No book is spared, it would appear, not the literal book that is scripture and not the metaphorical book of nature, where the very "marks," "images," and "characters" that confer readability implicate it in the unhappy fate of all writing. Not God's books and not even Homer's, the greatest of secular texts. Perhaps it is the sign of man's inanity and arrogance that these are precisely the books that give rise to the most outrageous misinterpretations. Montaigne complains that Homer is read differently by theologians, legislators, captains, philosophers, and men of science and adapted to their needs, and he remarks that a learned acquaintance who knows Homer as well as any man of their century draws from him support for the Catholic religion and claims that this was Homer's intention (586). And the essayist adds, as further proof of the problem, that what this man found in favor of his religion, readers before him had found in favor of theirs. As in the cases of scripture and of Plato, it appears that an essential authorial design is fragmented by the proliferation of readings and distorted in the appropriation that makes the text speak the languages of its readers and serve their purposes.

What emerges clearly from these examples is the tension between the assumption of an original written meaning or intention (or perhaps the *desire* for an original meaning) that is treated as timeless (and embedded in the materiality of writing that appears to transcend time: *scripta manent*) and the necessarily historical, contingent nature of man and his reading. Sebond's reading can claim to be ideal because it pretends to transcend history, it divines God's intention because it calls itself inspired by the transcendent divinity, but man on his own, in history, can read only by making the reading his own. Authors and texts may seek to impose their "intentions," but, for the reader who obtrudes upon the text, to impute intention is always and already to do a reading, and perhaps it is also a reading *of the reader himself,* insofar as reading reflects or confers (it is impossible to determine which) a specific historical identity and situation on / of the reader. The lesson of the history of reading reveals that all reading must obtrude regardless of the intention of the writer or reader, and even if the reader intends to honor that intention. Texts and readings can never make the truth known in any final or absolute way, as if they somehow could have the last word. Instead, they proliferate endlessly. In the example I have been discussing, the book of nature is followed in succession by Sebond's *Theologia naturalis,* the critics' readings of Sebond, Montaigne's "Apologie" responding to the critics, countless interpretations of the "Apologie" and the *Essais* in the four hundred years since their publication, and my own commentary, each establishing meaning by recounting a narrative of authorial or textual intent, and each in its own turn misreading and opening itself to further misreading.

.   .   .   .

Given the precarious status of authorial intention and the apparent inevitability of misreading, we understand the importance of the friend who might be able to safeguard the authority of the writer and ensure the integrity of the writing. We have seen the *Essais'* preoccupation with this reader, from the evocation of the intimate circle in the "Au lecteur" to the plaintive and generative apostrophe "O un amy," and to what could be called the constitution of the friendly reader in the person(a) of Marie de Gournay in "De la praesumption." The *Essais,* we might say, are above all written to or for this friend, but the form of the writing itself confirms that what the essayist desires he does not possess and what he seeks he cannot be certain he will find. When one addresses a friend, the essayist suggests in "Consideration sur Cicéron" (I, 40), one writes letters, not essays. Speaking of the fact that his own friends think that he has some ability in writing letters (although we must keep in mind that while he has friends he has no "friend": "O mes amis, il n'y a nul amy"), Montaigne raises the issue of writing when one has no one for whom to write:

> Et eusse prins plus volontiers ceste forme à publier mes verves, si j'eusse eu à qui parler. Il me falloit, comme je l'ay eu autrefois, un certain commerce qui m'attirast, qui me soustinst et souslevast. Car de

negocier au vent, comme d'autres, je ne sçauroy que de songes, ny
forger des vains noms, à entretenir en chose serieuse: ennemy juré de
toute falsification. J'eusse esté plus attentif et plus seur, ayant une ad-
dresse forte et amie, que je ne suis, regardant les divers visages d'un
peuple. Et suis deçeu, s'il ne m'eust mieux succédé. (252c)

And I would have preferred to adopt this form to publish my sallies,
if I had had someone to talk to. I needed what I once had, a certain relationship to lead me on, sustain me, and raise me up. For to talk to
the winds, as others do, is beyond me except in dreams; nor could I
fabricate fictitious names to talk with on a serious matter, being a
sworn enemy of any falsification. I would have been more attentive
and confident, with a strong friend to address, than I am now, when I
consider the various tastes [facets] of a whole public. And if I am not
mistaken, I would have been more successful. (185)

What sets the letter apart from other sorts of writing is that it is
addressed, written to someone "à qui parler," to someone with
whom the writer enjoys "un certain commerce." The name, the real
name of the true friend, gives the letter its privileged status. Personal,
private, the sign as well as the means of intimate communication, the
letter is a presentation or offering of oneself and a call for the return
of the other, in an endless process of profitable exchange that is indeed the ideal form of commerce. It is a variation on the portrait
model: the author present in his word, the word transparent in its
sincerity and naturalness, the reader receptive and comprehending.
In fact, portraits were exchanged in the Renaissance like letters; we
have only to recall the role that they played in the famous friendship
of Erasmus and Thomas More. Like books, letters arise from the need
to overcome absence, the distance that separates the self from another, but here "another" also means "another oneself." When the
letter makes of this "other" a reader, friendship is fulfilled through
the words in which the absent self inheres in a real and substantial
way.[8]

That Montaigne can no longer write letters after the death of La
Boétie, that the "commerce" of friendship cannot be replaced in any
meaningful way by the "negotiations au vent," or the true name by
"vains noms," by fictitious correspondents, signals the crisis in readership to which the *Essais* must respond. With the private realm
foreclosed, Montaigne becomes an essayist in the public domain,
where the reader is at the same time absent and other, where in a real

sense he is anonymous—that is, literally without a name. For the singularity of the friend is substituted a plurality of unfamiliar faces ("les divers visages d'un peuple"), multifaceted and of diverse aspects. This is the still recently formed readership of printed books that will have to be faced if Montaigne's intentions as author are to be safeguarded and his meaning preserved.[9]

We return here to the reader(s) that Montaigne has inscribed in his text and to the reading of itself that the text will enact through these readers. The familiarity and sympathy of the lost "ami" will be sought in those he must write down as his "amis" and in those readers to whom he must give names if he is to overcome the anonymity of his readership. Although several essays, as we have indicated, are in fact addressed to specific readers, all of them women whom Montaigne names, most of the writing will depend on more general, and more indirect, inscriptions to demarcate the reading activity. In this context we can identify the references to both the "suffisant lecteur" (I, 24, 147) and the "indiligent lecteur" (III, 9, 994) as examples of the way in which the writing gives "names" to its readers to guide the reading and make its own intentions known.

It is particularly appropriate that I continue my discussion with the essay "Divers evenemens de mesme conseil" (I, 24), for the issue of "various outcomes of the same plan" might be another way of putting our question about various readings (readers) of the same text. Through a series of historical readings and personal anecdotes Montaigne assays the consequences of man's decisions and actions to disclose that they lie beyond his control, that there is no way to determine their outcome. Beginning with the ways in which François de Guise and Augustus dealt with anticipated assassination attempts, he derives the general maxim, "Tant c'est chose vaine et frivole que l'humaine prudence; et au travers de tous nos projects, de nos conseils et precautions, la fortune maintient tousjours la possession des evenemens" (127a) ("So vain and frivolous a thing is human prudence; and athwart all our plans, counsels, and precautions, Fortune still maintains her grasp on the results" [92]). Further examples of the diverse effects of military strategies and of medical treatments also confirm that events take their own course whatever a man intends and in spite of precautions he might take. Fortune, then, is the name Montaigne gives to the discrepancy between intention and outcome, and it operates not only in the public realm, where "cette

own purposes, unmindful of the author's intentions or in spite of them—the issue of how what is in the text got there is a moot one. If the text is read as a portrait of the author, however, it is then essential to determine his intentions and to distinguish what can be ascribed to him and what cannot. While fortune's enhancements inadvertently enrich the text and add luster to the writer's reputation, they also obscure the reader's perception of the author's presence in the writing. When the text is taken as the author's, and the reading seeks to find and to judge him in his own right, the question of ownership becomes paramount.

In the context of discussion and conversation in "De l'art de conferer" (III, 8) Montaigne warns that the speaker should not automatically be given credit for all that he says that is valuable or good because "La plus part des hommes sont riches d'une suffisance estrangere" (936b) ("Most men are rich with borrowed capacity" [715]). The interlocutor should either deliberately oppose what is said or draw back, "pour taster de toutes parts comment elle [whatever truth or beauty has been proffered] est logée en son autheur" (ibid.). When it comes to books and to judging their authors, a similar caution is required: "Le subject, selon qu'il est, peut faire trouver un homme sçavant et memorieux; mais pour juger en luy les parties plus siennes et plus dignes, la force et beauté de son ame, il faut sçavoir ce qui est sien et ce qui ne l'est point" (940) ("The subject, according to what it is, may give a man a reputation for learning and a good memory; but in order to judge the qualities that are most his own and most worthy, the strength and beauty of his mind, we must know what is his and what is not" [718]).

The question of ownership (of what is one's own, "owned") thus becomes paramount and raises the central issue of borrowing, and borrowed capacity ("une suffisance estrangere"), an issue that is, of course, one of the major concerns of the *Essais*. It is figured in the quotations that Montaigne takes from others and inserts into his text and foregrounded by the many instances in which he draws attention to his practice. But while one can choose to cite other authors or not, as Montaigne says he does to "rehausser mon propos" (II, 10, 408c), one cannot chose whether or not to "borrow." Like the workings of fortune, which "lend" something foreign to the writing from "outside," this too is beyond man's control. "De l'institution des enfans" (I, 26) indicates clearly how the child is formed or composed from matter borrowed from elsewhere or from someone else, from the material of books, for example, and even in the case of lived experience, from attitudes toward that experience that derive from a long and rich intellectual tradition. And in "De la phisionomie" (III, 12), in which Montaigne claims that "Toute cette nostre suffisance, qui est au delà de la naturelle, est à peu pres vaine et superflue" (1,039b) ("All this ability of ours that is beyond the natural is as good as vain and superfluous" [794]), the sweep of his argument and the prominent place occupied by Socrates belie the absolute privilege given to nature over culture. In the Renaissance, making anything (and especially oneself) was never a making *ab nihilo*. Only God "created"; man "invented," coming upon things always through familiar ground. Given this view, Montaigne determines the measure of a man by the degree to which the borrowed material is made one's own, a process that the essayist and his contemporaries sought to naturalize through the traditional topos of the bee transforming pollen into honey. But clearly this is a problematical issue, as Montaigne's obsessive return to it reveals. He insists throughout the *Essais* that the subject be absolutely and exclusively himself and entirely himself in his writing, that he know what he is and what is his own ("ce qu'il est et ce qui luy est propre" [I, 3, 15c]), and this insistence returns like a refrain to betray the fact that neither the subject nor his text is ever wholly itself. There is always something foreign to the author, and to the subject of the text, always an "au delà" that exceeds his every act, a "superflu" that overflows like the ink of his writing to say more than he had it in him to say (beyond *his* "suffisance") or than he intended.[12]

If writing, or forming oneself, cannot be conceived without borrowing, without excess, then the task of the reader of the "portrait" becomes a formidable one indeed. How does one determine what is the author's own and what is borrowed? Although Montaigne suggests that the participant in discussion draw back to get a better "feel" ("taster"), in the same "De l'art de conferer" he evokes a wide audience of inexperienced readers (including himself) who have to consult "quelque sçavant" (940) when they come upon a striking poetic turn in a new poet in order to find out whose property it is. This may be a modest pose, or an ironic one, but it serves to underscore the difficulty of sorting out the issue of what I am calling the "excess." The reader of the portrait always faces a text that has been composed with foreign matter, matter that must be naturalized, but this effort must inevitably fall short. In "Des livres" (II, 10) Montaigne exploits this textual complexity by purposely concealing the identity of the authors whose ideas and inventions he takes over and by challenging his readers to seek them out: "Je veux qu'ils donnent une nazarde à Plutarque sur mon nez, et qu'ils s'eschaudent à injurier Seneque en moy" (408c) ("I want them to give Plutarch a fillip on my nose and get burned insulting Seneca in me" [296]). "I will love anyone who can unplume me," he says, "by clearness of judgment and by the sole distinction of the force and beauty of the remarks." But does such a reader exist?

Montaigne himself claims to recognize his borrowings, to find in what he refers to as his textual garden the flowers that stand out as too beautiful to be his own, although he says that he cannot often identify their author by name. But of course the full weight of the garden topos has been brought to bear precisely in order to persuade the reader that just the opposite obtains, that the text is indeed the place where borrowings are (can be) naturalized, where foreign flowers can be transplanted and take root to become one's own. If the text *is* a garden, as the metaphor implies, the reader will not finally be able to determine if what sounded like Plutarch or Seneca was actually, and profoundly, Montaigne's. But the essayist's own experience as reader suggests that the text as "garden" is no more than a rhetorical figure, one whose contingency cannot be hidden and that cannot itself overcome or hide difference. What his game of hide and seek discloses is the text's problematical status, its uncertain and unstable position between nature and art, a position that always exposes the reader as naïve and inexperienced and in need of some learned man to help him sort things out.

Perhaps in the case of specific borrowings, and in the spirit of play that Montaigne evinces in "Des livres," the author can confidently recognize what belongs to him and what does not. But generally speaking the essayist does not appear to enjoy privileged insight into his writing; as reader of his own text he must struggle, as other readers do, in his effort to interpret and judge the work and to take the measure of the man who has produced it. In "De l'art de conferer" Montaigne is less sure of himself: "Car ordinairement je m'aperçoy qu'on faut autant à juger de sa propre besongne que de celle d'autruy; non seulement pour l'affection qu'on y mesle, mais pour n'avoir la suffisance de la cognoistre et distinguer" (939b) ("For I notice generally that people are as mistaken in judging their own work as that of others, not only because of the affection that is involved, but also because they have not the capacity to know and distinguish it for what it is" [718]). And again he returns to the idea he expressed through the figure of fortune, that there is more in the text than the author has put there by himself. It is still called "his own work" ("sa propre besongne"), but it is judged or read no differently than if it were another's ("celle d'autruy"). Earlier, fortune was depicted playing a role in the composition of the work, coming from outside or beyond to add something in excess of the author's capacity and intention. Here, in the context of reading and judging one's own production, the essayist attributes an "excess" to the work itself, as if it had the power (and the fortune, he says) within it to write itself, in some sense. "L'ouvrage, de sa propre force et fortune, peut seconder l'ouvrier outre son invention et connoissance et le devancer" (ibid.). The work, by its own power and fortune, seconds the writer beyond his inventiveness and knowledge and outstrips him, it favors or assists him, but the favor is a paradoxical one for it alienates the writer from his own writing by going beyond ("outre") or ahead of him ("le devancer"), by adding on *its* own what is not *his* own. "Pour moy," Montaigne says, "je ne juge la valeur d'autre besongne plus obscurement que de la mienne: et loge les Essais tantost bas, tantost haut, fort inconstamment et doubteusement" (ibid.) ("For my part, I do not judge the value of any other work less clearly than my own; and I place the *Essays* now low, now high, very inconsistently and uncertainly" [718]). One's own writing ("la mienne") is just as removed, just as unmasterable, as the writing of another ("autre besongne").

·   ·   ·   ·   ·   ·   ·

Montaigne's text serves the purposes of our inquiry into the nature of writing and reading particularly well because only the writer as reader of his own text could sense so profoundly the excess produced by writing. Only by reading what he has written and not finding himself there can the writer experience the degree to which the text escapes him, goes beyond him, becomes something "other" than (to) him, whether we are referring to his intention, his knowledge, or his capacity to write. This sense of the otherness of the text comes not only from the impression that something foreign has been added to the writing but from the feeling that something personal has been lost in the reading as well. Montaigne talks about losing his original meaning, or what he intended, as he reads what he has written:

> Ceci m'advient aussi: que je ne me trouve pas où je me cherche; et me trouve plus par rencontre que par l'inquisition de mon jugement. J'aurai eslancé quelque subtilité en escrivant. . . . Je l'ay si bien perdue que je ne sçay ce que j'ay voulu dire: et l'a l'estranger descouverte par fois avant moy. Si je portoy le rasoir par tout où cela m'advient, je me desferoy tout. (I, 10, 40c)

> This also happens to me: that I do not find myself in the place where I look; and I find myself more by chance encounter than by searching my judgment. I will have tossed off some subtle remark as I write. . . . Later I have lost the point so thoroughly that I do not know what I meant; and sometimes a stranger has discovered it before I do. If I erased every passage where this happened to me, there would be nothing left of myself. (26)

> En mes escris mesmes je ne retrouve pas tousjours l'air de ma premiere imagination: je ne sçay ce que j'ay voulu dire, et m'eschaude souvent à corriger et y mettre un nouveau sens, pour avoir perdu le premier, qui valloit mieux. (II, 12, 566b)

> Even in my own writings I do not always find again the sense of my first thought; I do not know what I meant to say, and often I get burned by correcting and putting in a new meaning, because I have lost the first one, which was better. (426)

The common theme of these two passages, both inserted in very different essays composed earlier, is "je ne sçay ce que j'ay voulu dire," the reader not knowing in the present what the writer meant in the past. The repetition of "je" identifies the writer and reader as the same person, but the doubling of identity also distinguishes and fragments them, making them subjects of a different temporality (and textual function), so that the same person is also different persons. If past intention or meaning can be lost in the present, forgotten or erased so as not to be recovered, in what terms can we talk about its status, or that of the subject, for that matter? Montaigne does not wholly deny the idea of the writer's intention, for writing itself would be inconceivable without it, even though fortune, chance, the work itself may play their own roles. Nor does he totally exclude the possibility of its recuperation either by the writer/reader himself or by another ("l'estranger"). But the fact that the "stranger" is likely to find the intention before the writer himself signals the degree to which writing itself remains strange or foreign to any reading that seeks to master it, or, put another way, opens itself to all readings. Is intention only a trace in the writer's memory, the recollection of having had an intention—that is, a void that has itself become the sign of an intention whose content is always in some sense missing? Is it the reader's supposition of a writer's intention or meaning, an attribution that "invents" an author and invests the writing with value, or form, with a purpose that allows it to be intelligible and to be read? Is intention or meaning something the reader constructs as the act of reading itself? What we can say in this context is that any writing about intention, any "finding" or "recuperation" of meaning, is already a reading and, given the nature of reading, problematical, even (or especially) when the writing writes about itself, as Montaigne's does.[13]

In a sense then, the author is always to some degree "lost" in the writing, and to it, and what we call the "author" must be bracketed because it is always in some way an effect of the reading. But reading does not produce this effect gratuitously (my reading of intention suggests that an "author" is needed to guarantee form and to ensure the integrity of reading itself), nor does it produce it entirely on its own, from nothing.[14] Both the writer (the historical writer and the writer posited by my reading; it is no longer possible to distinguish them completely) and the writing are complicitous; they both participate in the invention of the author, just as they collude to produce the reader himself. The text as self-portrait is, of course, the most striking and explicit invention and the most direct effort to convince the reader that there is an author and that that author coincides with his text. But its implications are broad if one assumes that in some sense all writers implicitly inhabit their writing, that their intentions operate in what they write, whether the writer or his intention is openly in evidence or not.

Montaigne implies that he is to be found in the coherence of the text, a coherence imposed by the writing subject himself: "C'est l'indiligent lecteur qui pert mon subject, non pas moy; il s'en trouvera tousjours en un coing quelque mot qui ne laisse pas d'estre bastant, quoy qu'il soit serré" (III, 9, 994c) ("It is the inattentive reader who loses my subject, not I. Some word about it will always be found off in a corner, which will not fail to be sufficient, though it takes little room" [761]). According to these lines, the reader may have an active role to play in the articulation of that coherence, but he finds only what is already there, no matter what he finds, and whatever he finds serves among other things as a sign of the writer. The writing itself would thus be always entirely sufficient ("bastant"); if there were an aporia into which the reading fell, if there were a loss of subject, of meaning or of intention, the reader would have lacked diligence and would be at fault. Further on the essayist glosses himself to attribute to the writing qualities that guide understanding and stabilize meaning: "J'entends que la matiere se distingue soy-mesmes. Elle montre assez où elle se change, où elle conclud, où elle commence, où elle se reprend, sans l'entrelasser de paroles, de liaison et de cousture introduictes pour le service des oreilles foibles ou nonchallantes, et sans me gloser moymesme" (995b) ("I want the matter to make its own divisions. It shows well enough where it changes, where it concludes, where it begins, where it resumes, without my interlacing it with words, with links and seams introduced for the benefit of weak or heedless ears, and without writing glosses on myself" [761]). As if the matter operates actively, on its own—as a figure of prosopopeia— in the service of an integral Montaigne and his authoritative presence, the Montaigne who is present here as the desire, the will, or the intention that the writing function that way ("j'entends que").

This appears to be an uncanny strategy, one that allows the text to be open to the reader and at the same time makes everything attributable to the author.[15] Since there is no certain way for the reader to distinguish what belongs to the writer from what is excessive, no sure method to judge what fortune has contributed, or what the writing itself has produced—in a word, no way to master authorial intention or meaning—anything and everything recuperated through reading can accrue to the benefit of the writer. The reader changes register, stops, starts and picks up again, he supplies his own transitions, links, and seams, and he is only doing what the "text" intended. He makes associations, oblique or direct, among ideas in order to make meaning, and he produces only the meaning of the author: "Mes fantasies se suyvent, mais par fois c'est de loing, et se regardent, mais d'une veuë oblique" (III, 9, 994b) ("My ideas follow one another, but sometimes it is from a distance, and look at each other, but with a sidelong glance" [761]). The reader elaborates upon a suggestion or a fragment and sees what Montaigne meant him to see: "Ce que je ne puis exprimer, je le montre au doigt" ("What I cannot express I point to with my finger"). Anything that can be found, anything that can be said, is already there in the text because everything is in the text by design: "si on y regarde, on trouvera que j'ay tout dict, ou tout designé" (983b) ("If you look around, you will find that I have said everything or suggested everything" [751]).

I began just a few paragraphs ago to speak about the reader inventing the author for the purpose of reading, and I have concluded by talking about what sounds like an authoritative, omnipresent author who controls the reading and makes it appear that the reader is *his* invention, inscribed in the writing to guarantee its integrity and the truth of authorial intention and meaning. We can talk about the one only by talking about the other, for the two call for and necessitate each other and are not mutually exclusive but in a sense already inhabit each other. The writer would not need to insist on his true presence and to devise structural, thematic, and rhetorical strategies to protect himself and his work (word) if he were not faced with the potential threat of an obtrusive reader, if in fact he were not writing for that reader. The reader would have nothing to obtrude upon, nothing to thrust himself upon with undue pressure and without invitation, if the writing did not present itself as "something" (as author, intention, and meaning) and demand its due, and if it did not seek to resist the reading as unwarranted or unauthorized. This model of writing and reading is an agonistic one, a conflict for domination of the textual terrain. But it is a conflict that cannot be resolved because the property cannot be neatly partitioned or assigned. Reading, we might derive from Montaigne's *Essais,* is the recognition of the unresolvable and unmasterable nature of textuality and of the necessary tension between the competing demands of the author and the reader to impose their authority and their intentions.

·   ·   ·   ·   ·   ·   ·

The agonistic model thus emerges forcefully from my reading of Montaigne's text, and, while it overwhelms the notion of perfect communication between writer and reader, it does not eliminate it. There remains deeply embedded in the *Essais* a nostalgia for union, irretrievably lost and remembered as ideal, a nostalgia that betrays the hope, and the desire, for its return in the future. Sebond's divinely illuminated reading of the book of nature is an instance of complete understanding that once was possible but cannot be recaptured within the (textual) world Montaigne inhabits. The mystical relation with La Boétie in which the two friends came together, in the deepest sense, through their writing long before they met is another instance of communion in reading that the *Essais* cannot forget. Marie de Gournay's singular emergence in Montaigne's text as its perfect reader, drawn to the writer and loving him through the agency of his writing—that is, knowing him in his text before she, too, knew him in person—re-creates once more that fusion of souls that expresses the deepest wish of the essayist that his readers find him, and conjoin with him, in his writing.

As we saw in the previous chapter, Marie de Gournay becomes more than a textual projection, more than a persona that figures the essayist's wish; her own claim, and it is a powerful if problematic one, is that she realizes the promise and the hope that the writing announces. Reading Montaigne's text, she insists that she finds herself in the writer and the writer in herself, she imagines herself thinking his thoughts not only as her own, it would appear, but as if in some sense she were inhabited by them and by him. "Some people think that I usurp him," she says in her "Preface" that I quoted earlier, because she claims to reason and to think as he does, but the reverse could also be the case, that she herself is usurped, taken over by Montaigne and his thoughts. Taking Montaigne's own lead, Marie de Gournay attributes this spiritual mingling to the privileged relation that they share, but it is important to stress that this model of reading, however unique it may appear in the form in which it is expressed and practiced by Marie de Gournay, is not only exclusively personal or idiosyncratic. By attempting to live the project that the *Essais* can only nostalgically, and perhaps desperately, evoke, Marie de Gournay situates herself in what we can consider a modern lineage of readers who conceive of reading as the mysterious and not entirely fathomable union of writer and reader. We can draw a line that extends from Montaigne to a Rousseau (reader of Montaigne) yearning for what one critic calls "an immediate transparence of all beings to each other, which would enable them to understand each other in an ecstatic happiness," through the Romantics to modern phenomenological critics in order to trace an emphasis on the subjectivity of both writer and reader and to foreground their potential to meet and even join through the activity of reading.[16]

Among contemporary critics Georges Poulet has drawn this model with the boldest colors. Himself a reader of Montaigne, whom he considers to have given first expression to the essential experience of modern human consciousness, Poulet deems it possible for the consciousness of the reader to become one with that of the author as it is created in the work. Like the writing that Montaigne asserts is consubstantial to him, the literary work, Poulet claims, is impregnated with the mind of its author; to understand the work is to let that mind that reveals itself *in* the text disclose itself in turn *in* the reader. "From the moment I become prey to what I read," he writes, "I begin to share the use of my consciousness with this being whom I have tried to define and who is the conscious subject ensconced at the heart of the work. He and I, we start having a common consciousness." Thus it is that the reader understands and, to use Poulet's own terms, grasps the inner meaning of the work, its formal perfection, and the subjective principle that animates it.[17]

To read Poulet alongside Montaigne in this way is thus to theorize the essayist's highest aspiration for his work and for himself. And yet, as we have seen, even as it longs to be read as an essential experience of union, Montaigne's writing paradoxically undercuts its own desire and undermines the ground on which its readers, from Marie de Gournay to Poulet and beyond, have staked their claim to understanding. Montaigne's insistence on being in his writing and of a piece with it must be juxtaposed to his acknowledgment that his writing can never entirely escape what I have been calling a certain excess within which he must lose himself to his reader just as he loses himself there to himself. On the one hand, he encourages the reader not to linger over the forms and the words of his writing, its surfaces, so that like Poulet's reader the reader of the *Essais* will also be free to experience the author's interiority unencumbered by structural and stylistic properties (I, 40, 251). But on the other hand, the essayist's vigorous critiques of rhetoric belie his own fascination with it, and his repeated exhortations to resist the lure of the surface betray his own attraction to it and his need for it. These conflicted attitudes serve to remind us (and, I suspect, Montaigne himself) that the author's experience is never entirely accessible to the reader and that reading is always entangled in, and limited by, the words and the forms of writing. This may help to explain why, in Poulet's case, the critic seems to do away with writing, why he insists that the writing subject ultimately transcends the work to expose itself in its "ineffability" and why he posits the need for reading to "annihilate," or at least to forget the objective elements of the work.

Montaigne does not and, I would say, cannot relinquish the objectivity of the text, just as he cannot divorce himself from the material and physical dimension of human existence. Poulet sees the essayist as a precursor of Descartes, giving first expression to a modern consciousness detached from things but still "floating on the surface of the flux of phenomena." It will be Descartes, in Poulet's view, who completes this withdrawal by pulling consciousness back entirely from this flux and returning it to an initial moment of pure intuition.[18] But I would argue that Montaigne does more than just float on the surface; he actively engages the surface, whether it be the surface of phenomena or the surface that is language, because surfaces are his only link with interiority, however problematical that link may be. The (sur)face, we recall him saying in "De la phisionomie," is a weak guarantee, but it deserves some consideration. The essayist may distinguish himself *from* things to reflect upon them, but it is also true that he can only reflect himself *in* things, and no "things" are more central in this regard than his own body and the body of the text with which he is consubstantial, the words and the forms that compose his writing in all its objectivity. Montaigne may aspire, as we have seen, to silence and to transparent language, but he also expresses the need for words of "flesh and bone." I take Thibaudet's comment on Montaigne thinking his body as a gloss on his writing as well: "Montaigne ne penserait pas s'il ne se pensait, et il ne se penserait pas s'il ne pensait son corps" ("Montaigne would not have thought if he had not thought about himself [or thought himself up], and he would not have thought about himself without thinking his body").[19]

Bound to language in its materiality, incapable of transcendence in any absolute way and ultimately wary of it, Montaigne's writing both encourages and impedes the utopian desire for union with the reader. The *Essais* appear to engage and to perform the paradoxical encounter of that desire with what might be considered the fallen state of reading, and of writing, a postlapsarian and postboetian state. As if in an effort to alleviate separation and alienation, Montaigne implies that with application and with effort the reader can overcome idiosyncrasies of style and the obscurities and vagaries of writing itself to achieve a unified reading experience. When he says in "De la vanité" (III, 9) that he digresses by design and that his ideas follow each other, though sometimes from afar, "et se regardent, mais d'une veuë oblique" (994b), he may be inviting the reader into the text to make connections, to assume the oblique perspective that brings the relation between ideas into focus. In the manner of the painter, the essayist claims to write anamorphically, and the reader must actively seek the correct viewpoint in order to participate in the elucidation of the subject and its meaning. His own writing, he implies further on, resembles the flights and gambols of the poets and the prose of Plutarch, in which the author forgets his theme and smothers his subject in foreign matter, but the essayist insists that it is only the careless reader who loses his subject. This criticism of the "indiligent lecteur" obviously calls for a diligent reader (Latin *diligere*, to prize, love, take delight in doing), an assiduous and loving reader who, like a friend, finds what Montaigne himself has never lost, for there is always some word about it in a corner sufficient to make it known. And when Montaigne claims in the same context that the matter makes its own divisions and that he omits the words, the links, and the seams that would serve weak or heedless ears, his emphasis on what has not been "heard" calls on the responsive listener (reader) to fill in the words and the links as an interlocutor would do.

Thus encouraged by the essayist himself, modern readers have responded to the explicit structures and patterns that appear to invite them into the *Essais* by imagining a form of dialogue in which they participate with the text in the constitution of meaning. What more appropriate way to read a work that seeks explicitly to confound distinctions between writing and speech, as we have seen, and how better to engage a writer who claims to be speaking to the paper as he would speak to the first man he meets? Since Plato, of course, dialogue has occupied a privileged place in Western philosophy and literature as a way to truth and as the representation of that way, "en abyme" (even when that truth reveals itself ironically as indeterminate, as it could be said to do in some Platonic dialogues or as it does manifestly in the dialogues of Diderot, for example). From Socrates's dialectic method to the communication theory that underlies contemporary reader-response criticism, there extends a tradition in which forms of lively exchange and interaction define the scene of human understanding, its possibilities as well as its limitations. What has evolved through this tradition has been the displacement of dialogue from its presentation *within* the writing to its enactment *between* the writing and the reader. Montaigne clearly occupies a place in this history as an explicit exponent of reading as a form of interlocution where the writer (or the writing) and the reader engage each other through the textual medium. By considering the *Essais* in the light of that aspect of reader-response criticism that provides a theoretical ground for "dialogic" reading, the work of Wolfgang Iser, we can illuminate the practice Montaigne advocates for his reader and reveal in turn the limitations of the theory itself.

Drawing from the interactive model that Ingarden bases on the principle of textual indeterminacy, Iser posits a text that, like Montaigne's, must be completed or actualized by a diligent reader. Iser, of course, is concerned with fiction, and there are obvious differences between the gaps, interruptions, and blockages of narrative—the "inevitable omissions [by which] a story gains its dynamism"—and the open seams or the elusive subjects of a given essay or of Montaigne's work as a whole. But in both types of writing the gaps and seams do appear to invite response (Iser's term but also Montaigne's meaning) and to initiate "communication" between reader and text ("communication" is the key word in the subtitle of Iser's *The Implied Reader* and the essential ingredient of friendship in the *Essais* [I, 18, 184]).[20] When Iser speaks of the implied reader as designating "a network of response-inviting structures, which impel the reader to grasp the text," he glosses comments like those on the openness of writing in "De la vanité" and he evokes an active reader endowed with the diligence or the strong-ears Montaigne considers essential.[21] The open seams, the headings of subjects whose implications are only partially disclosed (I, 40, 251), words and ideas posited in passing, concepts and content sketchily developed ("ce que je ne puis exprimer, je le montre au doigt" [III, 9, 983b]), these openings represent what Iser calls the unwritten parts of a text that stimulate the reader's imagination and cause him to react by writing in what is missing.

Montaigne admits to holding back, to presenting stories upon which he does not comment, and to providing examples and quotations whose richness remains to be realized, so that what is unsaid might serve as so many seeds of further writing: "Elles [his stories and quotations] portent souvent, hors de mon propos, la semence d'une matiere plus riche et plus hardie, et sonnent à gauche un ton plus delicat, et pour moy qui n'en veux exprimer d'avantage, et pour ceux qui rencontreront mon air" (I, 40, 251c) ("They often bear, outside of my subject, the seeds of a richer and bolder material, and sound obliquely a subtler note, both for myself, who do not wish to express anything more, and for those who get my drift" [185]). While these lines apparently open the possibility that the reader who responds might produce innumerable essays of his own by plucking the text with a little ingenuity ("Qui voudra esplucher un peu ingenieusement, en produira infinis Essais" [ibid.]), the benefit may also accrue to the *Essais* by the extension of *its* meaning and the fulfillment of *its* intention. Montaigne specifically identifies a reader who "rencontre mon air," one who understands his sense, who gets his drift, and whose own "essais" bring out and develop that sense. Far from being an indifferent appropriation of Montaigne's text or an obtrusive or alien reading, this sympathetic response gives expression to what is "hors de mon propos" and brings it "inside" as Montaigne himself might have done. Here is an excess, or a beyond, that is domesticated by the reading, that can be brought in because in a sense it was always already there. The *Essais* and the reader's "essais" thus communicate with each other in a process that might be described, to use Iser's terms, as "the fulfillment of the potential, unexpressed reality of the text."[22]

Like Iser's implied reader, the reader of the *Essais* (who is also the writer of further "essais") appears to have entered into the reassuring community of dialogue, and the communion of meaning, where in benevolent interaction and partnership the sense (the seeds) of Montaigne's text flower(s). The reader seems to be drawn into the work, guided and stimulated by it, and he cooperates with that network of structures that invite his responses. Even when textual elements do not fit well together and appear to subvert the reader's search for coherence, or when competing "interpretations" arise, the spirit of this reading process is not disturbed. The critical act is one of organizing and reorganizing what Iser calls the data of the text, trying to "fit them together in the way we think the author meant them to be fitted."[23] The presence of discrepancies, he suggests, draws the reader into the text and compels him to conduct a creative examination not only of the work but also of himself. Apparently no text lies beyond the ultimate intention of the writer that it be a "fit" or beyond the ultimate competence of the reader to "fit it together" and, I sense, to find and to fit himself together in the process.

Yet it may be that the balance between text and reader, modeled in the *Essais* on the equality and exchange enjoyed in the communication between Montaigne and La Boétie, and theorized in Iser's work, represents an ideal, as absent from the text and perhaps from all reading, as the lost and unrecuperable friend himself. Even in Iser's formulation the ideal quality appears compromised by a pervasive and imposing textual system that always acts like the more forceful and demanding agent. According to the critic the text "must bring about" a standpoint for the reader, it must provide access to "what the reader is meant to visualize"; texts provide "guidelines," they provide "instructions," "predispositions," by which the reader is drawn "inescapably" into their world and "impelled" to grasp them. A tension exists between what the text prescribes through its structures—Iser calls this the "role" of the implied reader—and the disposition of the real reader, and it favors the side of the text: "Generally the role prescribed by the text will be stronger, but the reader's own disposition will never totally disappear; it will tend instead to form the background to and the frame of reference for the act of comprehending."[24] Iser clearly seeks to mitigate this imbalance because he needs a creative, interactive reader to formulate the unformulated "intentions" of the text. That is why he questions the desirability of Coleridge's "willing suspension of disbelief," takes issue with Wayne Booth's call for the reader to subordinate his heart and mind to the book, and cannot accept Poulet's demand that the individual disposition of the reader be shut out of the act of reading. Yet imbalance lies latent in his language, threatening always to overwhelm and to disrupt his precarious positing of equality. When he admits to the tension between text and reader, Iser cannot avoid suggesting that what is personal and historical about the reader fades or weakens, recedes into a background or marginalizes as a frame, although he must add, "never totally," for then the reader himself would disappear "totally," and with him Iser's act of reading as communication.[25]

The appealing idea of a partnership between the text that speaks for its author and the reader who both speaks the text and speaks himself in the process is thus a problematical one, and one that perhaps can never be more than a metaphor for the reader's desire to overcome the absence of the writer and the impersonality of textuality, to interact on equal ground and to share meaningfully in intersubjective exchange. Socrates argues forcefully in the *Phaedrus* (274d–277a) that writing can never enter into dialogue because it cannot respond to questions about what it is saying, and this view can serve to remind us of what we might call the single-mindedness (Socrates suggests it is stupidity) with which writing seeks to impose its own language, its own logic, its own "truth." Socrates's interest, of course, is to show writing up as the illegitimate child of the logos, and he allows that it can "speak" only to deny it the truth that characterizes "living speech" and to foreclose the possibility that writing can participate in that dialectic that opens the way to knowledge. In the context of my discussion of reading, I might extrapolate from Socrates's words that, rather than offering itself as a partner and making itself accessible to meaningful exchange, the text closes itself off, it speaks a monologue and recites endlessly what it is, and it provides no opening through which the reader can enter and interact. Unlike the true interlocutor of a spoken dialogue, the reader, for Socrates, can attempt endlessly to dialogue, but in the end he can only listen.

Reading Socrates's words in this way provides us with a radical statement of what I am proposing is the inclination of written texts to be overbearing and to dominate their readers. And yet there is nothing particularly radical in this idea, for the dominant reading mode today still gives priority to the author / text and persistently reads for the author's "message" or his ideas, and always with an expressed concern for the ways in which the writing expresses or fulfills his "intention." Even in Iser's case, where he tries to make reading approximate the face-to-face situation of social interaction, giving both text and reader equal weight, the critic cannot avoid describing the act of reading in terms that articulate control rather than communication. The structured gaps and blanks (structured by the writer? endowed with structural significance by the reader?) are the very elements of this control, for they provoke responses that are restricted and determined by the relationship between what is concealed and what is revealed, by what is implicit and what is explicit. One senses always, and in spite of Iser's lexicon of partnership and communication, that the reader consistently reacts at the behest of the text and that his formulations and reformulations, his perceptions and revisions, are always made in the name of grasping "the author's mode of experiencing" or the work as a "perspective intended by the author." Iser often characterizes the reader as creatively and imaginatively filling in the gaps, but this "creativity" is always reactive, always provoked, guided, and circumscribed by textual structures. He never speaks of an independent reader, one who might challenge the text or its assumptions or intentions, or read obtrusively against its structures. The text remains fixed and imposing, and the reader adapts, or, I would say, conforms; since the text cannot change, Iser says as if paraphrasing Socrates's words without intending his meaning, a successful relationship between text and reader can only come about if the reader changes.[26]

In a richly suggestive aside about speaking in "De l'experience" (III, 13), Montaigne claims that "La parole est moitié à celuy qui parle, moitié à celuy qui l'escoute" (1,088b) ("Speech belongs half to the speaker, half to the listener" [834]), as if to bolster the idea that the listener or reader plays his legitimate, subjective part in the equal exchange of dialogue. Or, as one critic has proposed, this phrase might also be read to affirm the reader's claim to "la parole," to allow that while the word belongs in the first instance to the speaker / writer it is also the rightful property of the listener / reader who may justifiably make of it what he wants.[27] If we replace the quotation in its context we can appreciate the degree to which Montaigne's words express not a sharing or a notion of equal access but a one-way process that seeks to control and dominate:

> Le ton et mouvement de la voix a quelque expression et signification, de mon sens; c'est à moy à le conduire pour me representer. Il y a voix pour instruire, voix pour flater, ou pour tancer. Je veux que ma voix, non seulement arrive à luy [his listener], mais à l'avanture qu'elle le frape et qu'elle le perse. . . . La parole est moitié à celuy qui parle, moitié à celuy qui l'escoute. Cettuy-cy se doibt preparer à la recevoir selon le branle qu'elle prend. Comme entre ceux qui jouent à la paume, celuy qui soustient se desmarche et s'apreste selon qu'il voit remuer celuy qui luy jette le coup et selon la forme du coup. (1,088b)

> The tone and movement of my voice express and signify my meaning;
> it is for me to guide it to make myself understood. There is a voice for

instructing, a voice for flattering, a voice for scolding. I want my voice
not only to reach my listener, but perhaps to strike him and to pierce
him. . . . Speech belongs half to the speaker, half to the listener. The
latter must prepare to receive it according to the motion it takes. As
among tennis players, the receiver moves and makes ready according
to the motion of the striker and the nature of the stroke. (834)

Montaigne's focus is first on himself as speaker / subject, on the
"moy" who guides his meaning to make himself understood, and on
the "I" who wills ("Je veux") that it be heard and that the desired
effect be produced on the listener. As one well-versed in rhetoric, he
knows that vocal tone and rhythm are expressive, that there are
different "voices" for different situations, and that these different
voices make different impressions and move the listener in different
ways. Clearly we are hearing the practiced writer speaking, the
writer who through the *Essais,* and especially in this moment,
chooses what he considers the appropriate voice and who modulates
and manipulates it to strike us, to pierce us sometimes, and to persuade us to his point of view and to his meaning.

When he comes to talk explicitly about the listener, Montaigne has
recourse to the figure of the tennis game, but not to elaborate on how
the game can be viewed as exchange between equals, or how the
receiver is also always (potentially) the sender—that is, the game as a
metaphor of dialogue. Rather, he chooses only the specific moment
when the player prepares to receive the ball, as in the moment of the
serve when he is entirely reactive. Three times Montaigne indicates
how the receiver is forced to adjust according to what is coming his
way, as if to stress that he must prepare to meet the ball as it "is":
"selon le branle qu'elle (la parole, la balle) prend," "selon qu'il voit
remuer celuy qui luy jette le coup," and "selon la forme du coup."
The flight of the ball, to paraphrase Iser, is fixed and does not change;
a successful game (that is, the reception of the author's meaning) can
come about only if the receiver moves to meet it. The notion that
speech belongs half to the speaker, half to the listener, implies that
the speaker / writer provides the motion and the form to represent
his meaning and that the listener / reader readies himself ("s'apres-
ter") and moves back ("se desmarcher") to "get" it.

I have in a certain sense been reading Montaigne's intended
meaning as my own interpretation of this passage, grasping his text
by bringing out its implications, making connections between the

explicit remarks on speaking and listening and the *Essais'* overriding concern with writing and reading, and formulating what is not entirely formulated in the text. This is reading as Iser intended, filling the gaps and blanks that prestructure the reader's role and allow him to assemble the meaning toward which the perspectives of the text have guided him. But we might also want to act more obtrusively and take the text where it apparently did not intend to go by giving expression to what remains unsaid in the tennis metaphor, to what the writing must ignore, eliminate, or marginalize—consciously or unconsciously—in order to pursue its intention or effect its program. This "unsaid" is precisely what the writer must not "say" and what the reader in his turn must not "say" if, to repeat Iser's formulation, he is to be guided by the perspectives of the text and assemble *its* meaning.

When I read Iser in this uninvited way, I uncovered in the formulation of the partnership between text and reader and in its language the specter of a domineering textual system that threatened to overwhelm the reader and dissolve the interaction between equals. Balance harbors within it a latent and disruptive imbalance. In Montaigne's case, if we play out the tennis match, the roles of sender and receiver alternate as the ball passes from one end of the court to the other, and in these successive reversals the potential for power and dominance changes hands. The author, or text, is no longer in the exclusive position of controlling the game of interpretation and meaning. The match becomes balanced and more complex as the receiver becomes the sender and attempts in his turn to force his moves on the other, to impose his motion and his form so that the other "backs up." What this indicates is that the reader does not have to fulfill a role implied by the text or play according to its rules, as Iser's reader seeks to do. Every text contains within itself the potential for obtrusive readings, every text exposes itself to the reader who repositions himself in relation to it and who repositions the intended meaning ("le coup") by getting in some shots of his own.

If we return once again to the question "To whom does the text belong?" and to the figurative language of ownership, we can read the "unsaid" in Montaigne's statement that "la parole est moitié à celuy qui parle, moitié à celuy qui l'escoute" as an assertion that the word represents contested property to which both writer and reader lay claim. All of the aspects that Iser describes, and that compose what we might call the intent of the writing (including the gaps that are filled to realize that intention), all of the forms, themes, and lexical elements that express the norms and values of the text, all this constitutes the claim by which the writer/text seeks to impose its meaning on the reader. My reference to the text as portrait was intended to convey this sense of the overwhelming presence of the writing and to reflect the demands it placed on the reader to be recognized and acknowledged for what it is. I might also have spoken of this as the rhetorical dimension of writing and referred to its persuasive intent and to the structural, thematic, and tropological elements (strategies) that act upon the reader to realize that intent.

One of the ways we acknowledge this control that the literary text seeks to exercise over the reader is to speak of readers as inscribed in the writing (or implied, as Iser does), or of writing that "reads" itself. Montaigne's reflections on his own writing, on its composition and expression, its meaning, its relation to his life, to the texts of others, to history, these are so many "readings" of the *Essais,* explicit readings that can serve to remind us of the hegemonic tendency that remains implicit in all literary texts. In fact, we might point to the variety of readings that Montaigne does—from the praiseworthy reading of the "suffisant lecteur" to the indifferent response of the "indiligent lecteur," from his call to seek coherence to his acknowledgment of the digressive, piecemeal quality of writing, from his own reading for the author's judgment to his willingness to fragment the other's writing and co-opt it for his own purposes—as illustrative of the fact that texts contain, and preempt, all readings and that the reader always fulfills his role by finding what is already there. This was the point of view of Heraclitus, that all things had in them the aspects that were found in them. The reader may give himself over wholly to the text by willingly suspending his disbelief, as Booth's reader does, or he may actively seek to fulfill this role, as Iser's does, or he may naïvely pursue what he takes to be his own reading, unaware that his activity has been anticipated and framed by the text, but in this general reading scenario the result is always the same: the writing imposes itself in each case.[28]

The text, we could say, is thus always something to be reckoned with, always some "thing" that cannot be ignored, disregarded, or eliminated in any simple way. But at the same time, if the reader is to be something in himself, if he is to be more than the instrument by which the text carries out its own program and actualizes itself, as much a product of the writing as the "meaning" he articulates, then he has to position himself "outside" of that meaning, he has to take an "unauthorized" stance and lay claim to the word on his own. I would argue that this is not a simple task, a task performed merely by saying anything at all about the text, as if the text could itself be saying anything at all, or, put another way, as if the text were nothing at all. The obtrusive reading always takes place against the pressure of writing's own claim to meaning, it confronts the text's effort to impose its intentions and must always take them into account.

Here we can return to Montaigne's tennis match and to the fact that in order to go successfully on the offensive, to return the ball forcefully and make his point, the receiver must first take account of the trajectory, the form, and the placement of the shot and react accordingly. The author, the text, intention, meaning, always clamor to get their due; the reader obtrudes, as I said, into "something" and then can seek to turn, to return, to overturn what is "there," but never without resistance. Writing can be recontextualized historically as Montaigne's friend did with Homer, rebutted as Montaigne does with Cicero the rhetor, or read against the grain, as numerous critics have done with the *Essais* themselves, but in each case the text will insist, as Montaigne's does, that it has been misread. The obtrusive reader reading against Montaigne's insistence on coherence and on a sort of unifying deep structure, for example, might find ample support for his own emphasis on fragmentation, on deferral, on open-endedness, and on contingency in the very gaps and indeterminacies that the essayist implies are only surface effects. In fact, this reader might claim that this surface was *also* the depth (that is, the meaning) and point to Montaigne's own strategies to conflate the two, as when he tries in "De la phisionomie" (III, 12) to make the face be the place where interiority is present and can be read.[29] But he will never be able entirely, and once and for all, to disprove the charge that he has been an "indiligent lecteur" or that he has had weak ears and has missed what the text has been "saying."[30]

If the text stakes its claim by seeking to *impose* itself and its meaning, a proper function of the obtrusive reader might be to *expose* the text in all its controlling practice, to disclose the rhetorical designs, the structural and thematic strategies by which the writing natural-izes its own activity and connects, substitutes, transfers, and represses elements of the experience that it seeks to encode, order, and organize. Even those self-reflexive texts that appear to expose themselves, to reveal the mechanisms of their production and to keep nothing to themselves, even those texts call for unauthorized readings. Self-reflexivity itself is a textual strategy that must conceal and suppress (time, an outside, history, ideology, the idea of the project itself) in order to represent itself. And when what I have been calling the obtrusive reader comes into his own in this way, the historical nature of both writing and reading becomes apparent.

From Montaigne's claim that every man bears within him the form of the human condition, and his insistence that his writing communicates what he calls his universal being ("mon estre universel" [III, 2, 805c]), we might infer the desire of writing to transcend the personal and to aspire to unified and essential meaning and truth. The obtrusive reader enters precisely to challenge that desire and to disclose the role that the cultural, the political, the social, the ideological play in the composition of the textual artifact. Precisely because writing strives to be natural and is thus willing to ignore or eager to conceal the assumptions and biases that condition both form and content, the reader intrudes to point up both evasive strategies and unexamined practices. But readings are themselves neither timeless nor self-evident, nor are they immune to self-serving blindness or to dissimulation. Readings, too, are grounded in person and in place, they are effects of a historical moment, products of the cultural, social, political, and ideological forces that shape thought itself. To enter uninvited into a text, to pass critical judgment as an obtrusive reader, is thus not to assume a privileged position outside of writing or outside of history. It is to open reading as writing itself has been opened, to disclose the reader as the writer has been disclosed, in all their power and their vulnerability.

4

The Presumption of Writing
Between Ovid's Children

Testis nemo in sua causa esse potest.

No one can be a witness on his own behalf.

Et n'est aucun si asseuré tesmoing comme chacun à soy-mesme.
(II, 16, 626)

And there is no witness so sure as each man to himself.

Nemo in sese tentat descendere. (cited in II, 17, 658)

No one attempts to descend into himself.

Montaigne undertakes explicitly to write about himself, but, after my discussion of textual progeny, of imposing texts and obtrusive readers, we might want to say that all writers write about themselves, whatever else they may write about. The work produced always reproduces the writer, however much he is "found" or "lost" there, it represents him as his offspring and speaks in his name in his absence and after his death. The diverse examples of the affection of fathers for their metaphorical children at the end of "De l'affection des peres aux enfans" imply that all "work," all actions and all deeds, are the other selves of those who produce them, especially the writings that are conceptions of the mind—as the long history of the topos of the book as child indicates. The metaphor is so pervasive that Montaigne can attribute paternity to those who might not have intended it or even thought of it; he can extend what he calls the affection that writers have for their writings and designate any writing as a child, that of Epicurus and even of St. Augustine. From this perspective Montaigne's declaration that he is himself the matter of his book and his claim that the text is his child announce the undeclared program of all writing and give his work exemplary status insofar as it explicitly foregrounds the activity by which all authors conceive of their subject—that is, the subject that is always also in some sense themselves.

While it might appear that writing could be taken as a form of self-conception that apparently concerns no one beyond the self, in effect Montaigne's effort to justify his activity also discloses its public dimension and his concern that his writing be considered presumptuous. Seeing himself in the eyes of his readers, the writer imagines that they will misinterpret his intention and misread his text, that they will mistakenly accuse him of self-aggrandizement, of writing to offer himself as exemplary or to satisfy his vanity. Perhaps if he wrote only for himself, or for his family and his intimate friends, the question of his audacity would not arise. But the *Essais* are a public text destined for a readership beyond this limited circle, and Montaigne's disclaimers of writing for such an audience cannot be taken entirely at face value. The rules of civility and decorum, he complains in "De la praesumption" (II, 17), do not allow a man to speak well of himself, nor do they allow him to speak ill either—that is, they effectively preclude speaking of oneself at all. But Montaigne does speak explicitly about himself, and we want to say as well that because he insists on writing at all he is always in some sense speaking about himself, always inscribing himself endlessly in his text, even when he appears not to be doing so. He thus finds himself, as he says, entangled in the laws of public ceremony and open, as all writers must be, to the charge of being presumptuous.

In "De l'exercitation" (II, 6) Montaigne raises the question again after making a personal anecdote the centerpiece of his essay: "La coustume a faict le parler de soy vicieux, et le prohibe obstineement en hayne de la ventance qui semble tousjours estre attachée aux propres tesmoignages" (378c) ("Custom has made speaking of oneself a vice, and obstinately forbids it out of hatred for the boasting that seems to be attached to bearing witness to oneself" [my translation]). Paradoxically, Montaigne acknowledges that custom is right to condemn as presumptuous the man who writes of himself, and he acknowledges its authority by addressing its concerns, by explaining and justifying his own activity. At the same time he holds that custom is wrong, that it imposes empty and superficial modes of conduct that mask what is natural and true and prevent man from expressing himself as he is. It may be presumptuous to write about oneself,

Montaigne allows, but he will not refuse any action that will display what he alludes to as this unhealthy quality since it is a part of him. Nor, he avers, does he want to conceal this fault, which he claims not only to practice but to profess (378). All public display of oneself, all writing, is "ventance," boasting of a sort, all "parler de soy," all "propres tesmoignages," are presumptuous, but they are to be performed, and both condemned and excused, as that which is both "propre" (one's own and therefore proper) and improper (in the eyes of others).

I am suggesting, then, that there is no other way to write except to write about the self and thus no other way to write except presumptuously, no other way to consider the performance of self-conception and self-perpetuation. It could not be otherwise as the author sends his progeny out into the world. Writing itself is always a public call and a public calling, simultaneously a call *to* the reader that demands that the writing be read and a call *from* the reader that elicits the text and demands that the writing be written. Without this fiction that brings the readership into being no writing can come into being. Montaigne claims that he and his text are not meant to be shown off in public like a statue mounted in the village square ("Je ne dresse pas icy une statue à planter au carrefour d'une ville, ou dans une Eglise, ou place publique" [II, 18, 664a]), but neither can his presentation resemble an intimate tête-à-tête, as the quotation from Persius that he disingenuously inserts would imply: "Secreti loquimur." Writing cannot be meant in any simple way, "pour le coin d'une librairie, et pour en amuser un voisin, un parent, un amy" (664a) ("for a nook in a library, and to amuse a neighbor, a relative, a friend" [503]). That is why Montaigne must come back repeatedly to the issue of his presumptuous writing, why the man who claims in all modesty to be capable of speaking only of himself must come back to excuse himself before his readers for presuming to speak at all.

Montaigne shares the anxiety of all writers about the public perception of their enterprise and thus makes the question of presumptuous writing an explicit subject of his discourse. The essayist anticipates the reception of his text and the meaning attributed to it (and to him) by his readers and responds in advance to their objections. But if he is concerned that others will misperceive him as presumptuous, he also worries that his presumption will cause him to misperceive himself, both as he writes about himself and as he reads his own text.

Here are the terms in which he defines presumption in the essay of the same title:

> Il y a une autre sorte de gloire, qui est une trop bonne opinion que nous concevons de nostre valeur. C'est un' affection inconsiderée, de-quoy nous nous cherissons, qui nous represente à nous mesmes autres que nous ne sommes: comme la passion amoureuse preste des beautez et des graces au subjet qu'elle embrasse, et fait que ceux qui en sont espris, trouvent, d'un jugement trouble et alteré, ce qu'ils ayment, autre et plus parfaict qu'il n'est. (II, 17, 631–32a)

> There is another kind of vainglory, which is an over-good opinion we form of our own worth. It is an unreasoning affection, by which we cherish ourselves, which represents us to ourselves as other than we are; as the passion of love lends beauties and graces to the object it embraces, and makes its victims, with muddled and unsettled judgment, think that what they love is other and more perfect than it is. (478)

Montaigne associates presumption with *philautia*, the classical concept of blinding self-love that was considered the source of folly, and of evil, by Renaissance writers and theologians. In a series of adages that Montaigne surely had read, Erasmus depicts philautia in the doubleness of its error, its excessive concern with the faults of others and its disregard of its own, recalling in its many reiterations (including Catullus, Persius, Horace, and St. Jerome) Aesop's fable of the man who keeps a double wallet over his shoulders with the faults of others in the front where he can see them and his own in the back where he cannot (I.vi.90). Montaigne himself frequently quoted Persius, and he found there the critique of self-love and the complaint, which he borrowed in "De la praesumption," that "no one attempts to descend into himself" (I will come back to this in some detail). In the *Satires*, this line is followed by, "They watch the wallet hanging on the back / Of him that walks before" (4.23–24). Like the distorting passion of those smitten with love for another, self-love troubles and alters the judgment, hiding its own defects and weaknesses, and it depicts the self to itself in flattering, and false, terms.

Everything is thus at stake in seeking to avoid presumption: for the philosopher who attempts to respond to the Delphic injunction and to know himself (only he who knows himself is worthy of being called a philosopher, Erasmus quotes Socrates as saying) and for the writer whose text both generates him and is his offspring, who both conceives himself as a text and seeks to read (and have others read) himself there. Presumption is thus doubly dangerous to the essayist, distorting his vision as he writes, blurring his vision as he reads. In "De la praesumption" Montaigne opens the wallet on his back. He confesses his faults ("quant aux bransles de l'ame, je veux icy confesser ce que j'en sens" [633a]), he dares to show himself as he is ("oser se faire veoir tel qu'on est" [647a]), and to make himself known ("pourveu que je me face connoistre tel que je suis" [653a]), so that in his openness and humility he will avoid presumption and assure the truth of self-presentation.

Montaigne thus confesses in "De la praesumption" to a profound dissatisfaction with himself and his work, to an inability to please, to the most common physical attributes, to a poor memory, to ignorance, to indiscretion and incivility. In fact, he goes much further as self-debasement becomes self-abnegation: "(a) De toutes les opinions que l'ancienneté a euës de l'homme (c) en gros, (a) celles que j'embrasse plus volontiers et ausquelles je m'attache le plus, ce sont celles qui nous mesprisent, avilissent et aneantissent le plus" (634) ("Of all the opinions antiquity has held of man as a whole, the ones I embrace most willingly and adhere to most firmly are those that despise, humiliate, and nullify us most" [480]). If the presumptuous man deludes himself by thinking too highly of himself, Montaigne will avoid the error by lowering his esteem, by bringing it as low as self-esteem has ever been brought: "Il est bien difficile, ce me semble, que aucun autre s'estime moins, voire que aucun autre m'estime moins, que ce que je m'estime" (635a) ("It would be very difficult, it seems to me, for any one to esteem himself less, or indeed for anyone else to esteem me less, than I esteem myself" [481]). Having affirmed man's nullity and emptiness, the essayist confirms his own and does so in a way that challenges any notion of the self as an origin or ground from which truth could be generated and imposed on the world, with the exception of the truth of man's own vanity. When in a confessional gesture of supreme self-denial Montaigne says that he disavows himself ("Je me desadvoue sans cesse"), he pulls away from himself and renounces himself, as if invoking the etymological weight of *avouer* (Latin *advocare*, to call or summon) to verify that the self cannot be called upon, that it cannot respond to any call except by the performance of its own nothingness. What alone can be called up are the faults of which Montaigne is guilty, and which he confesses: "coupa-

ble des defectuositez plus basses et populaires, mais non desad-
vouées, non excusées" (635c) ("Guilty of the commoner and humble
faults, but not of faults disavowed or excused" [481]). Herein lies the
response to the charge of presumptuous love for himself and of excessive affection for his textual child.

· · · · · · ·

Montaigne's lexicon of *affection* and *amour* that describes self-love
repeats the precise terms he uses to describe the feelings of fathers
for their children, for both physical and metaphorical offspring. To
love another does not appear to differ in kind from loving oneself,
even, or especially, when what one loves in the other is oneself. (How
could we possibly sort out the role of narcissism in love?) What sets
self-love apart as presumptuous seems to be a matter of degree, the
excessiveness that makes of it an affection that is "inconsiderée" and
produces an opinion of ourselves that is "trop bonne." This intem-
perance appears to be what distinguishes the infatuation of Pygmalion from the "normal" attachment of the poet for his work—"de
tous les ouvriers," Montaigne says citing Aristotle, "le poëte nom-
méement est le plus amoureux de son ouvrage" (II, 8, 402c)—the
poet, who along with Labienus, Lucian, Epicurus, and Epaminondas,
exemplifies that laudable affection of fathers for their children of the
mind. Is it then this excess of "passion amoureuse" rather than the
nature of its object that causes the essayist to condemn these "passions vitieuses et furieuses qui ont eschauffé quelques fois les peres à
l'amour de leurs filles" (402a) ("vicious and frenzied passions which
have sometimes inflamed fathers with love for their daughters"
[293]) and to cite Pygmalion as his only example?

Yet Pygmalion is a most complex example since it is precisely his
excessive love for Galatea that prompts the gods to act, precisely the
inordinate passion that led him to carress her ivory form and imagine
her loving response that caused Venus to answer his prayer and
bring her to life. Or rather that caused Venus to have Pygmalion
bring Galatea to life, since at his kiss the statue grew warm and at his
touch the ivory yielded, as Montaigne's quotation reminds us, just as
the stone had earlier yielded beneath his chisel. Here the "ouvrier"
as father loves his work beyond measure, with an affection that must
be considered as "inconsiderée." Here the sculptor fashions the work
as child, as daughter, as another himself, loves the work excessively

for having created it (Montaigne introduces this as another consideration: "Or, à considerer cette simple occasion d'aymer nos enfans pour les avoir engendrez" [399a]), and loves himself in the work. And this incestuous passion, which must be the height of self-love and presumption, finds the gods kindly disposed to honor a request so presumptuous that Pygmalion finally could not utter it: "If you Gods can give all things, may I have as my wife, I pray—" he did not dare to say, "the ivory maiden," but finished, "one like the ivory maid" (*Metamorphoses*, X.275–77).[1]

The figure of Pygmalion appears only twice in the *Essais*, first in the context I have described in "De l'affection des peres aux enfans," in which he is cited by name as an example of the "passion vitieuse et furieuse" that is the improper excess of the father's ("ouvrier") love for his daughter but also the paradoxical source of life itself. He appears again in the "Apologie de Raimond Sebond," but indirectly and without being named, and only to those who recognize the lines Montaigne quotes from Ovid of Hymettan wax softened by the sun and worked by men's fingers into different shapes. The simile that serves in the *Metamorphoses* to capture the sense of the ivory statue yielding beneath the touch of the impassioned sculptor, and that also functions as a metaphor of the creative process of the artist properly shaping his work, lends its resonance to the fashioning of self and text that is Montaigne's own essaying.[2] The striking relevance of these fleeting and understated appearances of Pygmalion to the themes of writing, conception, and self-love that I have been discussing and the curious ambivalence that suggests that the sculptor's story is both unpardonable and exemplary give Pygmalion an emblematic function in the *Essais* and help us address the problematic nature of presumption that appears to initiate and inhabit the project of writing about, essaying, oneself. The analogy between Pygmalion and Montaigne seems to suggest that the *Essais* are meant in a positive way to be the coming to life of Montaigne himself, that the essayist's desire to naturalize art is in some way an effort to approximate what Ovid calls the sculptor's "art without art." But the analogy also introduces the necessity of coming to grips with Pygmalion's love for Galatea, with his incestuous love for his creation / daughter and for himself in her, and with Montaigne's preoccupation with his own presumptuousness—that is, with *his* excessive affection for his creation (his daughter?) and for himself.

If Galatea could not have come to life without the sculptor's perverse and frenzied passion, we might speculate that Montaigne's textual child would not have been conceived and come alive without the audacious self-love that the essayist disavows in "De la praesumption." That this presumptuous obsession with the self gives rise to the writing is in fact literally true of that essay (and of all the essays), for he and his own presumption—whether he is guilty of it or not—are the subjects of his text. We might want to see in Montaigne's continual self-reference the most striking form of presumption, even and especially when he refers to himself to deny himself. Let me quote a passage representative of the monstrous (incestuous) presumption of saying "I," of imposing the "I" as the unique and exclusive linguistic and psychological center:

(a) J'ay le goust tendre et difficile, et notamment en mon endroit: je me (c) desadvoue sans cesse; et me (a) sens par tout flotter et fleschir de foiblesse. Je n'ay rien du mien dequoy satisfaire mon jugement. J'ay la veue assez claire et reglée; mais, à l'ouvrer, elle se trouble: comme j'essaye plus evidemment en la poesie. Je l'ayme infiniment: je me cognois assez aux ouvrages d'autruy; mais je fay, à la verité, l'enfant quand j'y veux mettre la main; je ne me puis souffrir. (635)

My taste is delicate and hard to please, and especially regarding myself; I am incessantly disowning myself; and I feel myself, in every part, floating and bending with weakness. I have nothing of my own that satisfies my judgment. I have clear enough and controlled sight; but when I put it to work, it grows blurred, as I find most evidently in poetry. I love it infinitely; I am a pretty good judge of other men's works; but in truth, I play the child when I try to set my hand to it; I cannot endure myself. (481)

Montaigne insists on the superficiality of his vanity just before the lines I have quoted ("J'en suis arrosé, mais non pas teint"), but the weight of the first-person subject pronouns opening each of his phrases belies his claim. Let me quote again the absolute terms in which he affirms his lack of worth; we can hear the presumptuousness of his claim that *no one* has a lower opinion of himself: "il est bien difficile, ce me semble, que aucun autre s'estime moins, voire que aucun autre m'estime moins, que ce que je m'estime." By presenting himself as the lowest of the low he does not escape the presumption of his self-conscious hyperbole; rather, he makes of himself the highest of the low, the best of the worst, because "no one" denies himself better than he does. And this same reversal operates over and again to make him the reference point for the norms and qualities that the essay ultimately values as desirable and redemptive. Every significant fault Montaigne confesses acquires positive worth, every self-abasing statement gives him exemplary status: ignorance becomes the source of wisdom, lack of memory the origin of self-reliance, incivility and the inability to please the marks of naturalness and sincerity, and his litany of faults the sign of that humility by which he redeems himself. Clearly, the denunciation of presumption is not the elimination of presumption.

The structure of Montaigne's avowal thus recuperates the very element it seeks to eliminate, the vain "I" that centers itself as the original effect of its vanity and must center itself again in order to disavow itself. This paradox, in which what saves is what damns and what damns saves, resembles that of Pygmalion's story, as Montaigne recounts it and as I have presented it, where what condemns the sculptor—his self-love expressed as his unnatural, incestuous passion for his image—is also what saves him, what brings the image to life. And Montaigne's case, as these analogies suggest, is based upon a similar paradox, for although he must censure the error of self-love that would represent himself to himself other than he is, only by erring in self-love can he represent himself to himself at all as the subject of his essays. Only his strong opinion of his lack of self-worth, he says, only his continual confession and self-abasement, allow him to avoid being deceived by what he calls "l'affection que je me porte singuliere" (657a) ("The singular affection I have for myself" [499]). It is equally clear, however, that only that "affection . . . singuliere" allows him to concentrate nearly all his affection on himself, to excite it so that he can seek to know himself and, as the writing in this essay seeks to imply, to be present to himself in himself and in his writing. In the lines that follow this statement of the double nature of self-love Montaigne's syntax turns back reflexively upon its subject in insistent self-reference:

Or mes opinions, je les trouve infiniement hardies et constantes à condamner mon insuffisance. De vray, c'est aussi un subject auquel j'exerce mon jugement autant qu'à nul autre. Le monde regarde tousjours vis à vis; moy, je replie ma veue au dedans, je la plante, je l'amuse là. Chacun regarde devant soy; moy, je regarde dedans moy: je n'ay affaire qu'à moy, je me considere sans cesse, je me contrerolle, je me gouste. Les autres vont tousjours ailleurs, s'ils y pensent bien; ils vont tousjours avant, "nemo in sese tentat descendere," moy je me roulle en moy mesme. (657–58a)

Now I find my opinions infinitely bold and constant in condemning my inadequacy. In truth, this too is a subject on which I exercise my judgment as much as on any other. The world always looks straight ahead; as for me, I turn my gaze inward, I fix it there and keep it busy. Everyone looks in front of him; as for me, I look inside of me; I have no business but with myself; I continually observe myself, I take stock of myself, I taste myself. Others always go elsewhere, if they stop to think about it, they always go forward; "No man tries to descend into himself;" as for me, I roll about in myself. (499)

Boldly claiming the infinite boldness of his self-condemnation, Montaigne performs the presumptuousness of his singular affection for himself: "Cette capacité de trier le vray . . . je la dois principalement à moy," he claims; "car les plus fermes imaginations que j'aye, et generalles, sont celles qui, par maniere de dire, nasquirent avec moy. Elles sont naturelles et toutes miennes" (658a) ("This capacity for sifting truth . . . I owe principally to myself. For the firmest and most general ideas I have are those which, in a manner of speaking, were born with me" [499]). Portraying himself as whole unto himself, enclosed within the circle of his self-reflexive gaze, speaking to himself of himself, the taster tasted (or, we might add, the writer written), Montaigne's affection for himself appears to affect himself and give him the unmediated sense of his own subjectivity. The essayist writes himself (down) as the experience of the reflexive gaze, the autoerotic gaze that makes of him a subject who both beholds and holds himself in the consciousness of his own presence and in the presence of his consciousness. In incestuous self-love, the work, the statue, come to life.

Is this not the expression of the most scandalous presumption? And of a presumptuous self-love that lies not outside the self as something that keeps the self from being itself but as that which composes interiority itself, that which gives rise to the sense of self and at the same time obscures it in presumptuous overestimation? The only way that the self can experience itself is in the experience of its presumptuousness—that is, in the emptiness of its vain and unnatural self-love, but no sense of self can come about without this error, this inflated and deceptive embrace of the self that Montaigne calls "un' erreur d'ame" (633). This "erreur" reveals the truth of the self in all its paradoxical complexity. Montaigne wanders from the truth about himself in the self-deception of his love for himself, but that error (Latin *errare*, to wander) also enacts the wandering through himself that he calls rolling about in himself, the wandering that both affirms himself and reveals his nullity, affirms himself *as* his nullity, and calls forth its bold condemnation. And here we might want to recall the story of Narcissus (readers have long been aware of the ways in which the narratives of Pygmalion and Narcissus reflect and refract each other) and say that perhaps Montaigne's double gesture of self-embrace and self-denial is what saves him from the fate of Narcissus and from the consequences of what I have called his auto-erotic gaze. When asked whether Narcissus would live to a ripe old age, the prophetic seer answered, "Yes, if he does not come to know himself," as if self-knowledge were possible only at the price of death. Montaigne's text reveals what Narcissus could not or would not "see," that the self cannot be possessed in any absolute way, that the movement that reveals it also conceals it, that self-knowledge is always a question of knowing and of simultaneously being ignorant of the self.[3]

Montaigne thus escapes the death that consumes Narcissus, the death that Ovid describes as the physical wasting away of the body, the golden wax melting in the gentle heat (we recall that the poet likens Galatea's ivory body to melting wax when the statue—the woman and art itself—comes to life), and that is the figure for Narcissus's confusion of substance and shadow. But we might ask if Narcissus dies because he comes to know himself, as the seer predicted, or if he dies because ultimately he does not know himself, because in the blindness of his self-love he remains ignorant of the truth of himself. Although at first Narcissus does not recognize his mistake, he does come to know himself as the image in the water and to understand his paradoxical position: "Alas! I am myself the boy I see. I know it: my own reflection does not deceive me. I am on fire with love for my own self. . . . What I desire, I have. My very plenty makes me poor. How I wish I could separate myself from my body! and, strange prayer for a lover, I would that what I love were absent from me" (III, 463–68). But the wish to separate himself from his body and to be absent from himself cannot be realized in life any more than his desire to be wholly present to himself. Paradoxically, Narcissus both "has" what he desires and is unable to possess himself.

Only in death can the prayer for release be answered, as Narcissus both realizes and is unwilling to admit. When his tears disturb the water, and the image vanishes, Narcissus once again cries out for the fulfillment of his self-love: "Where are you fleeing? Cruel creature, stay, do not desert him who loves you, cruel one!" (477–78). If the seer's prediction is meant to resonate with the words of the Delphic oracle, can we say that Narcissus knows himself in any real sense? He may overcome his initial blindness to see himself in the water, but he cannot "see" himself and understand the limitations of his nature, which is precisely what the oracle would have one know to know oneself. Narcissus dies because he remains trapped in the error of his self-absorption, because he "sees" only with his eyes. When Montaigne names Narcissus in the *Essais*, he depicts him as a victim of the senses (and a victim of the poet's recognition of the power of the senses): "Combien donnent à la force des sens les poëtes, qui font Narcisse esperdu de l'amour de son ombre" (II, 12, 594a) ("How much power the poets ascribe to the senses, who make Narcissus madly in love with his own reflection" [449]).

If Narcissus remains an essential subtext of the *Essais*, as the figure of the constricting and self-destructive side of presumption and self-love that does not know itself, Pygmalion plays a more complex role as both the author of the perverse and furious (self-) love for his creation and the author of the creation itself.[4] This double role allows the sculptor to escape the fate of Narcissus, for it is also the double role of the writer himself, of both Ovid and Montaigne. In his love for his work, his child, and for himself in it, the artist resembles Narcissus who is so taken with his own image. But where Narcissus is beguiled by a shadow of life and caught in the unnatural circle of his self-enclosed passion that can only result in death, the artist, as the story of Pygmalion reminds us, loves something outside of himself, even though it is also himself and even though this self is also his daughter. Pygmalion's Galatea originates in his revolt against nature, in his turning away from women toward art, but it is through that art that nature, and the sculptor's nature in the form of his love, and his desire work their life-giving transformation and soften the unfeeling stone. Art and nature are not antithetical in Ovid as they are not absolutely opposed in Montaigne. Art can be the way to nature, it can be the means to recuperate and embody nature, to give form and life to the child and to the self. "Si j'estois du mestier," the essayist says, speak-

ing of those who give an artificial color to common things, "je natu-
raliserois l'art autant comme ils artialisent la nature" (III, 5, 874c) ("If I
were of the trade, I would naturalize art as much as they artify nature" [666]). This is precisely the gesture that engenders the analogy
between real and metaphoric offspring in "De l'affection des peres
aux enfans," the gesture that makes intercourse with the muses a
natural intercourse and the child of the mind a child of nature as well.

Both times in the *Essais* when Montaigne evokes Pygmalion, he
quotes Ovid's lines in which Galatea comes to life under the caress-
ing hand of the sculptor, as if to insinuate his own handiwork as the
text taking shape beneath the pen and the self emerging through his
writing. The frenzied passion of Pygmalion for his "daughter" closes
"De l'affection des peres aux enfans" at the supreme moment of
artistic creation, the moment when it most closely resembles life-
giving creation itself: "Tentatum mollescit ebur, positoque rigore/
Subsedit digitis" ("The ivory grew soft to his touch and, its hardness
vanishing, yielded beneath his fingers" [X.283–84]). Later, in the
"Apologie de Raimond Sebond," in a passage that begins by paraphrasing Theophrastus to affirm how little man can come to know,
Montaigne changes perspective midway to depict how knowledge is
fashioned and passed from one person to another, from one generation to another, and finally from himself to his reader, and he concludes with the metaphor Ovid uses to depict Galatea's breast softening at Pygmalion's touch:

> Ayant essayé par experience que ce à quoy l'un s'estoit failly, l'autre y
> est arrivé, et que ce qui estoit incogneu à un siecle, le siecle suyvant l'a
> esclaircy, et que les sciences et les arts ne se jettent pas en moule, ains
> se forment et figurent peu à peu en les maniant et pollissant à plu-
> sieurs fois, comme les ours façonnent leurs petits en les lechant à
> loisir: ce que ma force ne peut descouvrir, je ne laisse pas de le sonder
> et essayer; et, en retastant et pétrissant cette nouvelle matiere, la re-
> muant et l'eschaufant, j'ouvre à celuy qui me suit quelque facilité
> pour en jouir plus à son ayse, et la luy rends plus souple et plus
> maniable, "ut hymettia sole/Cera remollescit, tractatáque pollice,
> multas/Vertitur in facies, ipsoque fit utilis usu." (II, 12, 560a)

> Having found by experience that where one man had failed, another
> has succeeded, and that what was unknown to one century the fol-
> lowing century has made clear, and that the sciences and arts are not
> cast in a mold, but are formed and shaped little by little, by repeated
> handling and polishing, as the bears lick their cubs into shape at lei-

sure, I do not leave off sounding and testing what my powers cannot
discover; and by handling again and kneading this new material, stirring it and heating it, I open up to whoever follows me some facility to
enjoy it more at his ease, and make it more supple and manageable
for him: "As Hymettian wax grows soft under the sun and, moulded
by the thumb, is easily shaped to many forms and becomes usable
through use itself." (421)

Once the context of the Latin quotation has been identified, the analogy between the essayist and the sculptor becomes strikingly apparent. Experience, knowledge, writing, the self are all like the artist's
material, all to be shaped and molded, sounded and tested, handled
and kneaded, to give them life. And Montaigne's figures suggest that
what is manipulated under the thumb of the artist as the work of art
is also manipulated as a work of nature, as the sun softens the wax
and as the bear licks her young at birth to transform the fleshy lump
into the cub who takes her shape (Montaigne would have seen this
topos in Ovid, XV.379–81). Again, nature and art intersect, interact,
in the conception of life itself. Only by fashioning a work of art, and
fashioning himself as a work of art, as both Pygmalion and Montaigne do in presumptuous self-absorption (and, we might add, as all
artists apparently do), can the essayist escape the fate of Narcissus.
Only by turning his gaze toward himself in the most outrageous and
incestuous desire to embrace himself can he experience the nature of
his own presumption, can he reveal the truth of his nature and come
to know himself. Only by writing, by engendering the metaphoric
daughter of the mind, can the artist exploit the power of the figure
and bring his art to life.

·   ·   ·   ·   ·   ·   ·

Narcissus and Pygmalion thus delineate the space of Montaigne's
presumptuous obsession with himself, they define the self-love that
lies between self-absorption and the death of the one and self-absorption and the transcendence through art into life of the other.
Within this space the self is essayed and the essays are written; only
within this space can art come into being. The hunter forsakes the
imperfect love of others and turns from the world, he turns toward
himself and finds himself in what he takes as the perfect love. But in
his self-love he loses himself, and in his self-consuming death he is
nowhere to be found. This is the danger that Montaigne seeks to

avoid, as our reading of "De la praesumption" indicates. The sculptor also turns from the world, from the degraded love of the women, but toward the ideal woman of stone he has engendered. Loving himself in his art and loving his art as if it were another, he overcomes the lifelessness of stone and returns both himself and his creation to nature. This is the ideal toward which the essayist strives.

And yet, the alternative represented by Pygmalion is not quite ideal for it is not without its darker side, a side that remains buried for three generations before its disruptive and destructive force erupts with disastrous consequences, as if history could no longer suppress or repress its secret. When Ovid turns directly from Pygmalion and Galatea to tell the story of their great-granddaughter Myrrha, his tale of her incestuous passion for her father discloses the truth of the relation of her ancestors, as if it were a reversed image that mirrored the sculptor's love for his daughter/statue. Both are stories of love between parents and progeny, and in spite of the differences between children who are natural or metaphorical, and of the differences between love requited or unrequited, favored by the gods or condemned by them, these are both narratives of incestuous desire.

In a narrow sense, Montaigne evokes Pygmalion in "De l'affection des peres aux enfans" to strengthen the analogy he has been developing between fathering physical children and producing the mind's progeny. The analogy holds, he seems to be suggesting by raising this limit case of parental affection, because, just as in natural parenthood, fathers in this "other kind" have also been smitten with a "vicious and frenzied passion" for their progeny. Witness what they tell of Pygmalion, he says. But more than the status of the figure is revealed by Montaigne's rhetorical strategy. What the reference to Pygmalion reveals is the complex nature of paternity, both real and metaphorical, its necessarily incestuous and self-enclosed character. Paternity, Pygmalion's story suggests, is more than a "paternal" narrative; it is a love story whose erotic dimension cannot be left out, and especially not out of Montaigne's story of textual progeny, even if he leaves it out himself. Pygmalion is not the polar alternative to Narcissus. While the hunter is completely overcome in his autoeroticism, the sculptor only provisionally triumphs in the erotic desire for the other, for the story of Myrrha discloses what in the tale of Pygmalion remains unsaid, that the desire for the other is another face of the impossible and inadmissible desire for the self. Montaigne condemns incestuous love in no uncertain terms, but, as in the case of presumption, its condemnation is not its elimination. Nor, in fact, can it be if art is to be brought to life, as our reading of the story of Pygmalion indicated, although the dark side of the passion has shown that the dangers to the artist and to his soul are real. Myrrha is haunted by her guilt and denied both life and death in order not to defile the living or the dead; she is changed into a tree, and, although she no longer has feeling, she weeps eternally. But the incestuous union of daughter and father, like that of her forebear, is productive and brings beauty to life: Myrrha gives birth to Adonis who, Ovid says, would have been praised for his beauty even by Jealousy personified.

Pygmalion thus reminds us that artistic paternity is not only a story of father and son but also a story of father and daughter that the patriarchal tradition and Montaigne himself have not been anxious to tell. In fact, in the Ovidian account that I have privileged in speaking about Montaigne, it is necessarily a story of father and daughter. The traditional, masculine gender of textuality, like gender itself, is a cultural construct, and culture and tradition in the West have conspired to have males produce male children. To protect long-standing privileges, woman has been elided: the father appropriates the conceptual function of the mother, the offspring is conceived as a son in the image of the father and becomes the sole bearer of the name. Perhaps, too, as long as the father produces the child, imagining that the beloved progeny is male allows the truth of Pygmalion to be repressed and blocks out the truth of Myrrha, the truth that at the source of art, and of beauty, may lie desire and the incestuous passion that we have identified as self-love. Montaigne appears to remain faithful to the traditional position on the issue of lineage and to conceive of his text as a son, but the *Essais* also disclose the inadmissible imperative that the text be a daughter as well if it is to come to life.

Writing, then, if we return to the example of Montaigne, is fraught with peril. It is not simply a question of condemning the trap of Narcissus and of celebrating the fate of Pygmalion, because one cannot avoid the implications of either story. Montaigne turns inward in response to the Delphic command ("Regardez dans vous, reconnoissez vous, tenez vous à vous" [III, 9, 1,001b]) ("Look into yourself, know yourself, keep to yourself" [766]), and in heeding its words in these essays of the self he risks losing himself in his narcissistic self-delusion. But by essaying himself as his art, by projecting an image of himself as his writing, he may also recognize himself in the oracle's words (and in his own) and find his presumptuous vanity and his emptiness as himself: "C'est tousjours vanité pour toy, dedans et dehors, mais elle est moins vanité quand elle est moins estendue. Sauf toy, ô homme, disoit ce Dieu, chaque chose s'estudie la premiere et a, selon son besoin, des limites à ses travaux et desirs. Il n'en est une seule si vuide et necessiteuse que toy, qui embrasses l'univers" (ibid.) ("It is always vanity for you, within and without; but it is less vanity when it is less extensive. 'Except for you, O man,' said that god, 'each thing studies itself first, and according to its needs, has limits to its labors and desires. There is not a single thing as empty and needy as you, who embrace the universe' "). The God seeks to turn man back upon himself from his audacious concern with the world so that he might know himself in his shame and humility. Yet Montaigne's experience reveals that man cannot return without presumptuous and incestuous self-love; without it he cannot create the image of himself to know, without it there will be no conception, no offspring, no art. The creation will reveal the vanity of self-love and the nothingness of the creator and his image. The self that must love itself cannot escape its own vanity, both its presumptuous self-absorption and its emptiness. It must, however, seek itself in its vanity, recognize and confess its nature. Although the confession of vanity, like the avowal of presumption, cannot be its elimination, it is the only way that the self can come to know itself.

When Montaigne writes about the nullity of the self he opens the possibility of the recuperation of the self, for the text that makes nothing of man is not itself nothing. On the contrary, its language declares itself as something, as a center that both affirms the nullity of the self and rescues it linguistically.[5] When Montaigne denigrates himself in the confession of his "erreur," he saves himself; his writing annihilates and by annihilating saves. But it is important to understand that the self that in its presumptuousness took itself for the center of language, for its origin and referent, has now become the subject of language and a metaphor of self. The self is displaced into language, it is figured by and through a series of chiasmic reversals where the denial of self becomes its affirmation and its affirmation denial, where text becomes self and the self a text. The writing reveals itself not only as the expression of the philosophical truth of being (as nothingness) but as the enactment of the rhetorical mode of substitution and reversal that produces the figure of self.

Montaigne's essays tend to underplay the implications of this displacement of the self and its recuperation through the rhetorical structure. Insofar as they lay claim to the essayist's unmediated presence, to the consubstantiality of writing and being, they must treat their language as a transparent medium, as no-thing in itself: at the center of language and as the center of language, the self pretends to be the same as its textual double. Is this not Narcissus's water as a transparent medium, a medium in which the self takes the image for itself, and where even the ripples in the lake disturbed by the falling tears do not draw attention to the facticity of representation and to the mediating function of the medium itself? In his claim to be confessing what he feels and to be saying what he thinks, Montaigne implies not only that consciousness and its thought are present in voice but that a certain kind of direct, unadorned, and self-effacing discourse—the spontaneous discourse of voice itself as the interpreter of the soul—guarantees its truth. The essayist's aversion to rhetorical speech, his scorn for a use of language—or a kind of language—composed of figures and tropes that can make things appear as they are not and that draws attention to itself, is a commonplace of the *Essais* that I have already examined in my discussion of the child learning how to speak.

In "De la praesumption" Montaigne specifically rejects a vain and debilitating concern with eloquence, grammar, and "les beaux mots" in favor of what he calls "la vraye philosophie" (660), which lives in the morals and the talk of peasants. Of course this is not "philosophie" at all in any conventional sense, just as the "peasants" are not historical peasants. These are figures based on a principle that reverses convention and, for the purposes of Montaigne's presentation, are intended to represent the spontaneous and natural expression of truth and being. Clearly, the denunciation of rhetoric is not the elimination of rhetoric, nor can it be, because rhetoric, like presumption and self-love, cannot simply be expelled or expunged. The self can be conceived only as an image projected, as I said, as a figure or a trope that allows form and meaning to be conferred. Rereading the passage in which Montaigne depicts himself rolling around in himself, looking within himself, considering, tasting, taking stock of himself, distinct from others and from the world (657), we can appreciate how the conception of self is generated by the syntactical and lexical oppositions between inside and outside, between self and other, and how the impression of the essayist's presence to himself derives from the carefully structured and balanced phrasing, and the play of antithesis, of hyperzeugma (each phrase with its own verb), of repetition, and the suggestive richness of rhyme.

We are in a sense again between Ovid's children, between the elusive watery image and the substantial ivory figure, between the mirror reflection of self and the sculptural refraction of self, between the destructive delusion of self-absorption and the productive illusion of art. If the essayist takes his rhetoric wholly as life—that is, if he overlooks the facticity of his self-creation—he falls into the scandalous trap of Narcissus. But if he takes his work as art alone and does not aspire to transcend it and bring it to life as Pygmalion did, he will remain trapped in his rhetoric or, we might say, trapped *as* his rhetoric. It is telling that in those instances in which he alludes to the sculptor, Montaigne evokes the moment when the statue undergoes its metamorphosis, when it is both inert and living at the same time, both art and nature. As if the work acknowledged its artificial, man-made quality, its contingency, its essential nontruth and simultaneously expressed its desire that it be something more, an authentic discourse, as solid as stone and at the same time representing its author to the life. The *Essais* will not, cannot, metamorphose into life as Galatea did, although Montaigne will insist that they are lifelike, consubstantial, but the writing will seek to be the place where form, subjectivity, and history converge, however problematical or unstable that convergence may be.

· · · · · · ·

In the midst of his most telling affirmation of self-affection—in the long passage in which he most assertively claims his self-sufficiency and presence to himself as he rolls about in himself—Montaigne quotes from Persius to distinguish himself from others: "nemo in sese tentat descendere" (658). No one, the grammar of the quote establishes categorically and unequivocally, no one attempts to descend into himself, no one moves from the outside or the surface to seek inner or deeper knowledge of the self. Misled by a presumptuous "affection inconsiderée" that gives him the false impression that he is the center of meaning, man goes out of himself to judge the world and to impose his meaning upon it. We recall that this line in Persius is followed by the image of the double wallet, the emblem of philautia, which blinds man to his own faults. Montaigne's striking figure in this same essay of those people perched astride the epicycle of Mercury to look into the heavens can stand for this obsession with all that lies beyond, an effect of "la trop bonne opinion que l'homme a de soy" that drives him to seek the cause of the ebb and flow of the Nile when he does not know the motion of what he moves himself, as the essayist puts it (634). And yet Montaigne does claim, and in this very context, to be looking within himself, as if in response to the Delphic injunction to be seeking that knowledge that will prove ultimately to disclose the nullity of both knowledge and self. He appears, in effect, to be the unique exception to Persius's rule and, in fact, to be the exception that proves the rule. How can Montaigne descend into himself when no one attempts to descend into himself?

The same grammatical sequence whose literal reading bars Montaigne from attempting to descend into himself engenders another meaning, a figurative meaning that is mutually exclusive and opens the possibility of self-knowledge. If we take *nemo* as a proper name (Nemo), as a persona called "no one"—as Renaissance tradition did in numerous literary and iconographic presentations—then the figure of the no one is the subject of the sentence and precisely the "one," the "no" one who is someone, the nemo, who attempts to descend into himself.[6] In the essay on presumption Montaigne has made himself into a no one, affirming his nullity. But as I have remarked, by displacing himself into his text as a self-negating nemo he allows himself to descend as a self-affirming nemo, a figure (of speech) born of the absurdity of language who does indeed come to know himself. Only by denying himself can the essayist find himself in his writing, only by asserting his existential nothingness can he claim something textually, only in the deceptiveness and the ambiguity of a rhetorical joke can he find the truth of his self. No one is someone, the quotation tells us, and nothing is something; the statement of nothing is something as a statement and the experience of nothing is in truth an experience. Rhetorically, syntactically, the essayist predicates something from nothing (affirming the difference between grammatical and logical subjects); writing reveals that the experience of the nothingness of the self is the truth of experience and the truth of the self.

Montaigne thus becomes a witness to himself and bears witness in his confession of ignorance, but it is a central lesson of the *Essais* that no one bears witness to himself just as no one descends into oneself. Although there is no explicit reference in the *Essais* to nemo as a witness, there existed, in fact, an ancient legal maxim that Montaigne as a jurist certainly knew and that brings this figure back to proscribe testifying in one's own behalf. This maxim might serve as a subtext for our reading, a text that like so many others reverberates beneath the surface of Montaigne's writing and is recuperated by the reading: "Testis nemo in sua causa esse potest" ("No one can be a witness on his own behalf").[7]

To say that "no one can be a witness on his own behalf" was to invoke a rule of law operative in certain provinces in sixteenth-century France and to raise the issue of the credibility of legal testimony. No one can be his own witness because testimony is valid only if it is disinterested, if the witness is not a party to the action, if he is located on the margins as a spectator and does not stand to gain personally from the story that is told. The witness speaks in the first person as an "other," he tells what he knows, what he saw or heard, and, to the degree to which he is removed, unrelated, a neutral, dispassionate voice, it is assumed he speaks truthfully. One's own testimony about oneself, then, is always suspect because it is always self-serving, it must always be taken as the expression of selfish interest, even when it is true. And then, as our discussion has indicated, it is always presumptuous to speak about oneself and to assume a public presence, always a sign of an exaggerated sense of oneself and an inordinate concern with oneself, even when one bears witness to one's nullity or speaks to humiliate or to debase oneself. Only in religious confession can one legitimately be a witness to oneself, but perhaps when one testifies before God the situation is different because God already knows what is being revealed. In a sense God has already himself been the witness who, in his omniscience and in his silence, assures the truth and opens the possibility that the speaker will be forgiven (for the sins of which he speaks and also perhaps for the sin of speaking of himself). In Montaigne's case, where the resonances are both theological and legal, the vocabulary of witnessing and confessing that is common to both tends to blur distinctions between the religious and the purely secular. What allows Montaigne to speak of himself if there is no transcendent other before whom he must speak? What right has he to speak in this way if there is no legal precedent that justifies that he speak of himself? The nature of Montaigne's speaking remains problematical, and this calls for some strategy to protect the integrity of the self-reflexive testimony.

We have seen Montaigne pause numerous times in the course of the *Essais* to consider the fact that he is speaking of himself, to confront what custom considers a vice and what he admits is presumptuousness. But who would speak of the private man, we heard him ask in "De la praesumption," if he did not speak of himself, if he were not his own witness (II, 17, 632)? Putting the issue in somewhat different terms, he wonders why it is not permissible for a man to portray himself in writing since King René of Sicily depicted himself in his painted self-portrait (653). In "De l'exercitation" (II, 6), after recounting the story of his fall from his horse as an example of how he has "practiced" death without actually experiencing it, Montaigne reacts over the final pages of the essay to an imagined reader who would hold it against him that he publishes what he writes about himself. The book might serve others, he claims; in any event it is a folly that will die with him, without any consequences; it is a new and extraordinary amusement, an activity that only two or three long-forgotten ancients had tried before him; in the other sciences man imparts what he has learned, why not in this one? But beyond these considerations, the figure of Socrates speaking of himself and leading his disciples to speak of themselves, seeking self-knowledge in response to the Delphic injunction, serves as the model and ultimate justification for Montaigne's self-reflexive discourse. We might say that Socrates spoke of himself because he was called upon to do so by the oracle, but it is also true that what allowed him to speak was the fact that he had nothing (good) to say about himself, that his self-study was the expression of his self-scorn. Anyone who knows himself in this way, Montaigne says in the imperative that concludes "De l'exercitation," let him make himself known boldly by his own mouth: "Qui se connoistra ainsi, qu'il se donne hardiment à connoistre par sa bouche" (II, 6, 380c).

No one, we might say, has the right to speak, or even the duty to speak, no one can testify in his own behalf. Making himself into a figure of the Socrates who resides in the pages of the *Essais* ("Montaigne est notre Socrate," Thibaudet said),[8] into a figure who responds to the call to know himself and who knows himself as nothing, Montaigne speaks as the avatar of this archetypal nemo. But only because he took himself presumptuously for someone can he now speak as a no one or have something to say about himself. And even as he now speaks in self-deprecating terms, he recognizes the audacity of speaking about himself at all, even or especially in these terms: "Mais, quand il seroit vray que ce fust necesserement presomption d'entretenir le peuple de soy, je ne doy pas, suivant mon general dessein, refuser une action qui publie cette maladive qualité, puis qu'elle est en moy; et ne doy cacher cette faute que j'ay non seulement en usage, mais en profession" (378c) ("But even if it were true that it is presumptuous, no matter what the circumstances, to talk to the public about oneself, I still must not, according to my general plan, refrain from an action that openly displays this morbid quality, since it is in me; nor may I conceal this fault, which I not only practice but profess" [273]). Presumption ("en usage") both engenders speech ("en profession") and is its content, but, while the profession of presumptuousness is a necessary remedy, it cannot be its cure since speaking, even in this way, is also a brazen act. Caught in this vicious circle, Montaigne must go on talking about himself until he runs out of paper and ink, as he says in "De la vanité" (III, 9, 945).

Often Montaigne characterizes presumptuous talk as a disease, as in this quotation ("cette maladive qualité"), yet the remedy he proposes is further talk: "Le supreme remede à le guarir [ce vice], c'est faire tout le rebours de ce que icy ordonnent, qui, en défendant le parler de soy, défendent par consequent encore plus de penser à soy" (379c) ("The supreme remedy to cure it is to do just the opposite of what those people prescribe who, by prohibiting talking about oneself, even more strongly prohibit thinking about oneself" [274]). But as in the case of confession where what damns is what saves, there can never be an absolute remedy ("le supreme remede") because the remedy is also the disease itself. Montaigne might say of presumption what he says of vanity and inanity: "De m'en deffaire, je ne puis sans me deffaire moy-mesmes" (III, 9, 1,000b). Yet this statement is not without its irony because it is precisely his vanity and his presumption that allow him to undo himself ("se deffaire") and a certain notion of self, to claim his total insignificance, his nothingness. And at the same time that vanity allows him to reassert the authority of a self that has descended into itself and now bears witness to itself, a self that founds itself on the claim that it is consubstantial with what

it asserts. Writing of his vanity in vain and presumptuously writing—
"Il n'en est à l'avanture aucune plus expresse que d'en escrire si
vainement," he says in opening "De la vanité" (III, 9, 945b) ("There is
perhaps no more obvious vanity than to write of it so vainly" [721])—
Montaigne both loses and recovers himself.

I should add at this point that the *Essais* appear to recognize explicitly the felicitous consequence that this paradoxical strategy allows. No man, Montaigne says, ever thought of himself as lacking in
sense; that would be a contradictory proposition because the admission of the lack of sense would prove that one is sensible. But it is
precisely this contradiction that Montaigne exploits and that he affirms by his quotation of the popular proverb, "S'accuser seroit s'excuser en ce subject là; et se condamner, ce seroit s'absoudre" (II, 17,
656a) ("To accuse oneself would be to excuse oneself in that subject;
and to condemn oneself would be to absolve oneself" [498]). While
French seems to preclude the absurd conflation of "no one" and
"some one," which Montaigne's recourse to the Latin *nemo* allows
(neither "personne . . . ne" nor the essayist's "jamais homme ne"
enacts the impossible ambiguity), the proverb restores the paradox
and allows the essayist to save himself by condemning himself. His
claim that he too is sensible—a common and vulgar claim, he says—
betrays his lack of sense, but his recognition of this lack recuperates
him and rehabilitates the quality of his judgment. Since so few men
engage in this sort of exercise, he adds, he hopes for little commendation and praise, and little renown.

There are implications in Montaigne's posture (posturing?) at this
point in the essay that are both disquieting and revealing and that he
does not, or cannot, explore. The proverbial status of "s'accuser seroit
s'excuser" suggests that it has already become a formulaic response
to error, an example itself of common sense but also a common and
unreflective gesture that pantomimes self-abasement as the desire
for pardon and absolution. Montaigne's open confession of his shortcomings is anything but formulaic, of course, yet at the same time as
the axiom speaks its commonly accepted truth it also trivializes and
degrades it as a cliché, and one that threatens always to undermine
confession and to expose its banality. Any such risk, however, might
be outweighed by the benefits for Montaigne's sense of self that
derive from the proverb *as* a formula. Constructed grammatically
and rhetorically on principles of equivalence, of reciprocity, and of

repetition, the axiom makes the self the active center of its own meaning, the agent of both commission and remission. The proverb encloses itself in its syntactical symmetry as the predicates respond to each other, it mirrors itself in the verbal reflexivity that returns the action upon the subject, and, in this linguistic circle where the self both initiates the action and becomes its object, where it errs, judges, and absolves itself, the self acts as its own author, the source of its self-sufficiency, in a specularity as unlimited as its infinitival form itself. We encountered this same recourse to the self-reflexive verbal structure before, and to its emphatic repetition, in Montaigne's most insistent statement of his introspective mode and of his claim to possess himself, which follows just two paragraphs later: "je me roulle en moy mesme" (658).

I took that paroxysm of self-reflexivity and self-absorption as an expression of the most scandalous presumption, and here again as he quotes the proverb Montaigne alludes to the presumptuousness of trusting in one's good sense, once more characterizing presumption as a disease. But in this context it appears against all prior evidence to be an unproblematic illness. Although it apparently is never where it is perceived, and in spite of the fact that it is tenacious and strong, the disease here dissipates under the first glance from the patient's eye, like a dense fog in the sunlight, he says. The image of the solar eye ("I") reflecting its illuminating and restorative rays on itself may be particularly reassuring, but its curative power must be suspect. Montaigne's own experience and the experience of his writing remind us repeatedly that the cure can never be absolute, indeed, that the writing, as his "profession," endlessly inscribes itself as both cure and disease. Perhaps when Montaigne mentions that he does not hope for much commendation and praise from this sort of exercise—from what he alludes to humbly as "les simples productions de l'entendement"—he not only draws attention to the rarity of his enterprise but betrays as well his own paradoxical concern with what others do indeed think of him, and with the praise that he will *not* receive. We might say that the disavowal of the interest in praise is the sign of its attraction. Thus, in the instant that the eye sees the disease clearly it also reveals its own blindness, its limitations, and discloses that the seeing (and curative) "I" is always also contaminated. When Montaigne allows that presumption is never where it is perceived ("c'est une maladie qui n'est jamais où elle se voit" [656c]), he admits that it

can never be mastered, that it will always be in play, even and especially when the eye (I) claims to have seen, known, and eradicated it.

.   .   .   .

In "De l'exercitation" (II, 6) Montaigne recounts an admittedly common story of his fall from his horse that provokes him to append a
long disclaimer of his presumptuousness. Speaking about himself
when custom considers "le parler de soy" to be unseemly and vain,
the essayist enumerates responses to the anticipated critique of an
imagined reader in order to defend and justify his discourse. Since
Montaigne often speaks about himself, and since here he does so
explicitly by way of example, we might wonder why this context
elicits such a vigorous and intense rejoinder to the charge of presumptuousness. Perhaps the very triviality of the narrative accounts
for Montaigne's reaction; would he have been less presumptuous in
speaking of himself if he had had a profoundly important story to
tell? The text seems to argue that in the quest for self-knowledge
nothing is trivial and that self-knowledge of a particular Socratic
kind is the highest form of knowledge and even justifies the risk of
presumption. In a sense Montaigne is defending his entire project in
these pages, for the practice of which his essay speaks is precisely the
activity of essaying itself, the writing by which the self tries itself out
in the effort to come to know itself. It is not coincidental that in this
text *exercer, essayer,* and *experimenter* (to experience), all privileged
verbs in the *Essais,* are both prominent and interchangeable. The
essayist's discursive practice of death in "De l'exercitation" both enacts and exemplifies those myriad other trials that are the substance
of the *Essais* and of the writer himself.

The seemingly trivial story of which he is the center thus provokes
Montaigne to defend his first-person discourse, to deflect the charge
of presumptuous writing, to claim here as elsewhere that what practice ultimately reveals to him is his emptiness and his nullity. But if it
is true, as he stated, that presumption is never where it is perceived,
then it may be that to address the audacity of "le parler de soy" alone
does not answer the charge. I would argue that where Montaigne
does not perceive presumption is also where it is in this case, in the
effort to practice death, to try out and to experience the passage from
which no man has ever returned, as he puts it. Like the philosophers
who prepared themselves for the rigors of fortune by going forth to

meet her and flinging themselves into the test of difficulties ("ils luy sont allez au devant"), the essayist intends to go forth, ahead of time, through his writing, his essay, to experience death. But to go forth in this way ("aller au devant") is to enact the very gesture of presumption itself, as its etymology reminds us: from the Latin *praesumere*, to take beforehand, to anticipate, or, in the French, *prendre d'avance*. Can Montaigne avoid the implications of this resemblance? Isn't the practice of death, that taking up of death beforehand that is the discursive essay, also the most presumptuous practice, and not only because Montaigne intends to "essay" what he claims—not entirely ironically—can only be "essayed" once ("mais, quant à la mort, nous ne la pouvons essayer qu'une fois" [371a]) ("But as for death, we can try it only once" [267])? Unmasterable and unknowable, both in the future and outside of time, death represents the ultimate essay (both trial, test, and discursive form), and it represents as well the most presumptuous essaying, both the most audacious and that for which we must go forth the farthest. But what does it mean to practice death ("l'essayer aucunement," Montaigne says, "to some extent," "in a way")?

Practice and experience form the soul and prepare it for action, Montaigne claims in opening the essay, and yet, "à mourir, qui est la plus grande besoigne que nous ayons à faire, l'exercitation ne nous y peut ayder" (371a) ("But for dying, which is the greatest task we have to perform, practice cannot help us" [267]). The temporality of practice confronts death as the end of time. Practice is always repetition and succession in time, the rehearsal whose series of recurrences has no necessary end, that anticipates the future and extends into it, that prepares and projects beyond itself towards some realization in a culminating "event" that is also another instance of the unending practice. But death is precisely that which cannot be repeated, that beyond which there is no beyond, temporally or spatially. Death annuls practice, it voids it in its own singular performance.

But even more than the status and function of practice is at stake here. Montaigne's entire project is grounded in the self-reflexivity of human consciousness—that is, on that doubling of the self that allows its division into apprehending subject and acting object. This is the writer written, the observer observed, which is the basis of the descent into the self as self-recovery and self-knowledge, and it is also the form of practice itself that prepares for future action. But this self-reflexivity is precisely what death does not allow. Montaigne recounts the anecdote of Canius Julius as one of those ancients who were such excellent managers (*mesnagers*) of time that they tried even in death to taste and savor it and strained their minds to see what this passage was ("que c'estoit de ce passage" [371a]). "Je pensois," Canius responded to a friend who asked what he was thinking as he was about to die, "à me tenir prest et bandé de toute ma force, pour voir si, en cet instant de la mort, si court et si brief, je pourray appercevoir quelque deslogement de l'ame, et si elle aura quelque ressentiment de son yssuë, pour, si j'en aprens quelque chose, en revenir donner apres, si je puis, advertissement à mes amis" ("I was thinking . . . about holding myself ready and with all my powers intent to see whether in that instant of death, so short and brief, I shall be able to perceive any dislodgment of the soul, and whether it will have any feeling of its departure; so that, if I learn anything about it, I may return later, if I can, to give the information to my friends" [267]). But death is not an instant, however brief, which might be seen (*appercevoir*) and in which one might see oneself, as Canius suggests; it is the end of all "instants," not in time but its end, the annihilation that voids both time and the self in time. And no one can ever come back to tell his friends about it, as Montaigne's quotation from Lucretius reminds us: "nemo expergitus extat/Frigida quem semel est vitai pausa sequuta" ("no one awakens from the icy end of life"). Here, it would appear, is one nemo that is an unproblematic negation.

Canius's problem, and Montaigne's as well, is the problem of the passage between time and nontime, between the self and the absence of the self: "et ont bandé leur esprit pour voir que c'estoit de ce passage" (371a); "quant à l'instant et au point du passage" (372a) ("they strained their minds to see what this passage was" [267]; "as for the instant and point of passing away" [268]). Can one pass between life and death so as to "see" and to "be" on both sides (and so as to see oneself "seeing" and "being" on both sides), as if the passage occurred at the very juncture of difference where difference is paradoxically overcome, where one is both in time and beyond, present to oneself at the very moment of absence, at once something and nothing? What is at issue, I would argue, is not only the passage from life to death but the passage from minute to minute or instant to instant that Montaigne evokes as the fundamental subject of his writing in "Du repentir": "Je ne peints pas l'estre. Je peints le passage:

non un passage d'aage en autre, ou, comme dict le peuple, de sept en
sept ans, mais de jour en jour, de minute en minute" (III, 2, 805b) ("I
do not portray being: I portray passing. Not the passing from one age
to another, or, as the people say, from seven years to seven years, but
from day to day, from minute to minute" [611]). If it were possible to
transcend difference, then through transcendence itself being, presence, and plenitude would be realized and Montaigne could say, "Je
peints l'estre." But eschewing transcendence and the transcendental
as an inaccessible "beyond" identical to itself, one and eternally continuous, Montaigne does not (and cannot) say this. Grounded in time
and space, he can only affirm difference, diversity, multiplicity, and
contiguity and portray the passage, the irresistible movement or displacement in time / space toward that which is necessarily absent or
deferred "over there," or in the next "minute." But what does it mean
"to pass" or to move through difference?

Canius, of course, cannot overcome the difference between life
and death, cannot possess them at the same time, or at least, Montaigne suggests ironically, he has not yet returned to tell us the news.
To pass from one thing to another over the border that separates
them is to experience separation itself, the gap or interval of their
differentiation. What we experience is precisely the "in-between,"
not as some middle ground that links two things or is both at the
same time but as the void that is the very condition of their difference.[9] And as the story of Canius also indicates, the passage never
culminates in fulfillment, it is never realized in any apotheosis of
knowledge, truth, or being. Either Canius cannot learn of death or he
is no longer around to tell us anything, which amounts to the same
thing. Death cannot be experienced "in itself" because it can never be
experienced as "present," in or as an instant (from the Latin, *in* +
stare, to stand upon, be present). What Canius's experience tells us is
that nothing can be experienced "in itself," whether we are speaking
of instants in life or the instant of death ("cet instant de la mort,"
which is either the last instant in life or not an "instant" at all). The
present instant, or the present self in an instant, or the place upon
which we are standing, can never serve as absolute ground, pure and
autonomous, because we can never be both inside it and outside at
the same time, because it is always already the lost instant of the past
that passes away and the absent instant of the future toward which
one passes. The richly suggestive sixteenth-century meanings of *le*

passage as the action of passing between two things, the place of passing, *and* the passing that is death itself imply not only that death is a passage—from life to lifelessness, or from terrestrial to celestial life, or the passage of the soul from the body—but that passing is also a kind of death, as if the experience of the "in-between" of passing were also the experience of the nothingness of death. Poulet also sensed the connection between death and the portrayal of passage when he was reading Montaigne: "passage, that is to say the very movement by which being quits being, by which it flies away from itself, and in which it feels itself dying. This decision (to portray passage) is thus joined to the deepest feeling of indigence."[10]

Nevertheless, Montaigne says, "il me semble toutefois qu'il y a quelque façon de nous apprivoiser à elle (la mort) et de l'essayer aucunement" (371a) ("It seems to me, however, that there is a certain way of familiarizing ourselves with death and trying it out to some extent" [268]). What cannot be tried out more than once can apparently be tried out, practiced, observed in its practice as if one could indeed awaken from the icy end of life. But in "quelque façon," "aucunement"; not death in itself but dying, or what Montaigne calls the approaches to death:

> Nous en pouvons avoir experience, sinon entiere et parfaicte, au moins telle, qu'elle ne soit pas inutile, et qui nous rende plus fortifiez et asseurez. Si nous ne la pouvons joindre, nous la pouvons approcher, nous la pouvons reconnoistre; et, si nous ne donnons jusques à son fort, au moins verrons nous et en prattiquerons les advenües. Ce n'est pas sans raison qu'on nous fait regarder à nostre sommeil mesme, pour la ressemblance qu'il a de la mort. (371–72a)

> We can have an experience of it that is, if not entire and perfect, at least not useless, and that makes us more fortified and assured. If we cannot reach it, we can approach it, we can reconnoiter it; and if we do not penetrate as far as its fort, at least we shall see and become acquainted with the approaches to it. It is not without reason that we are taught to study even our sleep for the resemblance it has with death. (268)

The sliding and hedging here is considerable and of consequence, for Montaigne can only try death out by mediation and displacement. He must displace the focus from death to its approaches and operate by the displacement that makes sleep a form of death. He admits that he cannot have a full and perfect experience and so claims a useful one; he well appreciates that he cannot reach death, or penetrate to where it "is," and thus suggests that it is enough to get close to it and to recognize it. But even with these qualifications and compromises, and this indirection, Montaigne's practice remains problematical be- · cause its weight is borne entirely by the common rhetorical figure of analogy, and by an analogy that is itself sustained by the authority of a common and collective wisdom. The nameless "on" of "on nous faict regarder à nostre sommeil mesme" speaks authoritatively precisely because its voice is anonymous, because it has no identifiable source in time or in space and consequently seems as old and as true as time or language itself.

On the basis of this authority Montaigne can make one further substitution, taking fainting and unconsciousness as a kind of sleep and thus as the surrogate of death; this loss of sensation, he says, brings one even closer to the "vray et naturel visage" of death. By this substitution, however, Montaigne himself issues the call for his own story, he opens the way to displace his experience into the text and himself into the "I" of narration. The practice of death is the mediated practice of writing. The "quelque façon de nous apprivoiser à elle et de l'essayer aucunement" is not only a "certain way" that tries out death's approaches but "another way" that is the written essay, the writing out (*essayer*) that in a way is also the trying out. The passage that is death is at the same time the written passage, just as the "essai" is both the trial, the weighing (Latin *exagium*, to weigh) of his judgment of things and the discursive form. We might object that Montaigne's practice is essentially a textual practice, his experience a linguistic one, and point, as I have done, to the role that rhetoric—in the unstable and questionable form of the trope and the axiom—must play to formulate and sustain his discourse. This in spite of Montaigne's own protestation in "De la ressemblance des enfans aux peres" (II, 37, 784) that whatever he is, he wants to be elsewhere than on paper. But the semantic richness of "passage" should serve to remind us that however insecure the linkage, only textual experience allows Montaigne to "experience" death, only the narrative gives meaning to the event of his fall, only the projection of the self into the fragmented, and doubled, persona and narrator of his discourse opens the possibility to essay an integral self, if only in passing. Only in the "passage," we might say, can the attempt be made to recover the instant of passage.[11]

Thus Montaigne narrates his own death (he was "tenu pour mort"; when he regained consciousness he "came back to life" [*revivre*], and when he lost it he "died again" [*remourir*]) and through the narrative experiences all that cannot be experienced in death itself. And he experiences as well the enormity of speaking about oneself in public, although his whole project depends on it. Montaigne carefully distinguishes himself from "le parler de soy" that is unexamined or uncritical and from those who under- or overvalue themselves; the former are stupid rather than modest and the latter stupid as well as presumptuous. He too presumes to speak about himself, but his is the only way the self can experience itself, it is the only way it can portray its thoughts ("Je peins principalement mes cogitations"), expose itself entire ("Je m'estalle entier"), and put down its essence to bear witness to what it is ("c'est moy, c'est mon essence"). And the lesson of *this* way, this practicing, essaying, writing of the self that Montaigne offers as the remedy for presumption, is the knowledge that the self is nothing, its knowledge nothing: "Nulle particuliere qualité n'enorgeuillira celuy qui mettra quand et quand en compte tant de imparfaittes et foibles qualitez autres qui sont en luy, et, au bout, la nihilité de l'humaine condition" (380c) ("No particular quality will make a man proud who balances it against the many weaknesses and imperfections that are also in him, and, in the end, against the nullity of man's estate" [275]).

Presumption is an error to be declared and recognized publicly, a disease whose ultimate cure ("supreme remede") is to continue to talk and to write about oneself, but an error and a disease that cannot be absolutely remedied by open profession and by being made into a profession, as Montaigne has done. Nor could it ever be, since it is *in* man ("elle est en moy"), it is the nature of man, and since it is never only where it is perceived, as my discussion of the presumptuous practice of death has indicated. But the presumptuous practice of death has led, by a way that is both circuitous and inevitable in the *Essais*, to the recognition of the nothingness of the self and thus to its recovery, to that knowledge of the self that, as in the case of Socrates, justifies making oneself known by one's own mouth. And the reverse is also true, that the self as nothing has informed the practice of death. Like the nemo who descends into himself and the nemo who is a witness on his own behalf, this nemo, this no one, because of who and what he is, *can* experience death and return from the icy end and can experience itself in its own nothingness. In the endless chiasmic reversals that discourse allows, the self uncovers and discovers itself "de passage," in the passages of its writing, in the passage that leads it and links it to the textual progeny it has produced and in which it is both nothing and something, lost and found, both dead and alive.

Echoes of Narcissus who loses himself in the desire to embrace his own image and of Pygmalion who finds himself in the image of the other he embraces. Montaigne's writing confirms that all along these were not two poles, two different stories, but two faces of the same story that reflect and refract each other. The essayist cannot in any simple way escape the fate of Narcissus by producing a work that is both other and himself, he cannot triumph over nothingness and death in any absolute way by conceiving textual offspring. He cannot be Pygmalion without also recalling Narcissus and anticipating Myrrha, because nothingness and death are also part of the sculptor's story. There is no transcendence to plenitude, to presence, to perpetuity. Montaigne can return from the nothingness of death only because he experiences his own nothingness as a form of death, he can find himself only because he loses himself, and he can find himself as something because he finds himself as nothing. The essayist as Narcissus and Pygmalion, as Ovid's child; the essay as son and daughter.

5

Monstrous Progeny

*Et [l'esprit] m'enfante tant de chimeres et monstres fantasques les
uns sur les autres, sans ordre et sans propos . . .* (I, 8, 33)

And the mind gives birth to so many chimeras and fantastic
monsters, one after another, without order or purpose . . .

*Que sont-ce icy aussi, à la verité, que crotesques et corps
monstrueux?* (I, 28, 183)

What are these things of mine, in truth, but grotesque and
monstrous bodies?

*Je n'ay veu monstre et miracle au monde plus expres que moy-
mesme.* (III, 11, 1,029)

I have seen no more evident monstrosity and miracle in the
world than myself.

At the end of "De l'affection des peres aux enfans," when Montaigne
turns from natural children to speak of the offspring of the mind, he
evokes progeny so worthy that their loving fathers were willing to
sacrifice all for them. These are children whose beauty and grace
redound to the credit of the father, children whose noble qualities
immortalize their progenitor because they reflect him faithfully. In
the natural order of things, the child reproduces the image of its
author; in this mirror the author's own worth can be read.

Montaigne's preference for textual progeny is philosophically and
theologically grounded in the privileged place in Western thought
given to mind over body, but in choosing time-honored writers and
artists to justify the priority that he gives to the life of the mind, and
to the work it generates, he also expresses and affirms a traditional
and classical aesthetic. As the discussion of presumption has indicated, however, and as the essayist admits in speaking explicitly of
his own work, not all children are beautiful or graceful, not all con-

form to conventional and valued norms, nor, he implies, should they. In fact, each of the three major essays devoted to children and their fathers opens with this particular essayist-father deprecating his offspring, and none more dramatically than the very text that seemed to posit the traditional norms themselves. Montaigne begins "De l'affection des peres aux enfans" by depicting his child as faulty, foolish, strange, wild, extravagant, bizarre, its face uncommon ("un visage si esloigné de l'usage commun"), its body ("subject") empty and vile. What I want to foreground is the incongruity that this essay holds in suspension, an incongruity that it does not or cannot resolve, with its uncommon opening juxtaposed against its ideal conclusion. The text itself seems to have two heads, or two bodies, each connected to yet at odds with the other, each representing a conflicting inclination of the writer and his writing.

We have in fact encountered diversity and disparity throughout the discussion, for it is a characteristic mark of Montaigne's writing. The work as a stable portrait and the expression of passage, as both faithful to its intent and given to treachery, as simultaneously seeking resemblance and performing difference, as both presumptuous and humble, rhetorical and plain, something and nothing, these are all expressions of a discourse at odds with itself, drawn simultaneously to the ideal and to the abject, to the high and to the low. The writing appears to be caught in the antagonism of these oppositions, but it also discloses their paradoxical, and necessary, affinity. In the oft-quoted analogy in "De l'amitié" between his work and a style of marginal decoration practiced by a painter he knew, Montaigne uses the term *crotesques* to express what he characterizes as the diversity and disorderliness of his writing. He draws from Horace the image of the woman whose body tapered off into a fish to affirm that his text indeed combines different and incongruent orders. In fact, it was precisely this sense of something that necessarily contains within what is foreign to it, an element that is both at home and an intruder, that characterized the Renaissance concept of the grotesque. The joining, the mixture, or the overlapping of disparate elements defies categorization, eludes naming, and thus escapes mastery. In Horace's example, what can this strange being be called except "grotesque," as a sign that it cannot be accounted for in the natural order of things? In Montaigne's textual variety and disparity, we cannot even tell which element is the intruder and which the home; is this a woman with a fish's tail or a fish with a woman's body?[1]

In this same context in "De l'amitié," and juxtaposed to "crotesques," the essayist also speaks of his writing as monstrous ("corps monstrueux"), a term that emerged when I spoke at the end of the first chapter of the seed that links the generations and carries resemblance between father and son. What a marvel ("monstre") it is that the seed operates in this way, I quoted Montaigne saying, and I suggested that the expression be taken not only figuratively to refer to the seed as a marvel but literally to make of it also a "monster." In this way I opened the possibility of diversity and of difference within the seed, harbored in the father as the origin of life itself, transmitted to the child as its legacy, always already present in the relation between them. We see from "De l'amitié" that the monstrous and the grotesque have the same face, the face of irreconcilable and necessary disparity and of difference itself. Individual essays, such as the two-headed text that joins the uncommon and the ideal in "De l' affection des peres aux enfans," as well as the varied corpus of Montaigne's text as a whole, each body bears the mark of the monstrous, each is a "corps monstrueux." It is the status and the fate of that monstrous textual figure and of the monstrous text that will concern me in this chapter.

· · · · · · ·

At telling thematic and structural junctures of the *Essais,* where the writer confronts the nature of his writing project and what it has produced, he returns to the figure of the monster.[2] Early in the book, in what is the second half of the one-page essay "De l'oisiveté" (I, 8), Montaigne describes the genesis of his text as his effort to record what he calls the chimeras and fantastic monsters produced (*enfanter*) by his mind. In the leisure of his retirement, he tells the reader, he had expected to spend the little of life he had left in rest and seclusion, and he intended that his mind would entertain itself in full idleness and, as he says, stay and settle in itself. What he anticipated was a mental life whose order reflected the design of nature and whose coherence bore the mark of reason. But to his apparent surprise, his mind engaged instead in tumultuous activity that conceived "tant de chimeres et monstres fantasques les uns sur les autres, sans ordre, et sans propos, que pour en contempler à mon aise

l'ineptie et l'estrangeté, j'ay commancé de les mettre en rolle, es-
perant avec le temps luy en faire honte à luy mesmes" (33a) ("So
many chimeras and fantastic monsters, one after another, without
order or purpose, that in order to contemplate their ineptitude and
strangeness at my pleasure, I have begun to put them in writing,
hoping in time to make my mind ashamed of itself" [21]). Beyond the
exercise of will and of intellect, beyond the control of reason, as if
discordant by nature, the mind generates uncommon notions, ideas,
imaginings that Montaigne will both deprecate and recuperate in
what appears to be the birth of the essays. The irrational, the multiform, and the disorderly may be, as his quotation from Horace implies, "like a sick man's dreams, vain imaginings," but they are
symptoms of a sickness Montaigne will not seek entirely to cure.[3]

The figure of the cure returns frequently in the *Essais* to suggest
that there are many sicknesses—presumption, jealousy, poverty, inadequacy, ignorance, sedition—that might call for remedy, but monstrous thought is not one of them. Here Montaigne will only record
and observe (*contempler*) or, we should say, read and recognize that
which he will not attempt to eliminate or hide. He proposes, in fact,
to shame his mind by conserving these otherwise useless fancies. To
do so, he must bring the chimeras and monsters to light and put them
on display, he must allow them to bear witness to the monstrousness
of the mind that produces them. This activity, remarkable also for
its passivity, for its acceptance of what one might expect to be disavowed or repressed, makes of Montaigne an essayist and of the
essayist a witness, a witness to the monstrous offspring of his mind—
both his monstrous thoughts and his equally monstrous text—and,
by extension, to his own monstrous nature.

Montaigne prefaces this personal narrative of his retirement and
the conception of his writing with references to the wild proliferation
of weeds on fertile, fallow lands ("terres oisifs"), to the disordered
production of shapeless masses and lumps of flesh by women who
have not been impregnated ("les femmes . . . toutes seules"), and to
the unruly fancies of the idle mind. Through the figure of analogy the
essayist identifies the mental with the agricultural and the biological,
naturalizing the workings of the mind through organic associations,
as if the rhetoric that both shapes and embodies the reasoning could
overcome difference to establish and sustain likeness: "Comme nous
voyons des terres oysives . . . ; et comme nous voyons que les

femmes . . . : ainsin est-il des espris" (32a) ("Just as we see that fallow land . . . ; and as we see that women . . . ; so it is with minds" [20]). Within this logical framework, lexical and structural repetition and metaphorical association link the three realms so that notions of birth and germination, idleness, seed, and monstrous offspring become elements of a common generation. What is needed in each case in order to produce proper and natural progeny ("faire une generation bonne et naturelle") is an intervention that tames and works its subject ("il les faut assubjectir et employer"; "il les faut embesoigner"; "si on ne les occupe à certain sujet, qui les bride et contreigne"); in the case of the land and of women this intervention takes the form of an impregnation, the introduction of the seed ("certaines semences," "une autre semence"). Analogously, the mind needs to be restrained, seeded, we might say, with a definite subject, pointed toward a fixed goal, in order not to throw itself in disorder into the vague field of imagination, not to produce mad or idle fancy in its agitation, not to produce sick men's dreams, not to be everywhere and therefore nowhere.

Reading the essay in this manner from end to beginning highlights the fact that the text itself is not consistent, that what is proposed as a remedy to the production of monstrous thought by the opening section is, in fact, denied or ignored by the closing paragraph. Montaigne's narrative of his own situation appears to describe a generation that resembles that of the land and the woman *prior* to intervention or impregnation from without, before the introduction of "certain seeds" or "a different kind of seed." His thoughts and imaginings are the precise analogues of the weeds and the pieces of flesh produced by the agent of conception on its own and without cultivation, an asexual birth in the case of the woman, generated from within by the wrong kind of seed, one's own. The essay thus eschews "une generation bonne et naturelle" and accepts what we are obliged to take as an unfortunate and unnatural birth, it recuperates what for all intents and purposes it should refuse, what is variously described in the course of the essay as "inutile," "informe," "folie," "réverie," "fantasque," "inepte," "estrange," "chimeres," and "monstres" and what it admits are objects of shame. The consequences of this attitude are momentous, for the birth of the monsters of the mind signals the birth, by self-generation, from within, of the writer himself and the conception of his text. Within the context of

Montaigne's account in "De l'oisiveté," if the monstrous fancies had not been born there would have been no need to write.[4]

This reading of "De l'oisiveté" thus affirms an extraordinary multiple and monstrous birth—of thoughts, of writer, of text. But there is something disconcerting about Montaigne's insistence on a program of "chimeres et monstres fantasques," because, in spite of all I have said about the grotesque and the monstrous in the *Essais*, the text does not literally "perform" it. Montaigne's mind does not throw itself in disorder into the vague field of the imagination, it does not lose itself in an undefinable nowhere, nor does it produce wild and unfettered thoughts without order or purpose, neither here in this essay nor in the work as a whole. In fact, the arrangement of general commentary and personal example, the form of analogy, the lexical and metaphorical patterns all structure the essay and suggest the operations of a careful ordering hand. This means that in spite of itself, or in spite of what I have read as the essayist's intention, the mind *is* imposed upon from without, occupied by a definite subject, or given a fixed goal.

Writing itself appears necessarily to act as that intervening agent, as that "other" or "different" seed, that through the orderliness of syntax, for example, shapes thought (even if at the time of the composition of the *Essais* French syntax is not yet quite fixed) or through the structures of rhetorical figures creates coherence. Writing about the need to have a subject to keep the mind from losing itself reveals itself as a subject that keeps the mind from running wild, like a *cheval eschappé*. Perhaps these are all implied in the expression "mettre en rolle," which with its suggestion of list or register by itself evokes the imposition of order. Later on, in "De l'exercitation" (II, 6), Montaigne will state explicitly that the public dimension of writing / reading requires that there be a certain decorum, a straightening up and arranging that would conflict with the notion of formless or haphazard thought: "Encore se faut-il testoner, encore se faut-il ordonner et renger pour sortir en place" (378c) ("Even so one must spruce up, even so one must present oneself in an orderly arrangement, if one would go out in public" [273]). The monstrous cannot be exteriorized, cannot in fact be known, in a pristine or original form. When it goes out in public, cultivation, or culture itself, we might say, intervenes to mediate its appearance.

Montaigne's project thus appears to some degree to betray its original intention. Rather than being directly and faithfully recorded, the monstrous is in some sense transformed or displaced in order to be expressed. But again, the displacement of the monstrous is not its elimination. Chimeras and monsters inhabit Montaigne's writing as the deviations from the cultural norms that early detractors of the *Essais* considered to be the great failing of his writing, the ways in which it contravened prevailing conventions of literary decorum by its disconcerting absence of strict, formal order and logic and its perverse content devoted exclusively to the self, often in the most intimate and physical way. I have emphasized Montaigne's affinity for the very structures of difference that define the grotesque and the monstrous, and I have foregrounded the multiple, the antithetical, and the contradictory within what is presumed to be a single and coherent order. As I speak about the presence of the grotesque / monstrous at this point, I am placing the emphasis on Montaigne's expression, on the rhetorical and the aesthetic dimensions of the *Essais*, to remind us that what I am calling the grotesque or the monstrous is also, and perhaps foremost, its textual representation. What is encountered and engaged by the writer, and by the reader, is not the referent itself but the mediating forms and figures of paradox, oxymoron, antithesis, contradiction. And because the monstrous is expressed and thus contained by the writing and its categories, what in itself escapes categories and eludes naming, what resists definition, can now be named and defined, although the name it bears is that of the unnamable itself. Or I should say expressed and *constrained* by writing and its categories, as the essayist himself admits. Montaigne's text enacts the tension between an artless and monstrous self and its necessarily artful and monstrous discourse.[5]

The monstrous thus appears to be situated between a deformed self that cannot be fully recuperated and a deforming discourse that cannot be fully recuperative. There is, in fact, an elusiveness about the monstrous in the *Essais* that is emblematic of the larger difficulty of situating and defining it. When characterized as deviant, anomalous, or different from the norm, it seems to be less something in itself and more a question of what it is not. The monstrous is that which does not conform to the law of nature that commands that like produce like, or it does not follow the dictate of reason that produces coherence. And yet, at the same time, it does resemble things in nature, although in uncanny ways, in unexpected forms, in unanticipated mixtures, and it does become the subject of a reasoned discourse that seeks to make it part of the larger order of things. In the effort to account for the monstrous, an effort that extended from the classical period through the Renaissance and sought essentially to locate and thus to master it, the urge prevailed to situate the monstrous in relation to nature, either beyond in the realm of the unnatural or within the domain of nature itself. The terms of the debate that informed that history are precisely those of the binaries natural / unnatural, inside / outside. There were those who sought to keep the monstrous *outside* so as to protect nature's order and congruity from an unthinkable internal inconsistency and contradiction. They argued that what was against or beyond nature's design was a sign or portent from outside sent by God. Others placed the monstrous *inside* the embrace of nature, as a function of nature, an effect of its intention, an example of its diverse abundance, or even as its mistake.[6]

Although the debate over the situation and status of the monstrous was carried on in these binary terms, both positions were fraught with problems that represented a challenge to the stability of the opposition. The monstrous that had its origin outside nonetheless entered nature, took its place and functioned there, however uncomfortable that place was or however mysterious the function. The monstrous that was a product of nature had in some way also to be different from nature itself, it had also to be distinguishable to be recognized as monstrous. What Montaigne's text confirms is that in the last decades of the sixteenth century the oppositional structure had weakened to a point where, instead of the monster exemplifying the difference *between* the separate and distinct realms of nature and the unnatural or the supernatural, it had become in some instances the sign of difference *within* nature itself.[7]

In "De l'oisiveté," wild weeds, shapeless flesh, and intemperate fancy all bear the name of chimeras and monsters, but the distinction between natural and unnatural does not itself remain clear or stable. In fact, the powerful images of monstrous generation, of earth and of woman giving birth, are taken from nature herself. The "vague champ des imaginations" and the mind "faisant le cheval eschappé" (obviously in that field) are both images whose effect, as I indicated, is to inscribe the operations of the mind in the natural order of things, however uncommon, disordered, or "unnatural" the essayist considers those operations to be. These tropological associations gather the essayist's unbridled thoughts and imaginings into the encompassing embrace of a nature rich enough, and diverse enough, to contain them.

The monstrous thus resides as difference within the order of nature, just as difference resides within the monstrous itself. Disparate and diverse forms, doubleness, mixed and hybrid orders, these are the variegated bodies and faces of the monstrous, of nature's monsters and of Montaigne's monstrous progeny. And at the source of monstrousness, in the multiform text as in multifarious nature, lies the complex seed. Let us return to "De l'oisiveté." The seed is integral to nature and to the existence and perpetuation of its life, and yet it also exceeds nature both as the unfathomable marvel that determines resemblance and the monster that embodies unlikeness. The vital profusion of weeds is produced by the "wrong" seeds; evidently there are "right" seeds, what Montaigne here calls "certain seeds." But it is clear that the distinction between right and wrong in this instance is relational, contextual, rather than categorical, that what matters about seeds and weeds is how they are valued—that is, what matters are differences that are cultural, and that are cultivated. Every seed has within it the potential to be the wrong seed or the right one, to produce a monster or a model. Every seed, we might say, is already within itself the right *and* the wrong seed.

Like the earth, the woman who produces monstrous lumps of flesh possesses a seed, and this seed too is emblematic of nature and of writing. Here the seed is also the "wrong" one for producing what Montaigne calls good and natural offspring. The woman needs to be "embesoigné" (fertilized, the translators say) by another or different seed ("une autre semence") to avoid the monstrous production. But "embesoigné" also suggests by its etymology a working or cultivation that responds to a need or a lack (*besoin*). Sixteenth-century medicine, as it was derived from Galen, did attribute semen to women, but it was considered colder and less active than that of the male and therefore insufficient, dependent on this "other" seed to produce "natural" progeny. The difference between "good" and "bad" seeds thus appears to lie *between* them, in the difference *between* the female and the male and their semen. But here again, as in the case of the earth's seeds, the difference *between* is also most significantly a difference *within*. According to Galenic anatomy, there was only a single male sex and sexual differences were considered to be matters of degree rather than of kind. In a world in which the body was thought to be more open and less fixed than it was to become in later scientific thinking, where, for example, female genital and reproductive organs were seen as internalized versions of the male organs, the female body and its semen were considered to be inferior forms of the male, different in degree rather than in kind. We recognize in this anatomical hierarchy long-standing ideological and cultural biases; in the next chapter I will use the single-sex theory itself to provide a critical perspective on these traditional notions of sexuality and gender. For the moment I want simply to underscore what we saw in the case of the earth's seed, that it is essentially the "same" seed that differs from itself, and within itself, the same seed that is either colder or warmer, and that produces either monsters or model offspring.[8]

What my reading of "De l'oisiveté" thus discloses is the presence of difference at the "origin," at the "seminal" moment, present in the multiple folds of a complex and diverse nature and of a complex and diverse text. Both nature and text encompass "within" themselves what is opposed to them, what contravenes their own laws, what is "unnatural" and monstrous. From this perspective the shameful monstrous offspring gain equal voice with what is born of a "generation bonne et naturelle," for they too, in their own right, hold a proper place in the order of things. This picture of a nature that can operate at cross purposes with itself, as if conflicted within, appears again in "De la punition de la couardise" (I, 16), in which the essayist explains the difference between faults of weakness and those of malice: "en celles icy nous nous sommes bandez à nostre escient contre les reigles de la raison, que nature a empreintes en nous; et en celles là, il semble que nous puissions appeller à garant cette mesme nature, pour nous avoir laissé en telle imperfection et deffaillance" (70a) ("In the latter we have tensed ourselves deliberately against the rules of reason that nature has imprinted in us; and in the former it seems that we can call on this same nature as our warrantor, for having left us in such imperfection and weakness" [48]). The same nature serves man paradoxically to originate the imperative for moral conduct and to justify his moral deficiency. In Montaigne's terms, nature reveals both a normative face and what he called an uncommon face, and, while the essayist will value the ideal face, he will seek especially to recuperate that other, meaner face of nature as the legitimate subject of his writing, the imperfect and uncommon face, the face that is ineptitude and disorder, unreason and imagination, ignorance and flattery, presumption and vanity—the faces of monstrous progeny.

In the light of this discussion with its emphasis on difference both within nature and within the text, Montaigne's comment that he writes down his monstrous thoughts to shame his mind is richly suggestive. If his thoughts are natural, if even as monstrous they have their rightful place in nature, they do not need to be excused or justified and should not be cause for shame because both they and the one who thinks them are innocent. If, on the other hand, they are cause for shame, the thoughts must contravene some law, derive from some flaw or wrongdoing, and thus themselves be guilty and produce guilt. In this case, the thoughts are in some sense unnatural. One way to resolve this bind would be to posit a fallen nature that produces monstrous thought "naturally" and that induces guilt precisely because it is fallen. But the *Essais* do not admit of a traditional Christian vision of a fallen nature that calls for transcendence. As in the figure of the essayist's thoughts as a sick man's dreams, visions from a sickness he manifestly does not seek to cure, Montaigne's shame does not have a curative or reformative effect, nor is it meant to. The monstrous thought itself is to be conserved and exposed and, we might even say, celebrated. And since the amphibious thought is both natural and unnatural, Montaigne wears his shame both as a sign of imperfection and a badge of honor.

Ovid's wisp of a narrative of the Propoetides, which introduces the story of Pygmalion, is a tale about shame that sheds light on its complex status in Montaigne's *Essais*. Having dared to deny the divinity of Venus, the women brought down upon themselves the wrath of the goddess and became the first to lose their good name by prostituting themselves in public. The narrator concludes with this descriptive line: "Then as all sense of shame left them, the blood hardened in their cheeks, and it required only a slight alteration to transform them into stony flints" (X.241–42). Since the loss of shame provokes the transformation into stone, we might infer from the story that shame itself is the sign of life and the sign of humanity. As long as they felt ashamed of their wantonness (monstrousness) the women survived, but when that feeling was lost, their life was lost as well. And as the Propoetides' public action was the source of their shame, so the essayist's shame signals the public dimension of the writing act. Writing, too, depends not only on being seen but on seeing and judging oneself in or through the eyes of the other, even, or especially, if the other has been interiorized, as Montaigne sees himself through the multiple readers he inscribes in his text and through himself as his own reader. The writing exteriorizes and materializes thought and self as a process of generation, it produces and records the birth of monstrous offspring, it bears witness to what they are and generates in its turn witnesses / readers who see them for what they are. The writer's shame is nothing less, or more, than the sign of the life of that thinking self and of its text, the sign of their monstrousness and of their humanity.

.   .   .   .

My reading of the *Essais* thus foregrounds the conception of what I have been calling the monstrous self and text; or, put another way, the *Essais* (and my reading) conceive of that monstrous self and text through writing. From its origin in the problematical seed, the monstrous is born as Montaigne's writing, disordered yet possessed of form, useless yet worthy, abnormal and unconventional yet normative in its own right, alienated from nature and a part of it, something that, for all its deformity and its vanity, Montaigne seeks to conserve and even to cultivate. The *Essais* themselves provide a striking emblem for the paradoxical doubleness and diversity that characterize this monstrous textual progeny: the Siamese brothers of "D'un enfant monstrueux" (II, 30). And the essay that shows them off reveals how showing off itself, as Montaigne does in the public register that he also calls his *Essais*, lies at the very heart of monstrousness.[9]

In a tone easily recognized as matter-of-fact, objective, even coldly analytical, Montaigne begins this short essay by describing in ample detail a strange child with one head and two bodies that he saw "the day before yesterday" being shown off for money. But the story that he claims is self-evident elicits two different commentaries. The first concerns prognostication. Montaigne refuses to "read" the child as an allegorical sign, to take him, for example, as a favorable portent to the king to maintain under the union of law the diverse parts and factions of the state. Predicting is risky business, he suggests, and quotes from Cicero's *De divinatione* to conclude ironically that it is safer to work backwards from the event, "à reculons," if one is going to hazard an interpretation. Montaigne's second commentary (which he adds to the text after the 1588 edition) juxtaposes multiple perspectives to reduce the monstrous to an effect of unaccustomed novelty. The monstrous is not monstrous either to God or to nature; man's limited vision and lack of experience alone induce him to astonishment and error and to the mistaken assumption that what he cannot account for has no place in the order of things natural or divine. "Nous apelons contre nature ce qui advient contre la coustume" (713c) ("We call contrary to nature what happens contrary to custom" [539]).

Montaigne's commentaries have the effect of neutralizing the monstrous, of removing the stigma of aberrance, and of eliminating its conventional referential value as meaningful sign that points beyond itself (as prophecy, prediction, omen). Recuperated into the infinity of God's creation and into the diversity of nature ("rien n'est que selon elle [la nature], quel qu'il soit" [713c]; "nothing is anything but according to nature, whatever it may be" [539]), the "monstrueux" has no special status, it belongs to the order common to all other things, even if its appearance flaunts what is customary or accepted. The monstrous is cut off from its etymological root, *monere* (to warn, advise). It is no longer God's way of using the supernatural as a sign that instructs or portends; it no longer subordinates itself through an allegorical or hermeneutical gesture to an exterior referent that it serves. Thus enclosed in nature, in its continuing strangeness, the monstrous signals nature's plenitude, but in effect, by circumscribing the monstrous in this way, Montaigne also limits and encloses it in itself. In its self-reflexivity it points to or shows itself, it is and means primarily itself. But what does it mean to say that the monstrous means itself? To respond we must return to the beginning of the essay to reread Montaigne's presentation of the "enfant monstrueux."

Montaigne begins in this way: "Ce conte s'en ira tout simple, car je laisse aux medecins d'en discourir. Je vis avant hier . . ." (712a) ("This story will go its way simply, for I leave it to the doctors to discuss it. The day before yesterday I saw . . ." [538]). The story goes its way simply, he suggests, it tells itself, because Montaigne's concern will not be with what it means, at least not in the conventional sense. While the "enfant monstrueux" does not need commentary, Montaigne will comment in order to foreclose the possibility of a certain kind of interpretive "commentary." If the medical doctors can reason and discuss causes and meaning, it is because the meaning of the monstrous is circumscribed by its natural and physical existence. Upon rereading, we understand that the essayist can only be the witness, can only recount what he has seen, matter-of-factly, coldly, objectively, because there is no other way to narrate, to speak about that which is only what it is. Since there is nothing else to say outside of the fact of that being, the narration can provide only the physical details of this strange child who has what appears to be a normal body to which is attached frontally a headless body, even to the extent of mentioning that the child urinates "par tous les deux endroicts" (713a). As "what it is," the enfant monstrueux is pure object, the object of Montaigne's eye as witness and of his narration that bears witness.

"Je vis avant hier," Montaigne tells his reader, and he tells what he saw: "un enfant que deux hommes et une nourrisse, qui se disoient estre le pere, l'oncle et la tante, conduisoyent pour tirer quelque sou de le montrer à cause de son estrangeté" (712a) ("The day before yesterday I saw a child that two men and a nurse, who said they were the father, uncle, and aunt, were leading about to get a penny or so from showing him, because of his strangeness" [538]). "De le montrer": to show the child off, to show him as spectacle, to exhibit him. But the child's monstrousness and his "showing" derive from something more profound than the pecuniary motives of the family. A richly suggestive etymology (genealogy) links *montrer* to *monstre* and anticipates Montaigne's own gesture of the circumscription of the sign. From *monere* the monster is born, and in an unexpected and perhaps monstrous back-formation the monster (*monstrum*) engenders in its turn the verb *monstrare*, "montrer," to show. A portent that points beyond itself to social, political, or theological meaning contracts, constricts, in a word, reduces, to the modest act of showing (itself). Montaigne's French captures and allows us to play on the homophony that we lose in English with the verb *to show*—although it is preserved in *to demonstrate*. We can say then that Montaigne's monster is that which is shown and shows itself, that which shows what it is, *that* it is. The essayist's own seeing and narrating reifies the monster and uncovers that what is proper to it is always already inscribed in its name. The monstrous child is spectacle itself.

By showing off the monstrous child for money, the father, uncle, and aunt apparently displace it from the object of *pure* display into a commercial object, from "show" into "sideshow." By paying to see, Montaigne participates in the new economy of the monster, the capitalist economics of commodification, of exchange (a "look" for a *sou*), the economics that here exploits the labor of the absent mother. Montaigne's representation of the episode (and the emphasis is on representation from the beginning, "Ce conte . . ."), in its objectivity and its visual detail, narrates the child as object of his gaze and as object of the writing, it recuperates monstrosity and reinscribes it as spectacle in / as the text, allowing it once again that exhibition that is only the performance of itself.

Immediately after presenting the child and arguing against prognostication, Montaigne briefly describes a shepherd from Médoc whom he also claims to have seen. As in the presentation of the child, and for the same reasons, observation replaces "commentary": "Je viens de voir un pastre en Medoc, de trente ans ou environ, qui n'a aucune montre des parties genitales: il a trois trous par où il rend son eau incessamment; il est barbu, a desir, et recherche l'attouchement des femmes" (713a) ("I have just seen a shepherd in Médoc, thirty years old or thereabouts, who has no sign of genital parts. He has three holes by which he constantly makes water. He is bearded, has desire, and likes to touch women" [539]). Although monstrousness is always a question of "showing" and of being seen, what shows and what Montaigne has seen when he claims to have "seen" the shepherd appear problematical. The child is made monstrous by his excess, by the useless supplement to his own already sufficient body that shows for all to see; the shepherd is made monstrous by his deficiency, by the lack of genitals that do not and cannot show ("aucune montre"), and this deficiency itself does not necessarily show for all to see. But in fact, it is precisely in the relation between what shows and what does not show, and in the incongruity between them, that we can locate the shepherd's monstrosity. When the shepherd is clothed, we might say that from the outside, on the outside, nothing shows but the conventional signs that he is a man: he has a beard, Montaigne says, has desire, and likes to touch women (and be touched by them, as Montaigne's expression also allows). On the inside—that is, concealed beneath his clothing although outside his body—we also have to say that "nothing" shows that he is a man and nothing shows that is a sign of masculine desire. But nothing in this case is also something, for what shows in the nothing between the shepherd's legs is both the monstrous absence of genitals and the incongruous presence of the beard, desire, and the wish to touch women. The testicles (Latin *testis*, witness) are the missing witness to the shepherd's virility, but precisely because they are missing they do, in fact, testify to the shepherd's monstrosity.[10] And when the shepherd becomes a figure of Montaigne's writing, when through the writing Montaigne can finally "see" all that there is to see, the man from Médoc shows all and shows off the monster that all can see. In this complex play of what shows and what does not, the shepherd shows himself, or itself, as strangely different within, a "man" and not a man, a creature double and diverse, not unlike the monstrous child, and not unlike the essayist and the writing itself.

· · · · · · ·

In "Des boyteux" (III, 11) Montaigne also speaks of strange and imperfect beings (the headless half of the "enfant monstrueux" was characterized three times as "imparfait"; the "boiteuses" of this essay have an "imperfection") and again attributes the wonderment they produce to their novelty, to the narrowness of custom, to the limitation and weakness of human reason. This too is an essay about seeing, and it is also about witnessing and bearing witness to phenomena that are often characterized as miracles (from Latin *miraculum*, object of wonder) and that the essayist, against the pressure of common opinion, would reinscribe in the domain of nature or on which he would reserve judgment altogether. Montaigne's plea for moderation in these issues, for a healthy skepticism that would make one wary of supernatural claims, derives as much from his wariness of his own personal inclination to hyperbole as from what he perceives as the common human tendency to make something out of nothing, to build worlds with words: "Nostre discours [both reason and language] est capable d'estoffer cent autres mondes et d'en trouver les principes et la contexture. Il ne luy faut ny matiere ny baze; laissez le courre: il bastit aussi bien sur le vuide que sur le plain, et de l'inanité que de matiere, 'dare pondus idonea fumo'" [1,027b] ("Our reason is capable of filling out a hundred other worlds and finding their principles and contexture. It needs neither matter nor basis; let it run on; it builds as well on emptiness as on fullness, and with inanity as with matter: 'suited to give solidity to smoke'" [785]).

In this later essay, Montaigne again seeks to neutralize and naturalize that which is perceived as strange, to domesticate it by making it familiar—in a word, to transform and thus to eliminate it: "On s'apprivoise à toute estrangeté par l'usage et le temps" (1,029b) ("We become habituated to anything strange by use and time" [787]). Grammatically speaking, through the action of the reflexive verb, man transforms himself, or is transformed, but *estrangeté* has undergone the most radical change: can strangeness still exist as such if it has become familiar? In the context of these two essays, "strangeness"—and here we must bracket it to indicate its own strange status—can be conceived only as a function of our own inexperience, as a function of time and "usage," as a misconception or misperception. Strangeness and the wonderment it produces are nothing in themselves, in a sense, are nothing to wonder about. As we get close to something strange, it vanishes: "Nostre veuë represente ainsi souvent de loing des images estranges, qui s'esvanouissent en s'approchant" (ibid.) ("Thus our sight often represents strange images at a distance, which vanish as they approach" [ibid.]). In "Des boyteux" Montaigne undermines the integrity of the eyewitness and of language that claims to bear witness to strangeness as he implicates knowledge in the unreliable realm of representation and its images, both visual and verbal. Neither what we see nor what we say escapes the deceptive performance of our own vanity or the distorting effect of image making. We might say that in challenging strangeness the essay testifies to the unreliability of testimony itself and bears witness to the deceptiveness of witnessing itself. But in a reprise of the formula that we have seen operative in the *Essais*, the challenge to strangeness is not its total elimination, nor is the questioning of the witness its absolute denial. Strangeness, testimony, and the witness remain central to Montaigne's monstrous project.

Montaigne testifies in "Des boyteux" to the limping and crippled vagaries of man's reason and to his self-deceiving nature, to his vanity, and he discovers that, rather than having been eliminated, wonderment and its object have been displaced from phenomena or events in the world to man himself. "J'ay veu la naissance de plusieurs miracles de mon temps" (1,027b) ("I have seen the birth of many miracles in my time" [786]), the essayist says wryly: man makes miracles, he conceives them in imagination and nurtures them by rhetorical prowess, props them up by public opinion, and authenticates them by calling on the testimony of the ancients. And in this vain and frivolous activity man reveals himself as the true miracle and displays the genuine estrangeté of his own wondrous ways.

Monsters and miracles are no longer seen outside ("Jusques à cette heure, tous ces miracles et evenemens estranges se cachent devant moy" [1,029b]), not only because their causes cannot be substantiated but also because the seeker of causes is himself the (unsought) cause, not only because the causes are not before man's eyes but because they are within him.[11] The marvelous, as Montaigne's language here reveals, has been appropriated as a function of man himself and of his vain and empty functioning: "C'est merveille, de combien vains commencemens et frivoles causes naissent ordinairement si fameuses impressions" (ibid.) ("It is a marvel from what empty beginnings and frivolous causes such famous impresssions ordinarily spring" [787]). Man, we understand, is the empty origin and frivolous cause, and he is the most extraordinary effect as well, and that, we also understand, is cause for wonderment.

The marvelous that man witnesses, the true miracle he sees, is thus himself, himself in his monstrous emptiness and vanity and, as we will see, in his ignorance. The monstrous, like the miracle, the monstrous *as* the miracle, is interiorized and personalized: "Je n'ay veu monstre et miracle au monde plus expres que moy-mesme. On s'apprivoise à toute estrangeté par l'usage et le temps; mais plus je me hante et me connois, plus ma difformité m'estonne, moins je m'entens en moy" (1,029b) ("I have seen no more evident monstrosity and miracle in the world than myself. We become habituated to anything strange by use and time; but the more I frequent myself and know myself, the more my deformity astonishes me, and the less I understand myself" [787]). With Oedipean irony, Montaigne discovers himself (and man) in his deformity (perhaps not coincidentally in the essay on "des boiteux"), and he uncovers himself as the very monstrousness he sought outside. And this estrangeté cannot be tamed or gotten used to, it cannot be domesticated, because it is already at home. At the end of "D'un enfant monstrueux" Montaigne's exhortation to universal reason sought to eliminate the monstrous as a factor of novelty and of wonderment: "Que cette raison universelle et naturelle chasse de nous l'erreur et l'estonnement que la nouvelleté nous apporte" (713c) ("Let this universal and natural reason drive out of us the error and astonishment that novelty brings" [539]). These lines suggest that the error of mistaking the unfamiliar for the monstrous is also the wandering (*errare*) of reason itself. And they imply as well that the astonishment provoked by what is an error is an error in itself. In this earlier essay, these errors of reason and astonishment, and astonishment itself, must be expelled from the mind and from human experience. In "Des boyteux," on the other hand, the astonishment (wonderment, I have called it, caused by the marvelous) provoked by deformity is authentic, and the deformity, we might say, is precisely that of reason in its natural "erreur et estonnement," in its limp. The novelty of *this* deformity can never wear off, never become familiar. Its strangeness can never vanish or be overcome: the closer one gets to it, the more of it one sees, the less one understands. "L'estonnement" thus becomes the genuine sign of a self that can only know that it does not know itself, that must forever in some sense remain alien to itself and experience that alterity as the inescapable, and imponderable, doubleness of its own monstrous nature. It becomes the incontrovertible sign of that lack of understanding, the sign of that monstrous deformity that is Montaigne's (man's) ignorance of himself.[12]

And ignorance, as "Des boyteux" makes abundantly clear, must be confessed. Speaking again of our ignorance of the causes and effects of things, and as always of our ignorance of ourselves, Montaigne attributes error to man's inability to see and to acknowledge himself for what he is: "[b] Il s'engendre beaucoup d'abus au monde [c] ou, pour le dire plus hardiment, tous les abus du monde s'engendrent [b] de ce qu'on nous apprend à craindre de faire profession de nostre ignorance" (1,030) ("Many abuses are engendered in the world, or, to put it more boldly, all the abuses in the world are engendered by our being taught to be afraid of professing our ignorance" [788]). The only possible way to avoid the abuses engendered by ignorance is to confess it, that is, to acknowledge it and to show it off. Montaigne thus professes ignorance, he admits and exhibits it, he makes a spectacle of it and of himself: "Qui veut guerir de l'ignorance, il faut la confesser" (1,030b) ("Anyone who wants to be cured of ignorance must confess it" [788]). Presumptuously making himself known as nothing, he performs the paradoxical status of nemo, and what he makes known as well as he shows himself off is the monstrousness of nemo and of his confession.

·   ·   ·   ·   ·   ·   ·

In a profound sense, neither the enfant monstrueux nor Montaigne has to *do* anything in particular to be known for what he is, he has only to *be* what he is and to be seen for what he is. The phrase from

"De l'exercitation" in which he claims that he has written down his essence rather than his actions ("Ce ne sont mes gestes que j'escris, c'est moy, c'est mon essence" [II, 6, 379c]) is often quoted to affirm that Montaigne is indeed in his writing and that he shows there. It is not sufficient to recount physical actions because they are as likely as not to be accidental to the self, the effects of fortune. The writer must record only himself ("moy"), his profound and authentic "self." Earlier we saw how Montaigne attempts to overcome factitious and deceptive language by conceiving of saying or writing (*dire*) as a form of action, a substantial making or doing (*faire*). But here he shifts emphasis from the activity of writing as a form of "doing" something to writing as the expression of "being" something.

"Being" in Montaigne's text is thus revealed in his confession that he knows nothing (of himself, of the world, of being, or of truth), does nothing (because of his "naturel poisant, paresseux et fay neant" [II, 17, 643a]), is nothing (as part of "la nihilité de l'humaine condition" [II, 6, 380c]). "There is nothing I treat specifically except nothing," he says (III, 12, 1,057c), "and no knowledge except that of the lack of knowledge," but more is at stake here than what some have taken for Montaigne's expression of a widespread Renaissance skepticism or his adherence to the Pyrrhonism of the ancients.[13] Because he dares to talk about himself, and in this way, the figure of the nemo does not lose himself, or being itself, in nothingness. What the juxtaposition of nemo and confession reveals is that Montaigne's confession seeks to be redemptive in a personal and secular sense. While in religious confession the self turns away from a personal ethos and identity to be reinscribed into the larger spiritual narrative of transcendence and salvation, losing itself to itself in order to find itself in God, Montaigne speaks a personal language of loss and of gain that returns him to himself and allows him to find himself, and his humanity, there.[14] By writing down his monstrousness in this way Montaigne provides a means for confronting the implications of his vanity and ignorance, that deformity that the essays cast as "physical" rather than metaphysical.

In my discussion of "De l'oisiveté" I insisted that Montaigne does not seek to cure his sickness or monstrousness. Here in "Des boyteux" he speaks again as if monstrous ignorance were some sort of malady, but in words we cited above he claims that confession is in fact its cure. The being that is both monster and miracle astonishes itself as it shows itself and thus embarks on the path toward recovery, toward the recovery of the self and of self-knowledge, and toward its moral recovery as well: "[c] L'admiration est fondement de toute philosophie, l'inquisition le progrez, l'ignorance le bout. [b] Voire dea, il y a quelque ignorance forte et genereuse qui ne doit rien en honneur et en courage à la science, [c] ignorance pour laquelle concevoir il n'y a pas moins de science que pour concevoir la science" (1,030) ("Wonder is the foundation of all philosophy, inquiry its progress, ignorance its end. I'll go further: There is a certain strong and generous ignorance that concedes nothing to knowledge in honor and courage, an ignorance that requires no less knowledge to conceive it than does knowledge" [788]). Through the text of confession, Montaigne's ignorance as "lack" becomes an ignorance as "fullness," an ignorance that claims for itself substantial "being" born of knowledge (*scientia*). Just as the *Essais* as confession allow for nothing to be something as well, so they allow for ignorance to be conceived in knowledge, to be conceived *as* knowledge. Thus they enact the curative and restorative power of writing and allow at the same time for Montaigne to be Socrates, as the closing words of "De l'exercitation" suggest: "Par ce que Socrates avoit seul mordu à certes au precepte de son Dieu, de se connoistre, et par cette estude estoit arrivé à se mespriser, il fut estimé seul digne du surnom de Sage. Qui se connoistra ainsi, qu'il se donne hardiment à connoistre par sa bouche" (II, 6, 380c) ("Because Socrates alone had seriously digested the precept of his god—to know himself—and because by that study he had come to despise himself, he alone was deemed worthy of the name *wise*. Whoever knows himself thus, let him boldly make himself known by his own mouth" [275]).

This is not the first time we have seen Montaigne propose that there is a remedy for what "ails" him, and it is not the last time that we will underscore the problematic nature of remediation. In the discussion of "De l'exercitation" in the previous chapter we heard him propose "le supreme remede" for presumptuous talk, but I insisted there that an absolute remedy was not possible since the cure—further talk—was also the disease itself. Here in "Des boyteux" the prestige that Montaigne imputes to himself through his association with Socrates cannot obscure a similar conclusion, that to know himself as monstrous in his vanity and ignorance and to confess it "par sa bouche" cannot eliminate or cure his monstrousness in any profound way. (I use "prestige" in this context and recall its etymology—from the Latin *praestigiae*, juggler's tricks, illusions—to expose the comparison with Socrates as a rhetorical move.) The path toward recovery—of self and of its moral health—is just that, a path over which the essayist travels (a familiar Montaignian metaphor) in a restless and errant movement that never concludes in full restoration or in complete rest. This is one of the profound implications of positing the "end" of all philosophy as ignorance ("l'ignorance le bout"), for this end is never really an "ending," it can never be known, possessed, realized once and for all.

Among other things, the *Essais* are the record of this endless movement toward a cure (or end), or it may be more accurate to say that movement "toward" is always at the same time movement "away." The more I frequent and know myself, we heard Montaigne say, the less I understand myself. Even though the confession of his monstrousness is made ostensibly in the humility of ignorance, it must always remain to some degree monstrous and presumptuous itself. The structure of confession recuperates the very element it seeks to eliminate, the vain and monstrous "I" that centers itself as the original effect of its vanity and the embodiment of its monstrousness, and that element must center itself again in confession in order to disavow itself. In a sense the confessor is both saved and dammed, since the confessional gesture must paradoxically exploit and repeat the error of presumption, the monstrous act of saying "I."

Perhaps by now we have sufficiently challenged Montaigne's own image of his writing as a "record" ("registre"), with its implications of a writing "après coup," "to record," since it has become abundantly clear that the writing *is* the movement itself, the experience that is both "toward" and "away," illness and cure. Although the essayist would exchange a deformed ignorance for an honorable and noble one, this momentous exchange cannot transcend the limitations of his language, his lexicon cannot carry him beyond "ignorance" and thus beyond monstrousness. Perhaps this is yet another sign that the malady or deformity he would seek to cure is not only *in* him, it *is* him, it is as much a part of his nature as the monstrous seed at the origin of life itself. To eliminate monstrousness would be to eliminate himself. Circumscribed by his ignorance(s), Montaigne can never fully recover; monstrousness has continually to be shown, the confession endlessly to be spoken, the text forever rewritten as both sickness and remedy, deformity and ideal form. Montaigne's experience of being is precisely the experience of this paradoxical doubleness that is the manifestation of the monstrous itself.

·   ·   ·   ·   ·   ·   ·

What I am describing as Montaigne's monstrous confession and his confession of monstrousness bears upon the relation between writer and reader that I raised in chapter 3. There, through the figures of the imposing writer and the obtrusive reader, I challenged the traditional view of the *Essais* as a congenial dialogue in which the essayist engages his reader-interlocutor and articulates his views and attitudes on a variety of subjects in order to enter into friendly exchange through the reading process. The present discussion appears in its turn to complicate the issue of communication, for it suggests that Montaigne does not write exclusively or even primarily to advance a discursive content, to talk, for example, about friendship, presumption, or experience. His ideas on this or that subject obviously say something in themselves, but they serve essentially as the means by which the essayist shows himself off. And as Montaigne reveals himself in this form of confession, as he seeks to expose himself through his words, and to be heard, or seen, what he needs is not an interlocutor but a listener, not an active reader but a passive one. The recurrent image of the *Essais* as the "registre" of the essayist's thoughts expresses both Montaigne's effort to manifest himself and the status of the text as an open record. By writing Montaigne makes a (public) spectacle of himself, and the notion of spectacle is important to express the fact that textuality exhibits both the writer and the writing itself to the reader / witness.

The status of the reader as witness to this spectacular confession, however, is not at all clear. When Montaigne asks in "Du démentir," "Et quand personne ne me lira, ay-je perdu mon temps de m'estre entretenu tant d'heures oisifves à pensements si utiles et aggreables?" (II, 18, 665c) ("And if no one reads me, have I wasted my time, entertaining myself for so many idle hours with such useful and agreeable thoughts"? [504]), and answers his own rhetorical question in the negative, he seems to suggest that once embarked on his enterprise he is entirely self-sufficient, that the confession speaks for itself and does not need to be read (witnessed) at all. He might be encouraged to say this because he is, of course, his own reader and able in a certain sense to dispense with others. He apparently does not need an other to confer absolution because the confession itself is already a kind of absolution, a way in which Montaigne frees himself (*ab-solvere*, to free, loosen from) to some degree from the bonds of ignorance and monstrousness. The paradox that to accuse and to condemn oneself would already be to absolve oneself does not escape him, as we saw. And this paradox is precisely what appears to operate here and to obviate the need for an "other," a witness, or a reader.

We have seen Montaigne dismiss his public reader once before, in the "Au lecteur," and so we should be alerted by the fact that that dismissal was also a paradoxical call to the reader and the sign of its appearance on the scene of reading. The readership constitutes a community of hearers who must be silent in order to hear and to witness as the essayist "witnessed" the monstrous child. In terms of his relation to Montaigne the writer of monstrous confession, the reader in the *Essais*—if there is one—thus cannot actively grant absolution, unless to be a witness, to listen to the confession—that is, to read—is already in some sense to absolve. And like all confessors whose primary task is to listen, the reader already knows what he is about to hear. The errors that Montaigne confesses are the errors of his humanness, errors he commits in common with those to whom he confesses, errors embedded in the human condition, in the human being. "Nous aymons à nous embrouiller en la vanité, comme conforme à nostre estre" (1,027b) ("We love to embroil ourselves in vanity, as something in conformity with our being" [786]), Montaigne says in "Des boyteux," using the first person plural not only to reveal that common character and fate but to underscore as well that it is already common knowledge.

When I argued in chapter 3 on behalf of an obtrusive reader I sought to provide a counter to the imposing text and to posit a model of reading that transformed the tension between them into a creative and dynamic force for interpretation. Here the text of confession exemplifies the weight claimed by the side of the writing and by its intention. The perspective of confession evokes a passive reading, as we have seen, indeed it could be said to necessitate it, and the reader who considers reading to be an invitation to generate *his/her* own discourse must not be allowed to drown out or to cancel out the silent reader required by the text for it to generate *its* own confessional discourse. This tension has been playing itself out in my reading, where I have sought both to be active enough to give the child, and Marie de Gournay, and the monstrous, and textuality itself their due and passive enough to let Montaigne's self-avowing writing speak for itself, in its own name. And I would reaffirm that this is the tension that characterizes—indeed, that allows for—all reading. Montaigne's confession of his monstrousness reminds us that reading always has to take into account that the text is something, intends something, and that its own role is to let it "be what it is" without the reading being anything itself. But reading cannot wholly abdicate its own voice and let the text speak entirely in *its* place; it would then be nothing more than recitation or "rereading" and not a reading at all. The reader's activity only begins, the active reading role begins (as did the essayist's and, I suspect, my own), with the reader's decision to make his/her own confession, that is, to write essays that are properly one's own and that disclose one's own deformity. In order to be something in itself, reading must also speak in its own voice, for itself. Like the writing subject, and the writing itself, reading must be double and deformed; when it speaks it must show (confess) its own monstrous nature as both something and nothing in order to be itself.

·   ·   ·   ·   ·   ·   ·

I want to recall the image of the Siamese brothers in "D'un enfant monstrueux," an image that emblematizes the monstrous text and the essayist himself. The perfect and imperfect bodies of the child(ren) joined in a grotesque whole evoke the co-presence of incongruous or incompatible elements that compose the monstrous confession. The humble avowal of ignorance cannot avoid being presumptuous, the remedy contains within itself an accompanying virulence, being is always a function of nothingness. The hybrid and the heterogeneous, the curious conjoining of natural categories that Horace rejected as an unacceptable perversion of the unity and proportion of true literary works, and that he depicted in the *Ars poetica* by the figures of a horse's neck coupled with a man's head and a woman joined to a fish's tail, these things Montaigne not only resituates within the order of nature but also within the aesthetic order, as the (dis)organizing principle of the *Essais*.[15] It is not coincidental that the hybrid tropes of paradox, oxymoron, contradiction, chiasmus, and irony, among others, operate so prominently in Montaigne's writing.

In the famous opening of "De l'amitié" (I, 28) where he compares his writing to the grotesque and fantastic images that fill the frame around a center destined to hold "un tableau riche, poly et formé selon l'art" (183a), the essayist quotes from Horace to figure his text in the precise terms that the Latin poet rejects: "Que sont-ce icy aussi, à la verité, que crotesques et corps monstrueux, rappiecez de divers membres, sans certaine figure, n'ayants ordre, suite ny proportion que fortuité? Desinit in piscem mulier formosa superne" (ibid.) ("And what are these things of mine, in truth, but grotesques and monstrous bodies, pieced together of divers members, without definite shape, having no order, sequence, or proportion other than accidental? 'A woman, lovely above, tapers off into a fish' " [135]). In my discussion of "De l'oisiveté" I called attention to the fact that Montaigne had quoted from the *Ars poetica;* there he quotes from the same passage from which he draws here. The Horatian image of hybrid shapes as the vain visions in a sick man's dreams served Montaigne to characterize the wild and foolish thoughts produced by the unbridled mind, which he then designated as the monstrous matter of his writing. What was striking there, as here, is that the essayist applies Horace's vocabulary, and its pejorative weight, to his own writing to insist that the text, like the self, must be double and diverse.

Montaigne's vision of the divided or double nature of man is not a static juxtaposition of incompatible elements as Horace's images of the hybrid text might imply (or for that matter as the image of the Siamese brothers might suggest). The horse's neck topped by a man's head, the lovely woman ending in a fish's tail, and Horace's unquoted examples—the harsh that mates with gentle, serpents that pair with birds, and lambs with tigers—all become in Montaigne's writing figures of a dynamic relationship defined by instability, change, and by what I have identified in the *Essais* as a central metaphor of the movement and variation of the self—that is, passage. What is at issue is the point or the moment at which the one thing passes into the other, at which it is at the same time both and neither of its composing and opposing parts. We recall that when Montaigne evokes Galatea, he chooses the precise point in Ovid's account when the statue metamorphoses into a woman. Looking at the lovely woman he draws from Horace in "De l'amitié," we would be unable to determine whether she was a woman changing into a fish or a fish changing into a woman. Are the Siamese brothers metamorphosing into a headless body, or is that body being transformed into its perfect half?

The opening of "De l'amitié" helps us to understand that it is precisely this issue of the mingling or the passage that lies at the heart of Montaigne's text. Montaigne appears to distinguish his own writing, the "corps monstrueux, rappiecez de divers membres," as the frame, the outside or margin of instability, but an instability that knows and keeps its place. In this picture change occurs but is contained, so to speak, kept outside and distinct from its other, "le plus bel endroit et milieu," as if the center—to which we might give the names truth, beauty, being, and so on—were the organizing principle that imposed a stable and incontrovertible order. However, the structured relationship of monstrous frame to artful center, the juxtaposition of radically different and separated contents and styles organized in a hierarchical relationship that subordinates outside to inside, collapses as the margin invades the center to mingle the incongruous and to confound distinctiveness. We have seen this process of dynamic mingling or cohabitation repeated endlessly in my discussions of the numerous configurations of the text as offspring and as monster: the father is in the son, the writer in his text, presumption in humility, the malady in the remedy, imperfection in perfection, with each, of course, also in the other. And the list could continue. In each case it is impossible to determine where the one begins and the other ends.[16] Taking the monstrous as perpetual becoming recalls the terms we used to characterize Montaigne's writing as movement both toward and away from a cure, an end, and it reminds us as well that the monstrous, and writing itself, can never be mastered, never be stabilized or arrested, because it is always "de passage," always passing from one state to another, always both dying and being reborn. Writing as passage, passages.

·   ·   ·   ·   ·   ·   ·

Reading the monstrous hybrid and amphibian images as expressions of dynamic change and instability allows us also to speak of a monstrous generation. Aristotle claimed that the law of nature decreed that like produce like, and where resemblance was the rule of generation difference became the scandalous aberrance from nature's own norm. Examples of women becoming fish and men metamorphosing into horses also describe generation. Here one form is perpetually giving birth to another, which, in its dissimilarity, fulfills Aristotle's definition of the monster as the offspring that does not resemble its parent. But I want to take this idea of monstrous generation one step further, because if we have understood that resemblance can never be absolute—recall the seed that both assures resemblance and introduces difference—it is also true that difference is not absolute either. In the static form that I have set aside, the woman/fish represents the grotesque coupling of two different species, placed side by side and connected as the contingent elements of a metonomy. In a sense the two elements remain separate; only in their contiguity do they form a third, monstrous whole. In the dynamic form in which the two species are continually merging into each other, losing themselves in each other, generating each other, the relation seems more than accidental, as if in some inexplicable way the woman and the fish did indeed share something essential. Here we might recognize the movement and the relation of metaphor that brings out, as Kenneth Burke suggested, the thisness of a that, or the thatness of a this. The fish emerges from the woman and does not seem to resemble her; but the fish also emerges as what we might call the expression of the woman's own "fishness," a quality that was always apparently latent in her and that needed only the monstrous birth to be recognized and affirmed. This monstrous metaphor should more aptly be called a catachresis, an extravagant, unexpected figure, and we might be tempted to dismiss it as abusive misstatement. But neither the catachresis nor the monster can simply be dismissed because, in its extravagance and abusiveness, each reveals what lies hidden or repressed within its singular and normative other. Just as every metaphor contains within itself the possibility of catachresis, its misstatement or its deformation, so every human carries within the possibility that it is also always a beast. The monstrous, as Montaigne said, is not alien and outside of us but the co-presence of the alien within us.

Monstrosity once again appears to be defined as a difference *within* rather than as a difference *between*, just as it was in the seminal case of the seed. In the Aristotelian terms with which we began, where the monster is that which does not take after its parents in any way, monstrosity is a matter of difference between parents and offspring, a matter of nonresemblance.[17] But the binary opposition between resemblance and difference, between likeness and unlikeness, is problematical, and this is borne out once again by the situation of the monster within. Montaigne does not discover his own monstrousness within until he produces his monstrous progeny outside. In a sense, the chimeric thoughts and monstrous fantasies that are his book/child surprise him by their difference, as we saw in "De l'oisiveté," their difference from what he expected his thoughts to be, or from what he knew himself to be. He has produced what for all intents and purposes is both like and unlike him, a monstrous child that is both him and not him, or we might say that the monstrous child is what has produced *him* as a monster, double and diverse. Father and child resemble each other, author and book are consubstantial. Father and child are different from each other, disparity constantly intervenes between author and book. The textual progeny is the form of the father in the world, and what it discloses in its own monstrous form is the monstrousness of its progenitor, *his* own doubleness shown off in the grotesque mixture that is the child itself. The father's real nature lies hidden, unrevealed by his appearance, until the birth of the strange child who both embodies and mirrors monstrousness, who bears witness to the heretofore unknown and unexpressed doubleness of the father.

Here the birth of the monstrous child reveals the most extraordinary secret about the father's real nature and the nature of his doubleness. From the beginning of this study I have spoken of the father, and, in a sense, primarily of the father, as the author of both child and text and, until the revelatory discussion of Pygmalion, characterized the progeny as male. There is historical precedent for this way of speaking, a long tradition of patriarchal privilege and appropriation that makes cultural conception a male birth, and it would appear that Montaigne contributes to that history and invites complicity on the part of his reader, as I have already suggested. And yet, an intrusive, active reading of the *Essais* that foregrounds male birth as a monstrous conception can confront and challenge this myopic perspective, and it can disclose secrets about sexuality and gender that the text "knows" and does not or cannot openly reveal, secrets that it hides or represses even as it lets it be known that it has secrets to tell. In the following chapter I will challenge the oxymoron of male birth in the *Essais* and examine the "secret" in detail. Here, by way of introduction, I want to suggest that when the monstrous child shows itself and its "father," it also shows that the complex question of gender, both of author and of offspring, lies at the very heart of its conception.

Let us return to the presence of the female at the birth of monsters and the monstrous text in "De l'oisiveté." The earth as mother and woman herself figure the generative power of the mind, and they produce grotesque offspring because they conceive on their own, without the benefit of the fertilizing male seed that compensates for their natural deficiency. The mind left to its own devices, *his* mind, Montaigne's analogy affirms, is like the female body that in its insufficiency or incompleteness gives birth to monsters that are themselves not whole or fully formed. But the mind that produces monsters is also like the female mind, for it was commonly held that the powerful force of the mother's imagination shaped her progeny and could have that precise deforming effect on the seed at conception and on the fetus in the womb.[18] Here, too, the very strength of the imagination indicates a deficiency or defectiveness, a lack of control of the exercise of reason that allows the mind to imprint its wild fancies and visions on the form of its physical offspring. And here as well the production of the monster is exclusively female. Not that the male is totally absent from conception, for he plays his natural part, but female imagination supplants him as the true source of the child.

In traditional patriarchal terms the resemblance of father and child signals not only the fact of paternity but its privilege. In the situation I am describing, the work of female imagination appropriates the male role in procreation, it displaces the male presence (it is perhaps not too strong to say "replaces" it), erases its trace, and produces difference. "We know by experience," Montaigne says, "that women transmit marks of their fancies to the bodies of the children they carry in their womb," as he tells the story of the birth of the hairy girl born to a woman who had in mind at conception a picture of John the Baptist in animal skins (I, 21, 75). The chimeras and fantastic monsters conceived as Montaigne's mind runs wild in the field of his own imagination, as we read in "De l'oisiveté," are just so many marks of the essayist's fancy and bear witness to the woman at their source, the female body and female imagination that preside at the birth of Montaigne's monstrous text.

We might be inclined to dismiss this reading of "De l'oisiveté," and the emphasis placed on the imagination, as just another fabulous tale, a tale told by a patriarchal culture to affirm the hierarchical differences between the sexes as the opposition between male reason and female fancy. Or a tale told by a fanciful, or overactive, reader. Montaigne characterizes the various stories he recounts in "De la force de l'imagination," including the one about the hairy girl, in precisely these terms, but he refuses to dismiss them. Fabulous testimonies, provided they are possible, serve like true ones, he says, they exemplify some human potential whether they actually happened or not: "I see it and profit from it as well in shadow as in substance." The criterion for "acceptance" is not truth but verisimilitude—that is, in Aristotelian terms the criterion is aesthetic, and I would add interpretive, rather than historical or referential. I am suggesting that there is something "likely" about the double gender that the monstrous shows, something that "could be" that is suggested by the network of associations that I have foregrounded. For the moment let us say that something is "showing" that we will attempt to see.

6

Fathering the Text
The Woman in Man

Nous sommes pere et mere ensemble en cette generation.
(II, 8, 400)

We are both father and mother in that generation.

The dominant Western patriarchal tradition has claimed and conse-
crated cultural production as a male preserve with authorship always a question of literary paternity and the text almost always a
son, although in a number of writings, such as Montaigne's "De
l'affection des peres aux enfans," some children of the mind are referred to as daughters. Classical writers—Plato, Ovid, Horace—speak
of their writing as male children going forth into the world, but it is
perhaps most prominently within Judeo-Christian philosophical and
theological discourse that genealogical and literary metaphors intersect, from there to make their way into the broader cultural and
ideological context. As God the Father engendered the universe and
man (Adam) and authored the book of nature and the Bible, so the
(male) writer appropriates both paternity and authorship, so he attributes to himself the conception of both physical and textual progeny. And there is more, for just as the divine creation complicates and
confounds the distinction between the literal and the figurative (between history and mystery, between embodiment and the Word), so
literary creation asserts that it too makes the word flesh, that writing
is an instance of procreation.[1] Authorship *is* paternity, and vice versa.
Montaigne too conflates father and author and affirms the fraternal
relation between the child of the body and that of the mind: "Et je ne
sçay si je n'aimerois pas mieux beaucoup en avoir produict ung [a
child], parfaictement bien formé, de l'acointance des muses, que de
l'acointance de ma femme" (II, 8, 401b) ("And I do not know whether
I would not like much better to have produced one perfectly formed
child by intercourse with the muses than by intercourse with my

wife" [293]). In spite of the reference to the muses and to the wife, the production of children, in the grammar of Montaigne's discourse, is predicated by a masculine subject.

Feminist critics have been sensitive to the male appropriation of the birth function in the metaphor of literary paternity and have insightfully examined its cultural and social implications. They have argued persuasively that the trope reflects the sexual divison of labor that has operated historically in the patriarchal order to exclude women from the creative arts: production/creation is an act of the male mind, procreation an act of the female body.[2] While the mind-body opposition is traditionally invoked to keep woman in her place, it also conveniently works to the benefit of the male through the metaphoric transfer by which he takes over the female bodily functions and fathers his texts. Without acknowledging either his debt to woman or to the effect of this figurative displacement, man imagines his mind pregnant with thought as if it were the womb itself. The writing of men is thus organicized, designated as "birth" within the natural order of things, so as to conceal or mask the abusive act of appropriation.

But of course there is nothing more unnatural than male birth, nothing further from the order of things or more monstrous. We should again speak of catachresis rather than metaphor to give voice as "misapplication," "misuse," to the otherwise unspoken scandal of the trope and to bring out the suppressed incongruity of the figure of fathering the text. To expose the scandal as a misappropriation, however, is not necessarily to eliminate it, since it may be that writing is already a presumptuous act of appropriation (of the word), an act that can only be justified, or rationalized, as natural by the further misappropriation of the womb. Catachresis is the red flag that signals the inappropriateness of this justification. Disclosing its own unnaturalness as a figure, it exposes the transfer as contrived and challenges all claims to a self-generative, phallic conception as factitious and self-interested.

All such claims are indeed challenged, including those implicit in Montaigne's reliance on figures of textual fathers and their progeny. We might be tempted to say that the essayist himself even recognized this and acknowledged the co-presence and perhaps the coupling of male and female when in "De l'affection des peres aux enfans" (II, 8) he represents himself and all writers as both father and mother of the child of the mind: "nous sommes pere et mere ensemble en cette generation" (400a). On the other hand, these words might simply express the conventional, patriarchal, and often misogynistic appropriation of which I have spoken. For the time being let me say only that whatever the "intention" of the historical Montaigne or the "meaning" of the first-person speaker in the text, I have read these words, and others like them, as nothing more or less than a possible breach in the traditional claim of phallic conception, as an aporia or a gap through which I can obtrusively assay their rhetorical, thematic, and structural implications within textuality itself. Entering the *Essais* in this way, I have found in their obsessive, self-reflexive preoccupation with writing that they problematize the opposition between male and female, complicate simple or exclusive notions of sexuality and gender, and in effect create and exploit the very conditions that allow textual production to be formulated as an androgynous act.[3] Without seeking to transform Montaigne into a protofeminist or to underplay the traditional patriarchal attitudes expressed in the *Essais,* the reading uncovers a more complex textual, and sexual, dynamic than the "father" figure and that of his "son" might have suggested at the outset.

.   .   .   .

Among the diverse examples on which Montaigne draws in "De la force de l'imagination" to illustrate the power of that faculty we find a striking series of metamorphoses by which women are transformed into men (I, 21). The essayist cites Pliny's claim to have seen Lucius Cossitus changed from a woman into a man on his wedding day. Pontanus and others, Montaigne continues, recount that similar metamorphoses have occurred in Italy in recent centuries. These "historical" metamorphoses lead him to Ovid and to the girl Iphis, whose prayer to the goddess asked that she be changed into a man in order to consummate her love for Ianthe. Montaigne recalls the story by citing the single line where Iphis realizes her destiny: "Vota puer solvit, quae femina voverat Iphis" ("Iphis the man fulfilled the vows made when he was a girl"). In the 1588 edition of the *Essais,* the essayist returns from this mythic archetype of sexual transformation to an example from contemporary history, to what he might even have confirmed with his own eyes. A version of Iphis, it appears, had materialized some years before just east of Paris in the town of Vitry.

Montaigne stopped there in 1580, early in the voyage he made to Italy following the publication of the first edition of the *Essais:*

> Passant à Victry le Françoys, je peuz voir un homme que l'Evesque de Soissons avoit nommé Germain en confirmation, lequel tous les habitans de là ont cogneu et veu fille, jusques à l'aage de vingt deux ans, nommée Marie. Il estoit à cett' heure-là fort barbu, et vieil, et point marié. Faisant, dict-il, quelque effort en sautant, ses membres virils se produisirent: et est encore en usage, entre les filles de là, une chanson, par laquelle elles s'entradvertissent de ne faire point de grandes enjambées, de peur de devenir garçons, comme Marie Germain. (99b)

> Passing through Vitry-le-François, I might have seen a man whom the bishop of Soissons had named Germain at confirmation, but whom all the inhabitants of that place had seen and known as a girl named Marie until the age of twenty-two. He was now heavily bearded, and old, and not married. Straining himself in some way in jumping, he says, his masculine organs came forth; and among the girls there a song is still current by which they warn each other not to take big strides for fear of becoming boys, like Marie Germain. (69)

Montaigne had recorded this story at the time in the opening pages of his diary, published posthumously (1774) as the *Journal de voyage.* Or, more accurately, his secretary recorded it as the third of three memorable "histoires" that the small entourage of travelers were told during their one-day stop in Vitry. "Nous ne le sceumes voir," the secretary reveals speaking of Marie Germain, "parce qu'il estoit au village," but the travelers were informed that Ambroise Paré in his *Des monstres et prodiges* (1573) had included this story, and they were assured of its veracity: "[ce conte] est très-certain," the secretary says, "et ainsi tesmoingné à M. de Montaigne par les plus apparens officiers de la ville" ("this story is most certain, and was thus confirmed to M. de Montaigne by the most recognized officials of the town").[4] When he revised his text of "De la force de l'imagination" upon his return from Italy, Montaigne added the incident of Marie Germain. Deleting the negative to transform what earlier in the diary "we" could not see ("nous ne le sceumes voir") into what he could himself have seen ("je peuz voir un homme"), Montaigne now produces an "eyewitness" account that lends veracity to the essay's bookish references, its literary and historical accounts of sexual transformation.

In its initial form in Montaigne's travel diary, the story of Marie

Germain makes no direct reference to the power of the imagination. Containing a few more details than the version in the *Essais* (it reveals, for example, that even before the sex change the young woman had more facial hair than most girls and was already known as "Marie la barbue"), the brief narrative tells the same story and concludes with the allusion to the song and the reference to Paré. The passage ends without further commentary, as abruptly as Montaigne's departure from Vitry: "De là nous partismes dimanche matin après desjeuné" (7). Paré's name, however, does lead us to the physiological subtext that serves to explain the transformation. In contemporary medical terms the incident illustrates the commonly held notion that men and women shared a single sex, with homologous sexual and reproductive organs distinguished only by their placement.[5] Women, Paré said, citing a tradition that extended back to Galen, "have as much hidden within the body as men have exposed outside." The single sex, the perfect sex, was indisputably male. Suffering from a lack of sufficient heat to force the genitals out, the physiologically inferior body of the female retained its (male) organs, in inverted form, within. Under extraordinary physical conditions, like the energetic effort made by Marie Germain in jumping, excess body heat could be generated to transform a girl into a boy.

Within the context of the single-sex theory, sexual difference is a physiological difference, the difference in the location and form of the male genitals. But the outside/inside opposition that is thus played out upon and within the body was also a culturally motivated difference, a difference that privileged the outside as the place of the penis and reflected the traditional hierarchical difference between the sexes. And yet, paradoxically, if biology was meant implicitly to reinforce and sustain the order represented by this cultural opposition, it could not do so in any absolute way. The body could never impose stability because it was not stable itself, it always risked turning inside out, as the example of Marie Germain shows. Or even outside in, because nothing in the logic of physiological transformation precluded men turning into women. We might explain the fact that cases of this sort are not recorded by adducing cultural reasons unrelated to the physical possibility itself. The position of the male within the cultural and social hierarchy depended on his maintaining his superior position; it was commonly believed that higher beings, including or especially men, could not turn into lower beings.

The song that Montaigne cites, perhaps as culture's response to this "natural" instability, reminds young girls to stay in their place (and it indicates *how* to stay there). Unless, of course, it is meant ironically, or inadvertently functions ironically, and by informing young girls precisely how they *can* change places ends up by undermining the fixity of place itself. The possibility of this second rendition suggests that the hierarchical grounding of culture (as well as the cultural grounding of hierarchy) contains within itself the very potential for its own undoing. In a society that imposes cultural, and categorical, distinctions between the masculine and the feminine based on the physical body, the chiasmic potential of the man within woman serves to unsettle the very grounds of opposition itself.

When Montaigne recasts the story of Marie Germain in the *Essais* as an effect of the imagination, he deletes the reference to Paré and in essence subsumes the biological into the cultural. What the song already implied was that physically acting like a boy could in itself produce anatomical changes within and without. What Montaigne now suggests is that acting like a boy in imagination, in thought, or in desire can also effect the change. For the girl to act "like a boy" is to transgress societal norms of behavior, to cross over gender-coded modes of conduct, to exhibit the signs of masculinity. It is already, from a cultural point of view, to *be* a boy, even if the body is not (yet) inscribed sexually as a male body.

Here the story of Iphis can be instructive. When Iphis bemoans her fate because she knows herself to be a woman in love with another woman she also opens the possibility that she may not completely know herself. "Consider what you were born," Iphis tells herself, "unless you are deceiving yourself, as well as everyone else." But is it entirely clear what Iphis was born as or what she is? Is it entirely certain that she is not deceiving herself? Sexually speaking Iphis is a girl, but both her face and her name are appropriate for a man, she dresses like one, and her reference to nature to situate her desire for Ianthe implies that that desire itself is masculine, and naturally so: "It is the ram which excites the ewe, the hind follows the stag, birds too mate in the same way, and never among all the animals does one female fall in love with another." Together with the female body there seems then to co-exist both upon and within the girl Iphis what could already be considered to be masculine, both naturally (her face, her desire) and conventionally (her name), even before she is transformed by the goddess into a man at the end of Ovid's story, even before she is endowed with a penis so that her love for Ianthe can be consummated. In the final act the goddess both weakens the female that was already there in Iphis and strengthens the male that was also already there. Without any mention of the genital addition, Ovid says that "Her face lost its fair complexion, her hair looked shorter, plain and simple in style, her features sharpened, and her strength increased. She showed more energy than a woman has—for she who had lately been a woman had become a man!" "Acting like a man" has indeed affected (effected) change. The goddess completes what was already to some degree a reality; the metamorphosis of Iphis was already written in her face, inscribed in her name, and confirmed by her love for Ianthe. The physical transformation resolves the double nature of Iphis by bringing out for all to see, and once and for all, the man within the woman (IX. 666–797).[6]

Montaigne's final comment in the passage on Marie Germain confirms in a hyperbolic (and perhaps ironic) way the transformative potential of desire and the desire for the (outside) penis:

> Ce n'est pas tant de merveille, que cette sorte d'accident se rencontre frequent: car si l'imagination peut en telles choses, elle est si continuellement et si vigoureusement attachée à ce subject, que, pour n'avoir si souvent à rechoir en mesme pensée et aspreté de desir, elle a meilleur compte d'incorporer, une fois pour toutes, cette virile partie aux filles. (99)

> It is not so great a marvel that this sort of accident is frequently met with. For if the imagination has power in such things, it is so continually and vigorously fixed on this subject that in order not to have to relapse so often into the same thought and sharpness of desire, it is better off if once and for all it incorporates this masculine member in girls. (69)

We might wonder where this sort of accident is frequently met. Villey suggests that the popularity of the texts of Pliny and Aulus Gellius made stories of sexual change the order of the day, to be found not only in Paré but in Vivès's *Commentaire de la Cité de Dieu*, du Verdier's *Suites des diverses leçons*, and Bouchet's *Sérées*, published later in imitation of Montaigne.[7] At the same time, we should not overlook the self-referential aspect of this remark, the fact that Montaigne's own writing (re)produces this sort of accident four times alone in this essay, and that it is here (especially) that "la force de l'imagination" transforms woman into the man within. Montaigne's concern expressed in these lines appears to be the tension generated by the discrepancy between the physical reality of the female body and the psychic reality of her desire for (that is, to be) a man.[8] All girls, Montaigne appears to say, are moved by the "same thought and sharpness of desire" (for the penis), all women are thus already avatars of Iphis, trapped in her body in the period when gender and sex do not coincide. Montaigne would resolve this tension not by triumphing over or eliminating the potency of imagination (or desire: can we ever uncouple the two?) but by surrendering to it and like the goddess allowing all women to enjoy the fate of Iphis. In a burst of phallocentric generosity that demonstrates the power of *his* imagination, Montaigne effaces sexual difference and the possibility of thinking differently by turning women into men.

The essay on the power of the imagination with its explicit reference to desire thus affirms how gender can be understood as a state of mind, and one not necessarily in accord with the state of the sexual body. The Médoc shepherd of "D'un enfant monstrueux" (II, 30), who appears as a monster of nature because he lacks male sexual organs, apparently deserves to be considered masculine because he exhibits the psychic signs of manhood: "he ... has desire, and likes to touch women" (713). His feelings and actions correspond to what society considers masculine, and he wears what appears to be the unfailing cultural sign of manliness, the beard, even more essential perhaps than the penis as the distinguishing mark of gender because it is always unmistakably visible "outside." It was, after all, the excess hair of Marie la barbue that betrayed the man within her and announced her gender even before she fulfilled her sexual destiny as a man. All of these examples affirm the power of the psyche (and of culture) to determine and to mark gender, although it is striking that neither psyche nor body is necessarily marked once and for all, that what I might refer to as the cultural and the natural are both susceptible to protean change.

What might have been considered an opening for creative self-fashioning appeared rather as an unsettling instability that threatened the integrity of both self and society, and it called forth myriad conventions and norms that functioned in the sixteenth century to preserve the cultural order and to keep things in their place. The song sung by the girls of Vitry ostensibly reflects their fear of becoming boys ("de peur de devenir garçons"), but that fear may very well be society's apprehension about its own stability. From sumptuary laws to the decorum in love making that made it "unnatural" for the woman to assume the active position on "top," rules in Montaigne's France enforced gendered behavior and supported the traditional hierarchical arrangement of the sexes. The second story the traveler heard at Vitry, and recounted in his *Journal de voyage*, the story of seven or eight girls who dressed as men and sought to live accordingly in society, underscores not only the problematical nature of gender but, in the stern reaction of society to transgression, the apparent menace that it posed. Living in a girl's body, the protagonist of this second story, who is named Mary, wears men's clothing, earns her living like a man, and, expressing desire conventionally coded as masculine, falls in love with and marries a woman. Montaigne's language reflects (produces?) Mary's transformation: when she arrives at Vitry, she is one of the girls ("l'une"), but as she settles into her masculine life there she becomes a young man in and through a gendered grammar ("jeune *homme* bien conditionné [élevé] et qui se rendoit, à un chacun, am*i*"). The subjects, the modifying participles, and the adjectives are all masculine, and they only revert to the feminine when Mary is unmasked, and judged, when Mary herself is forced to revert to the feminine: "elle avoit esté condamnée à estre pendue: ce qu'elle disoit aimer mieux souffrir que de se remettre en estat de fille" ("she was condemned to be hanged. She said that she would rather suffer that fate than return to being a girl").[9]

Mary thus "acts like a man," wearing the social signs of the masculine gender as her dress and her behavior. Gender, it would appear, is a matter of public performance, of acting, of being seen and "seen as," it is a matter of staging, of roles assumed and successfully played before others. Take Mary's marriage. Before others, Mary marries as a man, she performs what Austin takes as an exemplary performative; her ritualistic vow is both her entrance into the covenant and her entrance as a man. But when Mary's act is exposed her body is exposed as well, and the end of the story reveals that Mary was always also a woman, and that whatever social role she performed, sexually she had remained in her woman's body. Does Mary act like a man because she desires to be a man, because she experiences desire for a woman as if she were a man trapped in a woman's body? Or does she dress like a man as a "coverup" for a woman's desire for another woman? Are her clothing, her way of life, and the narrator's gendered grammar ruses that conceal her lesbian desire and "under cover" allow its inadmissible realization? Montaigne does not ask these questions but we must to pursue our reading.

Mary not only falls in love, she marries and lives conjugally for four or five months, with the consent of her partner, "à ce qu'on dit," the narrator adds ("according to what people say"). Mary had been engaged to a woman before, in Vitry, but there was some trouble between them and the relationship had not gone further, the story indicates, and itself goes no further. The narrator says, "*il* fiança," confirming Mary's social status as a man, but did the trouble arise from the troubling duplicity and doubleness of Mary's gender? When she went to Montirandet and married, what was the nature of this marriage, and to what precisely did her partner consent? In the unknowable space between her public persona and her private life, Mary remains an enigmatic figure of the complex social and biological issues that bear upon questions of sexuality and gender. And what remains as well, even or especially after the "question" of Mary has been resolved by her death, are the six or seven other girls who also dressed as men and who were not found out (at least the story does not mention how they turned out). These girls / boys are apparently still at large in society as unsettling reminders of the unsettled nature of sexuality and gender.

Montaigne says that Mary was hanged "pour des inventions illicites à supplir au defaut de son sexe" (for unlawful designs, devices, fictions intended to supplement, make up for, stand for, what her sex lacks). In a narrow, legalistic reading of this indictment, and in a particularly literal one, Mary might have transgressed the law against sodomy that was defined for women in Renaissance France as the use of prosthetic instruments of penetration.[10] In private she might have committed a criminal act by supplementing her body with a device, by illicitly "dressing" and performing in the intimacy of the love scene the role that society confers on men. But Mary also plays this role openly and in public, she carries her unlawful design further by dressing (without brackets) and performing like a man for all to see.

If we thus broaden the charge, Mary commits an additional crime, a cultural crime, a transgression against the established cultural and social order in defiance of the sumptuary laws and the rules of gender. This crime too was a codified, punishable offense. And if we pursue this opening of the indictment farther, we might also say that in dressing like a man Mary also commits a rhetorical crime, she illegally uses "inventions," or devices, to do what rhetors are often accused of doing, to convince the public that things appear to be what they are not. And in the process she exposes society's own and even more serious rhetorical crime, and she opens herself to retaliation by revealing that society's norms themselves are a fabric of artful, contingent relationships that function like language and rhetoric itself. Mary's cross-dressing reveals that sumptuary codes and rules of decorum (and the laws against sodomy) do not represent sexuality in any "natural," essential way, as society pretends, but are arbitrary signs that can with ingenuity be manipulated to produce desired impressions and effects. With the codpiece prominently displayed as if it were the penis itself, breeches, for example, were meant to function referentially, but like an element in the process of substitution by which sign systems operate, breeches can do nothing more (or less) than stand in for something else or perhaps for nothing at all. Society condemns Mary for being what we might call a rhetor of sexuality, for exploiting like all rhetors the gap between sign and referent, between signifier and signified, and for abusing the arbitrariness of substitution by passing herself off as a man. But Mary is also hanged for exposing the rhetorical nature of the social itself.

When justice claims that Mary's intention was to "supplir [suppléer] au defaut de son sexe," it raises the stakes of the affair. This formulation allows us to see that the real crime is not only, or especially, Mary's own—whether it be juridical, social, or rhetorical—but one in which she is complicitous with all others of her gender ("son sexe"). This is the crime by default of which all women are guilty, the crime of nature that is the lack of the penis ("le sexe"). That this fault is punishable by death is not peculiar to this time and place: in diverse societies throughout history female babies have been put to death for not being born boys.

This was the fault and the intended fate of Iphis. "A girl," Ovid has her father say, "is more of a burden, and fortune has not given me the means to support one. So, though I pray it may not happen, if a girl is born, she must be put to death" (IX.672). Mary is, in almost every way, the avatar of Iphis, I might even say the historical fulfillment of Iphis because she enjoys what her mythic counterpart could not without the intervention of the goddess: marriage and the consummation of her love. But Mary cannot live as Iphis because she is abandoned by the gods, caught in her performance, and unmasked as an actor. And she is caught as well in a bind that appears to be more than double and that defies escape. If she remains true to the masculine gender that was also in her name and on her face (for although the story makes no mention, Mary's name and face allow her to "pass" as a man and do not betray her) and in her desire, and she dresses like a man, Mary must die at the hands of society. But she endures the same fate if she remains faithful to the feminine gender that is also in her face, her name, and her body and tries to fulfill her lesbian desire under the cover of a man's dress. And yet if Mary tries to be true to society, and to the way society views her sexuality, her body, and she dresses and lives like a (heterosexual) woman, Mary betrays something deep within herself, she dies to herself, and by her own hand. Society will not see or cannot admit either of the two possibilities that the gods apparently acknowledged in Iphis, it will not see or admit lesbian desire, nor will it allow that even without the biological mark of maleness, the sexual sign of manhood, a woman might also be a man.[11]

. . . .

The stories I have been telling depict a protean world of dizzying instability, a world of both physical and psychic transformation, a surreal world where reproductive organs turn inside out, where self-images reverse, where men wear women's bodies and women wear men's clothing and might even wear their psyches. Neither biology nor gender offers a stable ground for sexual identity, since both body and mind can be transformed or transform themselves. The body, like the mind, it would appear, is both continuous and open, susceptible to movement along a range of differences that are ultimately only differences of degree.[12] In these stories body and mind are open only in the direction that changes women into men, although it seems clear that the structures themselves of both the single-sex anatomy and socially based gender would have permitted transformation in the other direction as well. Earlier I suggested that we do not hear about men changing into women because it was held that creatures cannot descend on the scale of being. But the need to objectify and metaphorize hierarchy may also betray this metamorphosis as man's most deep-seated fear (or deeply repressed desire), both social and psychological. Male-centered culture and ideology militate against it in the unspoken name of power and privilege and in the name of a stable male identity upon which power and privilege are based. And yet while this masculine taboo could not admit of "real" change in the world, it did allow for sexual inversion in the world of the imagination. Natalie Davis draws our attention to the fact that "switches in sex roles [were] a widespread form of cultural play in literature, in art, and in festivity," and, although she is interested mainly in the image of "women on top," she documents the prevalence in popular festivals and carnivals of the inversion where men take on the roles or dress of women.[13]

Whatever the demonstrable social and cultural ramifications of this transvestism (Davis suggests that males "drew upon the sexual power and energy of the unruly woman and on her license . . . to promote fertility, to defend the community's interests and standards, and to tell the truth about unjust rule"),[14] it surely also exerted some pressure on the tenability of a fixed gender opposition based on sexual difference. Men did not actually need to change into women for this contingency to affect both perception and understanding. Disguise and play are powerful elements that both reflect and shape our sense of the "real" and our relation to it. The ritual or festive appropriation of the feminine—not only of gendered elements such as dress but of sexually or biologically derived attributes such as unruliness as well—even (or especially) within its precise and controlled frame, performs at the very least a virtual transformation into the feminine. To "be" a woman is also to look like a woman, to act like a woman, even if it is only in "play," and even if the body would belie that claim. Iphis and Mary also played a role, that of the male, without the "proper" body, and although we might argue that their case is different because it is possible to say that they might have first felt like a man, the relationship of cause to effect is complex here. Should feeling be privileged over acting? Might we not say that all acting entails feeling like someone, whether that feeling originally informs the acting or is (also) generated by it?

If, then, the cases of Iphis and Mary, and of Marie Germain, can be used to argue for the presence and potential of the man within woman, the performance of male transvestism argues for an inverted and symmetrical presence and potential, that of the woman within man. I am imagining an inadmissible, repressed presence that is expressed symbolically as "play," a presence that must be denied because it threatens manhood as it is historically and socially constituted, a womanly presence signaled by the very fact that it is construed as "alterity," expelled, and scorned. Nowhere perhaps is the woman within man more forcefully and persuasively exhibited than in the figure of the pregnant male that inhabits both erudite and popular Renaissance culture. Harkening back to the seminal biblical image of what is taken as Adam giving birth to Eve, and connected to myths of the hermaphrodite and the androgyne that associate with man the generative powers of the female, the topos of male pregnancy represents the claims of patriarchy on its offspring, and over its women. But this figure of the life-giving father, which sustains structures of traditional and "natural" domination, also appears in parodic dress, as if to mock as unnatural the desire that usurps the role of the female. Male maternity is given expansive play by the carnivalesque imagination—in myths and popular tales, in literature and in the festival—as a representation of a world turned upside down. Here male pregnancy is inevitably derided as grotesque, the state of a swollen and flatulent body that conceives in the stomach (*ventre*) and gives birth through the anus to monstrous and misshapen offspring. And to books.[15]

The outrageous travesty of the birth of books may take as its object the serious and authoritative, "official" (in the Bakhtinian sense) version of male aesthetic production that proclaims itself a literary paternity. In this complex metaphor that has dominated Western patriarchal culture, the author is conferred status as a father, a progenitor, and procreator, "an aesthetic patriarch whose pen is an instrument of generative power like his penis."[16] And although images are often evoked of the writer enraptured by his muse or of the creative seed spilling out on the virgin page, these allusions only serve to reinforce the metaphor's expression of an autoerotic act, an act that eliminates and ignores the engendering function that is properly, and literally, the province of woman. Like God the father, man alone, and on his own, engenders himself as author and generates his progeny as if the word were made flesh.

The burlesque of male pregnancy takes aim at the pretentious assumptions of masculine autogeneration by invoking a paradigm of conception that is inconceivable without reference to woman. Releasing a parodic female from within the male, the caricature imposes on literary paternity the model of her body, it plays on the linguistic identity of womb (*ventre*) and stomach (*ventre*), confounds the birth and alimentary canals, and gives birth through an opening that confuses the vaginal with the anal. Male birth, the parody reveals, is always also or especially woman giving birth, no matter how much its female nature is distorted, ignored, or repressed. No doubt this representation can be read as a misogynistic statement: reproduction, it might be saying, is the province of lowly woman, and a man who desires that function—even figuratively—degrades himself unnaturally with monstrous results. And it might be a statement about the lowly status of writing as well. But the richness of the carnivalesque parody also allows us a reading that necessarily reintroduces the feminine into any representation of birth and generation, that reminds man that any claim to give birth—especially figuratively—also entails recognition, admission, of the woman within him. To be male and an author may mean that one must also be a woman; it certainly requires that one act and function like a woman, even when that action is degraded and produces only wind. When speaking of just this sort of figurative reproduction in "De l'affection des peres aux enfans" (II, 8) Montaigne couples father and mother, and this represents more than the simple co-opting for the male of the female prerogative. We may see here an expression of the androgynous being required for the generation of the children of the mind, an expression of the presence of the woman who also resides in man.

·   ·   ·   ·   ·   ·   ·

In a passage in "De trois commerces" (III, 3, 822) where he is discussing the tendency of scholars to parade their knowledge around indiscriminately, Montaigne imagines that they have penetrated even to the women's boudoirs ("les cabinets des dames") and filled female ears with bookish knowledge. Seduced by scholarly, pretentious writing, the women now even make love in learned style ("Concumbunt doctè"), he says in Juvenal's ironic words, when their style ought to be natural and their own. In a suggestive reprise of these tropes in "Sur des vers de Virgile" (III, 5), Montaigne opens the essay by announcing his own desire to gain access to the boudoir. He is annoyed, he says, that his work has remained outside like a piece of furniture in the public space of the parlor. Boldly proposing to speak of "l'action genitale," which is natural, necessary, and just, Montaigne now seeks to join the women inside, in private: "ce chapitre me fera du cabinet" (847) ("This chapter will put me in the boudoir" [644]).

Montaigne in the boudoir. We might imagine him there in his turn attempting to seduce the reader through his very different writing, attempting to caress and arouse her with his natural and intimate writing that, like the verses of the ancients he admires, would have fingers to excite ("Et versus digitos habet" [849]). Seduction may be his ultimate goal (and the ultimate goal of all literature; I will have to come back to this), but in this essay, where sexuality and textuality are inextricably linked, it is not at all clear that either remains fully potent, capable of vigorously consummating its performance. The essayist pictures himself, in his old age, lacking the virility of his youth just as his writing and, as he suggests, perhaps all writing in these modern times lack the force and plenitude of the great classical authors who serve as his models. Having gained access to the boudoir, where the scene of seduction ought to be played out, Montaigne uncovers his own sexual inadequacy instead, and he discovers as well the inadequacy of his language, what he calls at the end of his essay "un flux de caquet, flux impetueux par fois et nuisible" (897) ("a flow of babble, a flow sometimes impetuous and harmful" [684]).

At the end of his essay, this essay that focuses so insistently on covering and uncovering—on the public attitudes that conceal sex as shameful, on his own intention to speak openly of it, on the paradoxical way in which concealing is also, or perhaps especially, a means of revealing and deferment a way of exciting rather than postponing desire—Montaigne uncovers something else about himself, something else that comes out because he has inserted himself into the boudoir among the women. In a striking quotation from Horace by which he means ostensibly to contrast his own indecorous old age with that early age more appropriate to love, Montaigne reveals the truth of another male who is inserted into a group of women:

> Quem si puellarum insereres choro,
> Mille sagaces falleret hospites
> Discrimen obscurum, solutis
> Crinibus ambiguóque vultu.
> (Odes, II.5.21)

(If you should place him in a troop of girls,
With his ambiguous face and flowing curls,
A thousand sharp onlookers could be wrong
And fail to pick him out amid the throng.)

We might be tempted by the context of Montaigne's passage to see in this trope of hermaphroditic doubleness only an allusion to childhood as a time of undifferentiated sexuality that is left behind with the passage of youth. We would then take the essayist's attitude as one of nostalgia for a lost ideal, a time beyond recovery. There is certainly in Montaigne's words a strong expression of longing or regret, but I want to suggest that something else is also in play besides the sense of irretrievable loss, either of youth, or of sexual virility, or of the plenitude of language. What has been in play here all along in the women's boudoirs has been the act of uncovering itself, and here, at the end of the essay, what is uncovered is also the truth of sexual resemblance, of physical and psychic doubleness that also has its textual counterpart.

When he joins the chorus of girls the boy's resemblance to them is revealed, when he is among them what I referred to as the woman within is brought out. What was always there to be perceived but was perhaps overlooked or repressed is now seen openly, as if mirrored in the faces, the features, of the girls who stand beside him and whom he reflects in his turn. The boy has an ambiguous face, equally appropriate to a girl, recalling the double face of Marie la barbue and of Iphis, whose features, Ovid says, whether they were supposed to be those of boy or girl, would have been accounted handsome in either. Montaigne, too, has a double face, as the verses he cites from Catullus as he concludes his essay imply. To exemplify the way that his writing, this "flux de caquet," as he calls it with revealing irony, escapes from him in spite of himself, Montaigne evokes Catullus's maiden who inadvertently allows her lover's gift, the apple, to fall from beneath her robe where it was hidden. The essayist is like the girl, for both have allowed the apple, and love and desire, to be revealed—this is what Montaigne's essay has been about—but the writing in the boudoir has also revealed, through the paradoxical indirection (concealment?) of quotation itself, that the essayist is also the girl. In the boudoir, in the writing, Montaigne has discovered the woman within: "Je dis," he says to finish the sentence that frames

Catullus's words, "que les masles et femelles sont jettez en mesme moule: sauf l'institution et l'usage, la difference n'y est pas grande" (897) ("I say that males and females are cast in the same mold; except for education and custom, the difference is not great" [685]).

Montaigne thus appears to discover resemblance, a profound and originally shared nature hidden under the heterogeneity of traits that are both historical and cultural. Beneath contingent difference lies a single mold, the figure of apparent unity and identity. But this discovery also reveals that within the singleness of the mold, at the origin, an enigmatic difference remains, even if Montaigne insists that it is not very great. In the final analysis, nothing could be more foreign to the overall sense or design of the *Essais* than a totalizing sameness, a figure or expression that would be univocal or "unisexed." For long-standing structures that are binary and hierarchical, Montaigne repeatedly substitutes more fluid and flexible forms, forms of exchange and interdependence. Here the androgyne can serve again as an emblem of the essayist's paradoxical juxtaposition of unity (*mesme*) and diversity (*difference*), a side-by-side (or, more precisely, back-to-back) that is at once integral and double.

Nature, at the origin, derives then from a single mold that reveals itself also to be double. But my effort to interrogate the origin will be problematic at best, will fall short in determining in any precise way what is particular and what is shared in this single mold, or how same is also different in this enigmatic figure that both unites and distinguishes masculine and feminine. The origin, like being itself, is not recuperable and will thus ultimately remain unknowable and imprecise, as Montaigne suggests at the end of the "Apologie de Raimond Sebond": "Nous n'avons aucune communication à l'estre, par ce que toute humaine nature est tousjours au milieu entre le naistre et le mourir, ne baillant de soy qu'une obscure apparence et ombre, et une incertaine et debile opinion" (II, 12, 601) ("We have no communication with being, because every human nature is always midway between birth and death, offering only a dim semblance and shadow of itself, and an uncertain and feeble opinion" [455]). How did the androgyne speak and in what forms? How were its voices both common and divided? Human reason, Montaigne argues forcefully in this essay, and elsewhere, is incapable of reaching truth, as if reason and truth exist in an asymptotic relation where the approaching lines can never meet. And he argues as well that language and culture always intervene between man and what he seeks to know and understand, as if a deforming glass through which one only sees darkly. This conviction (reality?) informs his own figures of obscurity and shadows in the quotation above and the figure of uncertain and feeble opinion. And its consequences determine my own necessary recourse to figures, to cultural (that is, rhetorical) figures that may conceal as much as they reveal, to the oxymoronic figure "woman in man," with its chiasmic partner "man in woman," and to that equally "foolish," corresponding figure, the allusive and obscure enigma of the androgyne itself.

At the same time, and here we come upon one of the fundamental paradoxes of the *Essais,* and perhaps of much of Western thought, no truth or knowledge is possible *without* the mediating and deforming cultural glass, no experience of the world or of the self is intelligible outside of culture and its conceptual structures, outside of language, its lexicon, its figures. Truth and trope, we might say, are inextricably linked. That is why Montaigne's discourse on nature and nature's own discourse in the *Essais* are always bookish in nature, always to some degree borrowed, and why he (and I) must turn to rhetoric and its figures even or especially in response to the desire or the demand to speak a truth that is natural and naked. That is ultimately why we cannot establish definitively whether culture is a degraded image of nature or nature an idealized figure of culture and also why the question of the originary status of (androgynous) nature is ultimately indeterminable. At the origin, a single mold reveals its doubleness, and while the "origin" may itself have to be bracketed as a trope, as a cultural effect, it may still, if we can allow the last sentence in the preceding paragraph its own chiasmic reversal, reveal as much as it conceals.

What the originary figure of androgyny reveals is that the history of Western culture has been one of opposition between the sexes, a history not of different voices speaking in unity (as the figure of the androgyne might imply) but of conflicted and mutually exclusive voices. Plato's androgyne split in half by Zeus and the gods serves as a symbol that both resumes and anticipates that history, a history that will play out the widening of the gulf and not, as Aristophanes tells it in the *Symposium* (190e), the story of the desire for reintegration. The masculine is the voice of authority, of dominance, that of the warrior, a stifling voice founded on the principle of exclusion; the feminine is the stifled voice of otherness, that of a degraded body. But patriarchal culture's ruse has been to posit that opposition as natural, as inscribed in the nature of things, and from the origin. To foreground the arbitrariness of this polarity, to underscore its historical value as relative and relational, Montaigne cites these words from Plato and from Antisthenes directly after his reference to the single mold: "Platon appelle indifferemment les uns et les autres à la société de tous estudes, exercices, charges, vacations guerrieres et paisibles, en sa republique; et le philosophe Antisthenes ostoit toute distinction entre leur vertu et la nostre" (III, 5, 897) ("Plato invites both [sexes] without discrimination to the fellowship of all studies, exercises, functions, warlike and peaceful occupations, in his commonwealth. And the philosopher Antisthenes eliminated any distinction between their virtue and ours" [685]). Quoting from the philosopher, the essayist turns culture against itself, philosophy against misogyny and its own misogynous tendencies.

On this issue, and on so many others that are political, social, or anthropological, Montaigne speaks from the position of cultural critic, ready to expose the contingent and historical status of social attitudes. Although here he uses culture to undermine its own practices, his more usual recourse is to nature, which becomes in itself a powerful rhetorical trope to advance values that are posited outside of time and history and taken as essential and originary. In its most extreme expression, nature completely obliterates culture, in a sense stripping man of all that is accidental and contingent and returning him to his fundamental self: "Toute cette nostre suffisance, qui est au delà de la naturelle," Montaigne says in "De la phisionomie," "est à peu pres vaine et superflue" (III, 12, 1,039) ("All this ability of ours that is beyond the natural is as good as vain and superfluous" [794]). The argumentative and persuasive force of this strategy is undeniable, and yet the experience of essaying also reveals, as I have tried to suggest, that culture cannot simply be stripped off like a secondary or superfluous outside, that however dubious its moral worth, whatever its vices or virtues, culture participates in the constitution of being, it is also "inside" man, and with the same status as nature itself. In the context of the *Essais,* culture in the form of custom and usage becomes a powerful formative force equal to, and often indistinguishable from, that very nature Montaigne so often privileges at its expense. "Appellons encore nature l'usage et condition de chacun de nous," Montaigne proclaims in "De mesnager sa volonté" (III, 10, 1,009); or again in the same essay, " L'accoustumance est une seconde nature, et non moins puissante" (1,010) ("Let us call the habits and condition of each of us *nature*"; "Habit is a second nature, and no less powerful" [772]).

We might begin to sense that we are whirling in a vortex of concepts persistently differentiated and undermined from within and consistently interacting in an unstable and complex way with each other. Nature is simultaneously an originary moment and a rhetorical trope and culture both a deforming glass and an informing force. They oppose each other yet inhabit the same space, are bound to each other yet stand back-to-back in a relation of difference and resemblance reminiscent of the doubleness of the androgyne itself. From this perspective Montaigne's discourse must always be double voiced, or even multivoiced, he must always speak as both nature and culture, even when those voices are in conflict with each other or are conflicted internally. Thus, nature in the *Essais* can ground the equality of the sexes as it does in the image of the mold, or it can ground inequality through a discourse of originary difference, or, finally, either ground can give way in the contingency of the trope (of the mold, for example) and Montaigne's assault on rhetoric. Just as culture can be invoked to argue for sexual equality in Plato's name or to provide a litany of derogatory misogynous commonplaces. It should not surprise the reader that Montaigne's concluding reflections in "Sur des vers de Virgile" on the resemblance of male and female identify *institution* and *usage* as the culprits of difference in the name of an unnamed nature and that in other essays, and more frequently, nature itself confirms the inferiority of women and justifies their subordination, as if culture were simply carrying out its bidding after the fact.

My effort to read what I have called Montaigne's androgyny is thus complicated by the tangled, paradoxical relation between nature and culture in the *Essais*. I began in this section by establishing an interpretive space within which to posit Montaigne's discovery, or recovery, of doubleness. I have to acknowledge, however, that doubleness is challenged, and perhaps undermined, when the essayist speaks with the voice of the misogynous, patriarchal tradition, when he affirms male singularity and rejects, or even represses, the woman within. Moreover, it is impossible to determine fully whether androgyny is natural or cultural, originary or secondary, whether it has always been there waiting to be revealed, like the female side of the boy who joined the chorus of girls in Catullus's quotation. Nor can it be decided whether it is anything more, or less, than a consequence of the quotation itself, a rhetorical effect produced by Montaigne's text. And even if androgyny is a textual product, it is not necessarily less "real," since in the *Essais* writing generates life as much as life produces writing. But while the tangle remains indeterminate—that is, while it resists simplification and reduction—it does not remain impenetrable or unknowable. What we discern in the tangle in all its diversity and complexity is both the expression of the androgynous impulse and its misogynous counterdiscourse, a female voice seeking inclusion and a male voice bent on exclusion, voices of nature and culture, as I said, speaking for and against each other and themselves—in sum, the multiple and heterogeneous voices of the unruly brood clamoring simultaneously to be heard, echoing from within the trope of fathering the text.

·   ·   ·   ·   ·   ·   ·

Although mother figures are not absent from the *Essais*—there are figures mythic and historical, literal and figurative, and among them Niobe, nature, cowardice the mother of cruelty, and even Montaigne's own mother—the figure of the mother is clearly subordinate to that of father. In purely quantitative terms, words relating to mothers (*mère, maternel, maternité*) are outnumbered by those pertaining to fathers by more than two to one. In Montaigne's own case, his mother appears only twice in "De l'institution des enfans," and in passing, while his father, named thirty times in the essays as a whole, occupies an important place in the thematic and rhetorical dynamic of the essayist's discourse. And Montaigne's wife and the mother of his children? She appears a mere four times as spouse but only once as mother. We might want to take this as a consequence of the conventional patriarchal voice that frequently speaks in the *Essais*, and never more forcefully than in what it does not say about mothers.

What is not said about mothers in the *Essais* has to do with their singular, and privileged, ability to conceive and give birth. This is not to say that conception and birth are never mentioned but rather that mothers in Montaigne's text are less something in themselves than figures of a common humanity that respond to the thematic demands of a given essay, examples of gentleness or cruelty, of moderation or excess, of virtue or vice, of strength or weakness. When mothers are portrayed as something in themselves, when they fulfill the role that realizes their maternity, it is as nurturers whose concern and responsibility is to provide for their young children and assure their early education. Of the three essays dedicated to historical women, two of them speak directly to the women as mothers, directing and encouraging them to provide those essential elements of the formative years, education and affection. Even in this prominent role, and in this prominent place at the head of seminal chapters, however, maternity is diminished and ultimately displaced by the paternal figure. In "De l'institution des enfans" the male teacher (*gouverneur*) standing in for the father becomes the governing force in the child's life, and in Montaigne's own case, as he tells the story of his early formation at the end of the essay, his father completely overshadows, even effaces, his mother. In "De l'affection des peres aux enfans," the title itself tells all, for while speaking directly to Mme d'Estissac and praising her in the opening pages as a paragon of "affection maternelle en nostre temps," Montaigne is exclusively concerned thereafter with the father's affection for the child and that of his own father for him. And it is precisely at the end of this essay that he introduces the figure of the child of the mind and the affection it inspires in its author, that he ironizes his preference for the muses over his wife, and that he exemplifies intellectual conception as male birth.

In contrast to the tradition that consigns woman to procreation, the *Essais* elide the mother in physical birth as if to prepare her elimination from figurative birth as well. A broad space is thus cleared for a conception *sine matre*, without the mother, without the matrix. Ovid had compared the genesis of his poems to the birth of Athena from the head of Zeus: "Palladis exemplo de me sine matre creata/Carmina sunt; stirps haec progeniesque mea est" (*Tristia*, 3.14.13–14). Traditional medicine did not go quite that far, although it underplayed and undervalued the woman's role in conception. Life was considered to reside in and be transmitted essentially by the noble male semen; woman was often thought to contribute the less-perfect womb as the site of generation, the earthlike receptacle where the seed is planted, nourished, and where it grows. Again woman is relegated to the secondary role of nurturer.[17] Montaigne himself does go farther, however, when he speaks of the male semen as if it were the exclusive generative agent, the bearer of form, of mind, and of matter. Marveling over the way that the seed produces resemblance

in (male) children, the essayist invests it with broad life-giving powers: "What a prodigy it is," he says, "that the drop of seed from which
we are produced bears in itself the impressions not only of the bodily
form but of the thoughts and inclinations of our fathers! Where does
this drop of fluid lodge this infinite number of forms?" (II, 37, 763a).
What does the mother contribute, we might want to ask, but here, in
this essay entitled "De la ressemblance des enfans aux peres," she is
again elided. The question is moot because resemblance, like birth
and life itself, it might seem, occurs sine matre.

In what appears to be a reversal of the concept of birth sine matre,
we encounter in "De l'oisiveté"—that essay often taken as the representation of the origin of Montaigne's text and its programmatic
statement—figures of the birth of writing *sine patre*. Here, we might
want to say, is the mother we have been missing, the mother who is
always elided, and especially from figural production, but this is
woman alone, without the father—that is, without the seed that
makes the father what he is. This is the grotesque double of fathering
the text, a caricature of the self-generative male birth that takes itself
(seriously) as the paradigm of production. This is woman who gives
birth to lumps of formless flesh that are the very analogue of the
chimeras and fantastic monsters conceived by the writer's mind and
inscribed as the essays. Here, too, is the earth as fallow and fertile
mother, alone and self-seeding, self-generating, and producing wild
and useless weeds that are also figures of Montaigne's text. That we
encounter what we can call literary maternity may surprise us given
the long tradition that I have cited that relegates women to literal
maternity and, in the *Essais*, to nurturing. But perhaps we should be
less surprised, given that same tradition, that when she does enter
the realm of intellectual production woman gives birth to perverse
and grotesque offspring. Unless we recall the reading of "De
l'oisiveté" where we saw Montaigne recuperate the monstrous, and
monstrous writing, naturalize it, validate and appropriate it, ironically, as the only proper writing. There is, then, a kind of writing,
and the writing that Montaigne takes for his own, that can only be
figured by woman as mother and that must elide and ignore the
father and *his* writing.[18]

The mother thus reappears at the origin, at the conception of writing, woman and earth as figures of nature, incomplete yet self-sufficient insofar as they inseminate themselves to produce the monstrous offspring that Montaigne takes as the image of his own text;

figures of nature and of natural writing, a writing untouched and uncontaminated by that which appears to represent the male, culture, "science," "doctrine," or "art," a writing that Montaigne ironically valorizes through understatement, like the rhetorical trope of litotes where the least signifies the most and the worst the best. And yet, as I have acknowledged, the *Essais* also manifest abundant signs of a paternal origin, it also aspires to be culture's artifact and to embody *its* values, to demonstrate mastery, form, distinction. There are two tendencies in opposition in Montaigne's text, two tendencies that are also in apposition, and complementary, the inclination of nature and that of culture, what the essayist calls monstrous, fantastic, inept and what can be called rational, orderly, controlled.

Because it is not a simple matter to distinguish between the inclinations of nature and of culture—as I have suggested, each inhabits the other, each is a necessary and integral part of the other and inconceivable without it—we might ask where precisely the monstrous is located: in the image of the self-inseminating female of "De l'oisiveté" as Montaigne explicitly states or in that of the self-inseminating male as the grotesque parodies of literary paternity imply? Generation sine patre represents the chimeras and monsters of imagination and libido, but does the birth sine matre not also represent monstrous desire both psychic and biological? And are the *Essais's* values absolute or exclusive? Does the emphasis on formlessness, strangeness, and imagination eliminate the desire or the need for form and judgment? Clearly both the mother and the father generate Montaigne's text, each without the other and also in some way with it, each always also present in the absence and the presence of the other. Let me return once again to the epigraph to this chapter, "Nous sommes pere et mere ensemble en cette generation." Speaking of the birth of that other, and noble, self that is his text, Montaigne apparently appropriates the female prerogative, but we might choose to recognize the admission that writing is always, even in spite of itself, "pere et mere ensemble."

·   ·   ·   ·   ·   ·   ·

The duality of writing (and of thinking, since *essayer* is always both at the same time), its necessary yet inconceivable juxtaposition of male and female, can be read in a richly suggestive image, easily overlooked, that occurs in the "Apologie de Raimond Sebond." In this most skeptical of essays, where Montaigne shows up the emptiness of traditional knowledge and argues that the proliferation of philosophical schools has only produced uncertainty, he evokes the figure of Socrates, the Socrates whose questions, whose doubts, put everything in question and who troubles the minds of his interlocutors: "Le conducteur de ses dialogismes, Socrates, va tousjours demandant en esmouvant la dispute, jamais l'arrestant, jamais satisfaisant, et dict n'avoir autre science que la science de s'opposer" (II, 12, 509c) ("The leader of his dialogues, Socrates, is always asking questions and stirring up discussion, never concluding, never satisfying; and says he has no other knowledge than that of opposing" [377]). In the context of the "Apologie" this Socrates both performs and confirms the uncertainty and vanity that afflict man's quest for knowledge, although it is clear that the philosopher's lack of resolve, his restless movement and self-critical judgment, indeed, his very sense of uncertainty and of his own vanity are qualities that both tradition and the essayist prize and validate. They are also the qualities that compose that learned ignorance that makes him most human, qualities that Montaigne associates with Socrates as the embodiment and the model of nature, as we saw in the reading of "De la phisionomie" (III, 12). And I want to suggest as well that these "natural" qualities can also be associated with that which the text takes as female, with a certain formlessness, with parts rather than the whole, with endless motion (*émouvoir*) that is also emotion, with action that is also agitation, with internal contradiction (*s'opposer*). Perhaps in this light it is not surprising that, as Montaigne develops the passage, the generation of thought (*disputer*) resembles birth and Socrates, the "conducteur" of the dialogues, is figured as an intellectual midwife.

In fact, Montaigne has borrowed this Socrates from Plato's *Theaetetus*, where the sage reminds his pupil that his mother Phaenarete was a midwife and then develops the figure of midwifery to show that he is indeed his mother's son (149a–52). The essayist's transposition is also a story of the birth of thought, and it is the story of the double birth of Socrates as the physical and spiritual offspring of Phaenarete, although the mother, and the maternal origin of the art, remain unnamed:

> Socrates disoit que les sages femmes, en prenant ce mestier de faire engendrer les autres, quittent le mestier d'engendrer, elles; que luy, par le tiltre de sage homme que les Dieux lui ont deferé, s'est aussi

desfaict, en son amour virile et mentale, de la faculté d'enfanter; et se contente d'aider et favorir de son secours les engendrans, ouvrir leur nature, graisser leurs conduits, faciliter l'issue de leur enfantement, juger d'iceluy, le baptizer, le nourrir, le fortifier, le mailloter et circonscrire: exerçant et maniant son engin aux perils et fortunes d'autruy. (II, 12, 509c)

Socrates used to say that the wise women [midwives], on taking up the practice of making others give birth, abandon the practice of giving birth themselves; that he, by the title of wise man that the gods conferred on him, has also done away, in his virile and mental love, with his faculty of begetting, and contents himself with aiding and favoring with his help those who are in labor, opening their organs, greasing their conduits, facilitating the issue of their offspring, judging it, baptizing it, nursing it, strengthening it, swaddling and circumscribing [circumcising] it; exercising and employing his skill upon the perils and fortunes of others. (377)

Here again we encounter the traditional separation of labor and the appropriation of the woman's natural and physical prerogative, the metaphorizing of generative power as the male conception of thought. Again we encounter male birth and the birth of the male ("circonscrire/circoncire"), sine matre, with another phallocentric twist, the elimination and replacement of the literal midwife—the "sage femme"—by the figure of the "sage homme," although this displacement is not exclusively figurative since men actually began to supplant women as practitioners of that "art" at the beginning of the sixteenth century and to turn it into a "science" and a profession. And yet it matters greatly that Socrates takes a woman's place, that he takes up woman's work, however metaphorical that work may be. I want to stress that in French the pun (paronomasia) on *sage* reveals the profound truth of the identity of Socrates; it reveals that only by becoming a "sage-femme" can he become a "sage-homme," only in this conflation of woman and man, of physical and intellectual, can he acquire that *sagesse* that is proper to the name of Socrates and thus give birth to himself. The wise or knowledgeable woman (Phaenarete and Socrates himself) produces the knowledgeable man, the man who is wise because he knows himself, for Socrates, in his sterility, is not only the midwife but also the improbable father to his students and himself. At the end of "De l'exercitation" Montaigne confirms what was already at stake in Socrates's genealogy, that "sage" was Socrates's name.[19]

Clearly, then, we cannot uncouple the male and female that appear to generate both wisdom and writing (the two are always intertwined in Montaigne's *Essais*), to be present both at their conception and at their delivery. Socrates gives up the feminine faculty of begetting and, in his virile (masculine) love of wisdom, exercises his feminine trade as "sage-homme." But even as a "sage-homme" he does not completely give up the faculty of begetting, as he claims. Socrates is more than a facilitator; he is always in some sense the origin of thought and of wisdom, and precisely because he claims that he cannot beget anything, that he has no wisdom in him to which he could give birth. And in the self-reflexive writing of the *Essais*, the feminizing of Montaigne's own body and mind enable him to write about himself and to aspire to be wise, as if the feminine body and feminine knowledge were the enabling conditions of writing itself. The mind must become the womb and, pregnant with its own thought, deliver itself of what it knows; acting as its own midwife to open its "nature," the mind then opens its mouth and says that it does not know. Speaking of that same Socrates who is worthy of the name of "sage" because he knows that he does not know, Montaigne invites he who knows himself in this way to boldly make himself known "par sa bouche" (II, 8, 380c).

A knowledge that proclaims paradoxically that it does not know issues from the open mouth, as if from the birth canal. A knowledge that proceeds from the model of Socrates's midwife, from the oxymoronic foolishness of "male midwifery," proclaims its own folly. Here among images of conception and birth, of delivery and midwives, of the mind as the feminine body, the figure of the mouth, talking endlessly, talking in and of its ignorance and its foolishness, also announces itself dramatically as woman. It is an old commonplace, the image of the garrulous woman, excessively talkative because she is woman: verbosity as physiology, lodged in and as a woman's body. When the feminine figures the opening of Montaigne's writing in "De l'oisiveté" it figures as well the excessiveness and lack of restraint that will mark that writing itself as feminine. The earth in that essay lies fallow, but it teems with weeds; the woman on her own also engenders excess; and the mind, prey to unbridled imagination, gives birth to countless chimeras and fantastic monsters. When Montaigne recuperates excessiveness and appropriates uselessness, when he forgoes traditional notions of order, moderation, and control in favor of a production that knows no apparent measure, that is apparently boundless, we might say that he performs and valorizes a certain conventional form of the feminine, brings it in from the margins to which it had been shunted and where it was scorned and oppressed.

Perhaps the term *dilation,* whose semantic richness Patricia Parker found to be pervasive in the Renaissance as an informing principle in hermeneutics, in rhetoric, and in obstetrical, judicial, and amatory writing as well, can be used to express the varied and dynamic production we are describing and the aesthetic that informs it.[20] Associated with expansion, opening, abundance, excess, increase, deferral, the multivalent dilation was frequently linked to figures of the feminine and the feminine body. In my discussion we have met dilation in the swelling of the childbearing body and in the figure of the mind pregnant with thought; we have seen it in the openings, in the cervix, the mouth, and the parodic anus, that dilate and open up, that enlarge to permit passage; and, finally, we have encountered it in excessive birth and in the expansion produced by what issues forth, the increased number of children, weeds, and words. Montaigne's image of himself writing "sans cesse" is a figure of dilation, his digressive style and his apparent unwillingness or inability to conclude is a form it takes, his seemingly endless additions to the ever-expanding body of his text is another. In this manner of writing and rewriting, we might see dilation as his effort to compose according to the Renaissance criterion of *copia* and to realize an aesthetics of inventive richness and verbal abundance. And it is also true that as he dilates he risks falling victim to its excess and to copia's potential for empty rhetoric.

Erasmus draws attention to the danger of prolixity in the opening line of the *De copia verborum* where his enthusiasm for the magnificence of speech when it "surges along like a golden river, with thoughts and words pouring out in rich abundance" is tempered by his awareness that this "godlike power of speech [might] fall into mere glibness, which is both silly and offensive."[21] Here too, in the silly glibness of discourse, we might see a not particularly well-disguised reference to the feminine and to its tendency to be garrulous. In traditional terms, when the excesses of copia are not regulated or mastered, discourse runs the risk of resembling a woman. In the dialogue of Erasmus's *Ciceronianus,* when Bulephorus cites criticism of Cicero, he recalls judgments accusing him of a smoothness that was considered feeble and effeminate, a style that lacked virility and was not manly. Speaking to the inept and slavish Ciceronian Nosoponus, Bulephorus says at one point, "Surely you don't think that something that was considered rather unmasculine in Cicero could be thought right and proper for Christians, . . . whose behaviour should be totally dissociated from anything that borders on artificiality and theatrical pleasure?"[22] When Montaigne examines his own writing in "Consideration sur Ciceron" (I, 40, 251) he highlights the substantial or "thick" ("drue") nature of his material, a certain restrained yet potentially expansive development, and the necessary rather than ornamental function of his stories and quotations. With this emphasis on substance rather than decoration, and on measure and control as opposed to a facile and superficial expansiveness that he treats ironically as "la vertu parliere," the essayist exploits a critical language that endows his writing with virtues that have a decidedly masculine ring. The quotation from Seneca with which he ends his passage makes this explicit: "Elegance of style is not a manly ornament" ("Non est ornamentum virile concinnitas").

It would appear, then, that there are two modes of discourse, two styles of writing squarely in opposition: a controlled, concise, and substantial discourse that is associated with the masculine and an abundant, sweeping discourse, given to excess and to superficiality, that is named feminine. But both writing theory and practice reveal that the opposition is not absolute, that its terms are not mutually exclusive but rather two sides of the same coin, two tendencies of any discourse, and of discourse itself. Erasmus recognized that what he called the compressed style and the contrasting abundant style depend on the same basic principles (*De copia*, I, 5). In Plato's dialogue, he says, Socrates "accurately deduces that the same man is capable of either lying convincingly or of telling the truth; in the same way the craftsman in words who will be best at narrowing down his speech and compressing it will be the one who is skilled in expanding and enriching it with ornament of every kind." And Erasmus saw as well that overabundance is an irrepressible inclination within abundance itself and not some "otherness" that could be absolutely repressed or eliminated. Quintilian, he explains, censured Stesichorus for overabundant and extravagant expression, but at the same time he had to admit that it was a fault that could not be totally avoided (I, 4). Stesichorus commits a compositional and stylistic error, and even an

error in judgment, but this error also enacts the natural and ineluct-
able errance of language, its wandering off in excess and in emptiness. Terence Cave's seminal reading of Erasmus in the *Cornucopian
Text* uncovers the essential and inextricable duality, and duplicity, of
copia.[23]

Montaigne's text uncovers it as well and confers gender upon it.
The discourse of the *Essais* is always multiple, diverse, masculine and
feminine, voices juxtaposed and speaking simultaneously, voices
speaking separately as well as within each other, recalling the harmony of the androgyne but also its confused and monstrous hermaphroditic double. These Renaissance paradigms provide us with
pertinent examples of the dynamic coincidence of the ideal and its
"other," the monstrous that it harbors within its own nature. The
androgyne, the figure of ordered difference, is systematically confused with the hermaphrodite in the sixteenth century, and in this
conflation it reveals its other side, a side of incongruous forms and
blurred distinctions, abhorred as grotesque and unnatural by contemporary culture and placed by conventional medical wisdom in
the category of monster. Plato's androgyne, which could be divided
into two discrete halves and, with a bit of rearranging, be united
again as one, shows itself in the looking glass also to be Ovid's Hermaphroditus, the creature who distorts the clarity of sexuality and
gender and obscures identity itself. As Hermaphroditus metamorphoses into him/herself, the poet says, "two bodies knit in close
embrace: they were no longer two, nor such as to be called one,
woman, and one, man. They seemed neither and yet both" (IV.377–
79).

Montaigne's language provides a striking example of this concur-
rent and conflated gendering.[24] Abandoning Latin, which he considers his mother tongue ("qui m'a esté donné pour maternel") although it is not the language of his mother (or of his mother country),
Montaigne adopts his father's native tongue and that of the father-
land, French, which he calls "gratieus, delicat et abondant," clearly
marking it as feminine (II, 17, 639c). Of course, he does not entirely
abandon Latin. This is, after all, the language of his intellectual fathers and of the tradition that nourishes the *Essais*, a language that
speaks eloquently not only in abundant quotation and innumerable
paraphrase but in Montaigne's rhetoric as well, even though he
claims no longer to be able to speak it or to write it well. And then
there is Gascon, his regional dialect, which he characterizes as "beau,

sec, bref, signifiant," qualities that make it a masculine language, "[a] à la verité un langage masle et militaire, . . . [c] puissant et pertinant" (639) ("indeed a more manly and military language, powerful and pertinent" [484]). Montaigne describes Gascon in these terms to set French off as feminine, but he also speaks his regional dialect in the *Essais*, as he imagines his critics reminding him: "Quand on m'a dit ou que moy-mesme me suis dit: . . . Voilà un mot du creu de Gascoingne" (III, 5, 875b) ("When I have been told, or have told myself: . . . 'Here is a word of Gascon vintage'" [667]). Although he refused to excise what he considered a fault of habit rather than an inadvertent error ("This is the way I speak everywhere," he insists), after his death Marie de Gournay and his friend Pierre de Brach would edit his Gasconisms out of his text and in the process edit out of his language some measure of its "masculinity."

Montaigne's use of French would appear to reflect his claim to prefer a humble and everyday style appropriate to the modest, even lowly, subject of his essays, himself, a Ciceronian style often called *mollis*, soft, which is the sign of the feminine in the *Essais*.[25] But the poetic discourse he admires in "Sur des vers de Virgile" (III, 5), and to which he also aspires, is a language "de chair et d'os," of flesh and bone, a substantial masculine language. The language of the great poets, Montaigne says, "est tout plein et gros d'une vigueur naturelle et constante" (873b), copious, naturally vigorous, but also unmistakably full and forceful like the erect phallus. This is *not*, the essayist makes a point of saying, a "soft" eloquence (*molle*), feminine, or effeminate and limp. And, not surprisingly, this "phallic" language "remplit et ravit, et ravit le plus les plus forts esprits," seizes the reader, carries *her* off, penetrates and fills *her* with ecstasy in the fulfillment of its manliness. This is, of course, the male writer's fantasy as the expression of his sexual desire, his language acting as surrogate to perpetrate the forceful possession and subjugation of the reader as female, to make her submit to the will and the intention of the text. Montaigne quotes Seneca to speak of the writing of the admired poets: "[c] Contextus totus virilis est; non sunt circa flosculos occupati" ("Their whole contexture is manly; they are not concerned with pretty little flowers" [*Letters*, 33]). This text, like its cognate *contextus*, is manly, virile, not occupied with little flowers because it is occupied with deflowering.

I want to come back at this point to the question of seduction that I raised earlier, of Montaigne's seduction of the women in "Sur des vers de Virgile" and of the seductive intent of literature. Montaigne penetrates into the women's boudoir in what looks like the opening of a scene of seduction and that could be read as an allegory of his desire to seduce his reader. The offer of the book, and of reading, Starobinski reminds us, is a symbolic seductive act; it creates the relationship (*commerce*) that comes closest to that of the love relationship.[26] But speaking to the women of "action genitale," of intimate things in the privacy that facilitates the "faveur" of acquiescence and provides its "saveur," the essayist discloses that he is not quite up to it, that in Horace's borrowed words he is "even for one encounter, limp" (III, 5, 886). Advancing age and approaching death appear to have rendered seduction improbable, just as they have transformed its very suggestion into an act of harmless, even charming, flirtation. And yet the essayist's physical impotence does not preclude the potency of his text, indeed, it may even be the condition that produces its virility, as if the weaker and emptier Montaigne gets the stronger and stouter his writing becomes. It might be that the impotent figure Montaigne strikes is just that, a figure, a flirtatious trope in the essayist's rhetoric of seduction and an element of its power.[27]

We thus encounter in Montaigne's text the paradox of an improbable seduction, a seduction that both denies and performs itself, that announces and masks its desire, and that reveals and conceals its (rhetorical) strategies. It is a seduction that also dreams of being more than itself, a seduction that fantasizes not only about leading or misleading the reader (*seducere*, to lead away) to itself but of moving vigorously toward the reader, ravishing her (*rapere*, to seize) with the violence of rape. In the expression of this fantasy of forceful possession Montaigne's text reveals its profound masculinity. Perhaps in this light the essayist's ubiquitous admiration for military virtues and his love of a "soldierly" discourse ("le parler que j'ayme . . . plustost soldatesque" [I, 16, 172a]) are not innocent or neutral textual elements but reflections of this masculine desire for conquest. And yet, the operation of strong elements that connote a "manly" posture or discourse, elements that Montaigne qualifies as "vehement," "brusque," "difficile" (172) and that are not only military but judicial and aesthetic as well, cannot obscure the real presence of the feminine in the *Essais*. We cannot say that Montaigne's text is masculine in any exclusive way or that it seeks exclusively to act upon a feminine reader, because the opposite also appears to be true.

The complex gender coding of the *Essais* marks them as *both* masculine and feminine but not according to any simple binary structure. The feminine presence is itself double, manifest in the textual dilation (in all of its variations) that Montaigne seeks to associate with his writing and to embody in it, but that presence also appears in the very textual qualities from which Montaigne seeks to dissociate himself, from affectation, from artifice, from rhetoric, and that are also in his writing. The rhetorical trope can serve as the emblem of this feminine doubleness, of an expansiveness, an instability, a diversity that Montaigne would embrace and a shiftiness, a deceitfulness, a superficiality that he would reject. But shiftiness and deceit, artifice and the art of rhetoric itself, are the very elements of seduction, and thus the precise instruments of seduction that the essayist employs are the same affectation, artifice, and rhetoric he scorns. If the *Essais* sometimes appear as a generous masculine text offering to male readers a "token" of friendship, it also expresses itself as a forceful, aggressive masculine text bound on ravishing its female reader. And our own reading suggests that it may well also be a seductive feminine text seeking to affect a male reader, a text that displays itself, and seeks to make itself known, and desired, as an object of affection.[28]

.   .   .   .

We saw Montaigne intimate that women have been seduced by the learned men who have gained access to their boudoir ("cabinet"), that they have been beguiled and enticed by what is always only the display of knowledge (the "parade de . . . magistere"). The essayist seeks to dissuade them from study in "De trois commerces" (III, 3) or, perhaps more accurately, in his turn to seduce them away from it by praising their beauty. Even when the women apply themselves, he suggests, their knowledge remains superficial (like the learned men and their "parade") because they are incapable of appropriating it, making it their own: "la doctrine," he says, "qui ne leur a peu arriver en l'ame, leur est demeurée en la langue" (822b). Montaigne urges them to exploit what is already their own and to show off their beauty.

Reflecting the traditional cultural opposition of female body / male mind, learning here remains on the surface of the female body, on the surface that *is* the female body, Montaigne appears to say, in the (wagging) tongue and in its empty speech, rather than attaining the deeper intellectual or spiritual reaches within, as it does, allegedly, in the male mind or soul. We might be concerned that in this serious (masculine) statement that represents the tongue as a synecdoche for the feminine body and for the excess and emptiness of garrulous woman, Montaigne himself "shows off" (like a woman?), he plays on the homophony of "l'ame" and "langue" and puns in a facile and entirely conventional way on the two meanings of "langue," speech and tongue. In this talk of glib and wordy talk, the essayist appears himself to speak with a marked facility, but we have encountered this rhetorical antirhetoric before. In another rhetorical flourish that also paradoxically condemned the play of language, the essayist had used the Athenians and the Lacedaemonians to set "une continuelle exercitation de la langue" against "une continuelle exercitation de l'ame" (I, 25, 143a) and to valorize magistrates over rhetoricians, doing over saying, and things over words. In the gender-coded semantic and structural network in the *Essais*, Athens and its rhetoric are feminized and opposed to the masculine and soldierly Sparta, the place where children could be sent not to learn the effeminate linguistic arts (rhetoric and dialectic) but "la science d'obéir et de commander." Here in "De trois commerces," in a move replete with misogynist overtones but not unequivocal in its own expression, Montaigne proposes that instead of covering themselves with the beauty of a knowledge that remains always borrowed, and alien to them, women concern themselves with what is indeed already their own, their body, and that they content themselves with displaying ("faire valoir") those riches that are natural to them, that is, their own beauty.

Montaigne thus elaborates the pervasive rhetoric of inside and outside, extending the opposition between "l'ame" and "langue": learning for women is artificial, it is appearance ("mine") instead of what is real ("substance"), a form of concealment that is also makeup ("fard"). There is nothing benign about this artifice, this surface that is superfluity itself; it is dangerous, and even deadly, an outside that buries and entombs women within and under it ("elles sont enterrées et ensevelies soubs l'art" [822b]). Within themselves women have all they need to have, the argument goes, and there they also know all they need to know.

This, of course, is the general lesson Montaigne draws in "De la phisionomie" when the model of Socrates allows him to state that man does not need learning to live "à l'aise" because it is already in him: all knowledge that is beyond what is natural, he claims, is vain and superfluous. Yet this central structuring opposition in the *Essais* between outside and inside—and the dual admonition to turn away from what is borrowed, or artificial, or superficial, and to turn back toward what is substantial and one's own—is complicated by the fact that in this case of the women the outside *is* the inside. What is properly women's own, what Montaigne calls "leurs propres et naturelles richesses," is their body in all its exteriority—that is, the body itself in its external, physical beauty, on display ("faire valoir") outside in that most outside of worlds, the social world governed by seeing and being seen, that is the scene of seduction. In this paradoxical reversal that turns outside in, or inside out, the nature of woman is realized in public when she shows herself off, confirming and valorizing herself as the object of the masculine gaze and of masculine desire.

What do women need, the essayist asks rhetorically, except to live beloved and honored? And for this, he adds, they possess and know only too much. But what is it that women know and that allows them to realize their nature, what is it that they know but do not know that they know and that Montaigne has to tell them because they do not know themselves well enough ("C'est qu'elles ne se cognoissent point assez")? What is it that he says only has to be awakened and rekindled in them and that he (here) brings to light as if he had already looked within (them? himself?) and knew?

> Baste qu'elles peuvent, sans nous, renger la grace de leurs yeux à la gaieté, à la severité et à la douceur, assaisonner un nenny de rudesse, de doubte et de faveur, et qu'elles ne cherchent point d'interprete aux discours qu'on faict pour leur service. Avec cette science, elles commandent à baguette et regentent les regens et l'eschole. (823b)

> Enough that without our help they can adjust the charm of their eyes to gaiety, severity, or sweetness, season a 'no' with harshness, uncertainty, or encouragement, and that they need no interpreter for the speeches we make in courting them. With this knowledge they hold the whip hand and master the schoolmaster and the school. (624)

Women do not need rhetoric and other learned disciplines, including law and logic, "drogueries si vaines et inutiles à leur besoing," because they already possess a "science," but that innate "science" is already also a rhetoric, a "science" that is also paradoxically an art,

but an art that is not (just) an art. This is a rhetoric of the eyes and of
the voice, a bodily rhetoric that is an art of seduction and of persuasion, a powerful rhetoric that empowers woman and allows her to
hold the whip hand, as Montaigne says, and to master the school-
master and the school. It is a sign of the complexity of gender coding
(and of its contingency) that Montaigne must speak of that which is
most feminine in terms that are traditionally coded as masculine, that
apparently in spite of himself he must use terms of knowledge ("science"), of commanding ("commander"), and of ruling ("regenter"),
as if masculine and feminine were not mutually exclusive and the
coding itself open rather than absolute. But Montaigne's argument
also sustains the logic of the code when it concedes poetry to women,
if they want to compete on masculine turf, because of all the bookish
arts (from which women have been excluded), poetry most resembles their conventional image and is arguably the most rhetorical.
"C'est un art," Montaigne says, "follastre et subtil, desguisé, parlier,
tout en plaisir, tout en montre, commes elles" (823b) ("It is a wanton
and subtle art, in fancy dress [in disguise], wordy, all pleasure, all
show, like themselves" [624]).

   While we might again emphasize that a traditional patriarchal
view dictates Montaigne's distinction between female body and
male mind and provides him the banal image of seductive woman,
and that it furnishes as well the association between woman and
rhetoric and between woman and poetry (and all literature), much
more is at stake here than the essayist's reiteration of a conventional
misogynist line.[29] To whatever degree Montaigne's comments in "De
trois commerces" represent a depreciation of women, they are also,
and perhaps most profoundly, an anamorphic image of himself and
his writing, an image of himself within that of woman that requires
only that we change perspective to see Montaigne in it. Isn't he, like
woman and like poetry, "parlier" and "tout en montre"? In his own
shift in perspective immediately following his comments about these
others in "De trois commerces" he begins again to speak about himself: "Ma forme essentielle est propre à la communication et à la
production: je suis tout au dehors et en evidence, nay à la societé et à
l'amitié" (823b) ("My essential pattern is suited to communication
and revelation. I am all in the open and in full view, born for company and friendship" [625]). The essayist who vigorously eschews
essences reveals that his own essence is that of revelation itself. Here

we find confirmed the figure of Montaigne as monster, the monster whose nature or essence it is to show himself, to be "tout en montre." The writer who forcefully condemns outsides and surfaces shows himself as a man of the outside, and shows up on the outside, "en evidence." Claiming "production" as his own, Montaigne lays claim to the book he has produced to show himself off and announces that he has produced himself as its subject, both fashioned himself and shown himself (the sixteenth-century judicial sense of *production*). Isn't this assertion that his nature is to be "tout au dehors et en evidence" what we now can call the feminine in him, the condition of his monstrousness and of his confession, and of the realization of his project?

We have already identified multiple examples of Montaigne's intention, his desire, and his need to be shown, and known, from his initial statement in the "Au lecteur" that he would have preferred to portray himself "tout nud," to the indelible "Je suis affamé de me faire connoistre," and to the countless references to confession, profession, bearing witness. And to confess, to profess, and to bear witness to himself is to make himself the center of his discourse, to talk incessantly about himself, insistently to exercise his "langue" so that he can also, and especially, exercise his "ame." This is the only way he can show himself, it is the only way he can come to know himself, but it is also the way that produces a presumptuous and immoderate discourse. In the passage at the end of "Sur des vers de Virgile" that was discussed earlier, where Montaigne characterizes his text as a flow of (feminine) babble, he states that male and female are cast in the same mold. Garrulous woman; the art of poetry "parlier"; the talkative essayist who could go on until he runs out of paper and ink: paraphrasing Montaigne, we can now say that the difference among them is not great. The difference, as we have said, is within; it is not an external opposition of separate entities.

Let me take this resemblance a bit further. In the *Essais*, woman is figured synecdochically by her cosmetics (*fard*) and by bodily adornments like jewelry and clothing (*parure*), elements that are related to the semantic cluster art, artifice, surface, outside, rhetoric. And while the great poets are capable of writing in a full and vigorous masculine language, poetry also participates in this feminine configuration, as when it is described as an art particularly suited to women, not only "parlier" but "desguisé," decked out, or made up (III, 3,

823). Montaigne, too. He suggests as much in the "Au lecteur" when he wraps himself in decorum to explain that he cannot show himself "tout nud" and in "De l'exercitation" when he openly confesses that he dresses himself up to go out in public, that he adorns himself because he constantly describes himself (II, 6, 378c). This is not a choice but an obligation and a necessity, what might be called the law of transformation that is in force when one goes out, out from the inside, from the apparently privileged place of the self, into the social space. And although Montaigne inveighs consistently against all that transforms and deforms the inside, the natural, and against all that dissimulates or that conceals from the outside, in this case he cannot avoid the transformation, nor does he seek to. The essayist may lose something of himself as he dresses himself up, adorns himself, like a woman, as a woman, but it is precisely because he loses himself in this way, because he goes out the way a woman does (or is), "paré(e)," that he also finds himself and finds the feminine in himself. In order to be himself and to be within himself, in order to know himself within, Montaigne must go out in public through his writing, he must show himself in his text, as woman, inside out.

This paradoxical figure of Montaigne helps to explicate a particularly enigmatic reference in the *Essais*, the statement that occurs in the context of Montaigne's advice to women to reject book learning and display their own natural riches where he insists that women's role is to honor the arts (or to do them honor) and to make up makeup ("C'est à elles d'honnorer les arts et de farder le fard" [822b]; "It is for them to do honor to the arts and to decorate decoration" [624]). In a general sense we understand that this line reinforces woman's association with the various faces of the outside, and especially the face that is made up or artificial. It appears to affirm as well that her proper place is on the outside and in its service. But Montaigne's phrase, "farder le fard," is a curious formulation that appears to pile artifice upon artifice. And it is a striking paradox that natural beauty would serve the arts and artifice, that it would embellish what is already embellishment, as if the natural itself could be a cosmetic ("fard") for what is already cosmetic and also remain itself, as if an inside could also be an outside and be the outside of what was already itself outside. How can we keep track of this bewildering series of reversals? Aren't things turned inside out once again, just as they are when Montaigne proudly states that he is *naturally* of the outside, and when we saw how the inside of woman was properly the outside? Doesn't this turning inside out once again confound the absolute distinctions between what is natural and what is artificial, what is inside and what is outside? And what is masculine and what is feminine? Neither Montaigne nor his text can be situated confidently at one pole or the other because he and the traditional binaries that he negotiates are both double and diverse, as he says both of understanding and of things in the doubled rhetoric at the end of "Des boyteux," the essay where he confesses his own monstrousness: "Il n'est rien si souple et erratique que nostre entendement: c'est le soulier de Theramenez, bon à tous pieds. Et il est double et divers, et les matieres doubles et diverses" (III, 11, 1,034b) ("There is nothing as supple and as erratic as our understanding; it is Theramene's shoe, good for either foot; it is double and diverse, and matters are double and diverse" [792]).

I want to elaborate on the reference to Theramene's shoe by way of a conclusion to this discussion, which I entitled "Fathering the Text: The Woman in Man" because the figure of doubleness has dominated the discussion of gender and sexuality just as it has been a dominant figure throughout my discussion of textual progeny and of monstrous offspring. As a shoe that is neither left- nor right-footed, the versatile buskin served in literature and in proverbial speech as a metonymy for an unreliable and inconstant man, as Erasmus notes, one like Theramene the Athenian rhetorician who sat as it were on two stools, now on one and now on the other, or rather on both, trying to please two opposing parties (*Adages*, I, i, 94). But Erasmus recognized that the expression "cothurno versatilior" was also itself a buskin since it could be used either in this disparaging sense or in a good sense. "One might call a man a *cothurnus* because he had easy ways, a certain mobility of intellect, and a capacity for getting on with all kinds of people," Erasmus adds in a display of his own rhetorical versatility and intellectual agility. Because it is a form without a specific content, the buskin can be simultaneously both this *or* that and this *and* that. In the separation of form and content that it performs, in the absence of a fixed identity or essential meaning, Erasmus extends the buskin as a protean figure, like the Ulysses he evokes, "play(ing) any part to perfection."

In this display of words and figures changing sides, turning, as it were, inside out, Erasmus includes Suidas's comment that the buskin was of a kind that both men and women could wear. In itself the reference multiplies the idea of versatility—just as the shoe fits either the right or the left foot so it fits either a masculine or a feminine foot—but it can also serve as a suggestive reminder that the concepts of masculine and feminine themselves can fit either "foot," or sit, to use Erasmus's figure, on one stool and then the other, and on both as well. Masculine and feminine in the *Essais* are also cothurni, versatile, double, like the buskin and like the concepts of right and left themselves, whose meaning, we might say, is contextual, differential, relational rather than referential. The writer is by turns father, mother, masculine, feminine, androgynous, or hermaphroditic; single, unified, conflicted and confused, no one and some one, monstrous. Textuality is also masculine and / or feminine, spare and dilated, rhetorical and antirhetorical, vigorous and soft, misogynist and generous, a writing whose effort to impose itself acts like a traditional male posture and whose desire to seduce might easily be taken for traditionally female, a writing that does not seek to overcome or remedy its doubleness, its monstrousness, but to show it and to celebrate it.[30] And what of the gender of the reader, since it too, changes shape like the "cothurno versitilior"? The reader is an androgynous friend, the surrogate for La Boétie in the person of Marie de Gournay; the reader is both the object of seduction, a woman reader in the boudoir desired by the figure of a masculine writer and a masculine reader led on by a rhetoric figured as feminine; and, finally, the reader is a female to be ravished by a vigorous written discourse, a male to be overcome by the imposing textual will, and an obtrusive reader who could be either male or female, sitting on one stool or the other. When Montaigne couples father and mother, male and female, to characterize the generation of the child of the mind he provides the double and diverse emblem for literary conception, for the unruly textual brood it engenders, and for the monstrous writer and reader who give it life.

Notes

INTRODUCTION

1. E. R. Curtius sketches the outlines of an early history of the metaphor of the book as child in *European Literature and the Latin Middle Ages,* trans. W. Trask (New York, 1953), 132–34. He indicates the trope's infrequent appearances in antiquity (in Plato, Catullus, Ovid, Petronius, and Synesius), the intermediary role Ovid played for the Latin Middle Ages, and the popularity of the metaphor in the Renaissance and Baroque periods (with quotations from Ronsard, d'Aubigné, Shakespeare, Bacon, Cervantes, Donne, and Stigliani). He ends with references to Lessing, Schlegel, Manzoni, and Ranke.

2. References to Montaigne's *Essais* are to *Les Essais de Michel de Montaigne,* eds. Pierre Villey and V. L. Saulnier (Paris, 1965). Full citations are by book, essay, and page; in a string of citations to the same essay, those following the first full citation are shortened to page number only. The letters *a, b,* and *c* are the customary symbols used to refer to the editions of 1580 (a), 1588 (b), and 1595 (c). English translations are from *The Complete Essays of Montaigne,* trans. D. Frame (Stanford, Calif., 1958).

3. One child in Montaigne's writing to whom I pay less attention is Michel himself, as the son of Pierre Eyquem. Antoine Compagnon has analyzed this dimension of Montaigne's family story, how the literal relation to the father leads necessarily to the generation of the figurative offspring, writing, in *Nous, Michel de Montaigne* (Paris, 1980). See esp. pp. 170–230. I will deal only in passing with Montaigne's relation to his father, but I will directly address the role of Montaigne's "daughters" in considerable detail in this study.

4. See J. Derrida's seminal discussion of the invention of writing in the *Phaedrus* as a family affair in "La pharmacie de Platon," *La dissémination* (Paris, 1972), 71–197. In *Distinguo: Reading Montaigne Differently* (Oxford, 1992), Steven Rendall speaks of Montaigne's use of the metaphor of the book as child and recalls Socrates's story in the *Phaedrus* to introduce his discussion of reading and interpretation in the *Essais* (pp. 73–78).

5. Geoffrey Harpham, *On the Grotesque: Strategies of Contradiction in Art and Literature* (Princeton, 1982), 178–179. Harpham makes a strong case for reading the grotesque, or what I am calling the monstrous, as not only "outside" of art but "within" it, as exemplary of contradictions central to art itself.

6. Critics have begun to address questions of gender in the *Essais.* See esp. R. Cottrell, "Gender Imprinting in Montaigne's *Essais, L'esprit créateur"* 30, no. 4 (Winter 1990): 85–96; L. Kritzman, "Montaigne's Family Romance," in

The Rhetoric of Sexuality and the Literature of the French Renaissance (Cambridge, 1991), 73–92, and "Montaigne's Fantastic Monsters and the Construction of Gender," in *Writing the Renaissance: Essays in Sixteenth-Century French Literature in Honor of Floyd Gray*, ed. Raymond La Charité (Lexington, Ky., 1992), 183–196; C. Bauschatz, " 'Leur plus universelle qualité, c'est la diversité': Women as Ideal Readers in Montaigne's *Essais*," *Journal of Medieval and Renaissance Studies* 19 (1989): 83–101.

CHAPTER 1

1. The concept of "oratio speculum animi" has significant status in the sixteenth century, and this has perhaps encouraged the reading of the *Essais* as the mind's own discourse. Sainte-Beuve was an early exponent of the coincidence of mind and expression in Montaigne: "pensée, image, chez lui, c'est tout un" (*Port Royal*, eds. René-Louis Doyon and Charles Marchesne [Paris, 1926–32], 3:54). Thibaudet followed this lead: "Non un style construit, mais un style qui coule, qui se meut—un esprit en marche" (*Montaigne*, ed. F. Gray [Paris, 1963], 493), and Floyd Gray makes a similar case in his *Le style de Montaigne* (Paris, 1958): "il faut y voir [in Montaigne's style] une création qui exprime l'être de Montaigne dans tout ce qu'il a d'organique" (13). More recently, although with a different tack, Gérard Defaux's emphasis on Montaigne's text as the image of his soul makes the idea of style transcend the status of literary construct or mere mimesis: "Montaigne est celui qui écrit comme il parle; celui aussi qui, quand il écrit, pratique ce qu'on pourrait appeler une 'écriture de l'âme' " (*Marot, Rabelais, Montaigne: L'écriture comme présence* [Paris, 1987], 206). In *The Cornucopian Text: Problems of Writing in the French Renaissance* (Oxford, 1979), Terence Cave demonstrates that confidence in the coincidence of mind and expression in the French Renaissance was also challenged by writers such as Montaigne.

2. See especially Jean-Yves Pouilloux, *Lire les "essais" de Montaigne* (Paris, 1969); Richard L. Regosin, *The Matter of My Book: Montaigne's Essais as the Book of the Self* (Berkeley, 1977); Terence Cave, *The Cornucopian Text: Problems of Writing in the French Renaissance*; Michel Beaujour, *Miroirs d'encre* (Paris, 1980); Lawrence Kritzman, *Destruction/Découverte. Le fonctionnement de la rhétorique dans les Essais de Montaigne* (Lexington, Ky., 1980); Robert Cottrell, *Sexuality/Textuality: A Study of the Fabric of Montaigne's Essais* (Columbus, 1981); Gisèle Mathieu-Castellani, *Montaigne. L'écriture de l'essai* (Paris, 1988); François Rigolot, *Les métamorphoses de Montaigne* (Paris, 1988); and Steven Rendall, *Distinguo: Reading Montaigne Differently*.

3. A great deal has been written, of course, on "De l'institution des enfans," but these studies tend to overlook the child as such to draw out Montaigne's ideas on pedagogy. An important exception in dealing with the child in the *Essais* is Antoine Compagnon's *Nous, Michel de Montaigne*, in which the central concern is the essayist's successful production of the textual "child." Compagnon sees the generation of the *Essais* as the response to Montaigne's unfulfilled role as both literal father and son and the means by which he

overcomes the ontological impasse created both by his Pyrrhonism and his nominalism. While I share with Compagnon the seriousness with which he takes both the literal and figurative child and the care he gives to the analysis of their relationship, my own interests differ in their focus on general problems of authorship, textuality, and reading and on issues of monstrosity and sexuality that the subject of children in the *Essais* allows me to raise. See also L. Kritzman, "Pedagogical Graffiti and the Rhetoric of Conceit," *Journal of Medieval and Renaissance Studies* 15 (1985): 69–83; Rendall, *Distinguo: Reading Montaigne Differently,* chap. 5; and Gisèle Mathieu-Castellani, *Montaigne: L'écriture de l'essai,* 221–40.

4. Roy E. Leake, *Concordance des Essais de Montaigne* (Geneva, 1981), 403–5.

5. Paolo Valesio examines Montaigne's antirhetorical rhetoric in *Novantiqua: Rhetorics as a Contemporary Theory* (Bloomington, Ind., 1980).

6. In his seminal *Ramus, Method, and the Decay of Dialogue* (Cambridge, 1958), 283–84, Walter J. Ong notes that the Puritans, who bring out the full implications of Ramus's notion of the plain style, speak of the ideal style in terms of light whose medium of transmission "seems to act as though it were not there."

7. In *The Matter of My Book* I explore in some detail the rhetorical and thematic implications of "dire," "écrire," and "faire." See esp. chaps. 6 and 9. Paolo Valesio draws attention to this passage from "Du pédantisme" as an example of rhetoric used against itself in *Novantiqua,* 43.

8. In *Montaigne: L'écriture de l'essai,* Gisèle Mathieu-Castellani explores the rhetorical and epistemological implications of Montaigne's discourse about the body and of what she calls the body's own discourse, the role it plays in the apprehension and appropriation of reality, and in the activity of writing itself. See especially 135–253, entitled "Ecrire le corps."

9. For my observations on the complex and indistinct notions of child and childhood I am indebted to Philippe Ariès, *L'enfant et la vie familiale sous l'ancien régime* (Paris, 1973), esp. his first chapter entitled "Les âges de la vie," 29–52, and to Georges Matoré, *Le vocabulaire et la société du seizième siècle* (Paris, 1988), 137–39, under the heading "L'enfant."

10. Matoré, *Le vocabulaire et la société du XVI siècle,* 138.

11. See, among others, A. Wilden, "Par divers moyens on arrive à pareille fin: A Reading of Montaigne," *Modern Language Notes* 83 (1968): 577–97; D. Frame, *Montaigne's Essais: A Study* (Englewood Cliffs, N.J., 1969), 10; A. Thibaudet, *Montaigne,* 143ff; M. Butor, *Essais sur les Essais* (Paris, 1964); J. Starobinski, *Montaigne en mouvement* (Paris, 1982), 52–86; F. Rigolot, *Les métamorphoses de Montaigne* (Paris, 1988), 61–95; and my *The Matter of My Book,* 7–29.

12. Benveniste analyzes the difference between verbs of active and middle voice in "Actif et moyen dans le verbe," *Problèmes de linguistique générale* (Paris, 1966), 1:168–75. See Roland Barthes, "To Write: An Intransitive Verb?" in *The Structuralist Controversy: The Languages of Criticism and the Sciences of Man,* eds. R. Macksey and E. Donato (Baltimore, 1970), 134–56.

13. There are two other direct addresses to women in the *Essais:* to Mme.

de Grammont in the twenty-ninth essay of Book I, in which Montaigne offers "Vingt et neuf sonnets d'Estienne de la Boetie"; and, in the "Apologie de Raimond de Sebond," to an unidentified "vous" who is thought to be Marguerite de France, the future wife of Henri de Navarre. In both cases Montaigne speaks to the women of his writing.

14. My view that the women Montaigne addresses are marginalized, either written out of his text or subsumed by the essayist, differs from that of Cathleen Bauschatz in " 'Leur plus universelle qualité, c'est la diversité.'" She argues that Montaigne's women readers are prominent in their own right as his exemplary audience and that the essayist associates with them and with a feminine perspective on a variety of issues. As I suggest here, and as I will seek to demonstrate in detail in chapter 6, Montaigne does in fact recuperate the feminine for himself, and most strikingly as an element of textual engendering.

15. M. Foucault, "Language to Infinity," in *Language, Counter-memory, Practice: Selected Essays and Interviews*, ed. D. F. Bouchard; trans. by D. F. Bouchard and S. Simon (Ithaca, 1977), 54.

16. Natalie Zemon Davis has examined these issues in Montaigne as she considers the differences between the ways historians and literary critics have traditionally read. See her "A Renaissance Text to the Historian's Eye: The Gifts of Montaigne," *Journal of Medieval and Renaissance Studies* 15, no. 1 (Spring 1985): 47–56.

17. In *Nous, Michel de Montaigne*, Compagnon argues that paternity is a universal law in the *Essais*, the source of life and continuity for the father, and that the seed is its agent. He also explores in suggestive detail the relationship between Montaigne's failure to produce a son and his effort to produce a text, between the way he both betrays and remains faithful to his father as he becomes an author. See esp. his concluding chapters entitled "Tel père, tel fils: Une ontologie de la semence" (170–93) and "Le livre et l'enfant, le nom d'auteur" (194–230).

18. The model for the analysis of metaphoric contamination is Derrida's discussion of the two kinds of writing in "La pharmacie de Platon," esp. 164–80.

19. In the "avant-propos" to his *La nature et les prodiges: L'insolite au seizième siècle en France* (Geneva, 1977), viii, Jean Céard defines the many faces of the unwonted and the unusual and in the process defines the monstrous in terms of familial resemblance: "un monstre, en ce que sa configuration n'est pas conforme à celle de ses parents, est insolite."

CHAPTER 2

1. On Montaigne and La Boétie see, among others, Wilden, "Par divers moyens on arrive à pareille fin"; Butor, *Essais sur les Essais*; Thibaudet, *Montaigne*, 143ff; Starobinski, *Montaigne en mouvement*, 52–86; Rigolot, *Les métamorphoses de Montaigne*, 61–78; and Regosin, *The Matter of My Book*, 7–29. S.

Rendall (*Distinguo*, 73–94) examines the implications of what he calls "expropriation" for Montaigne, using the model of La Boétie's text, but he does not center Marie de Gournay in the story as I do.

2. Marie de Gournay is beginning to receive the attention she deserves both as a writer in her own right and in her complex relationship to Montaigne. See especially M. H. Ilsley, *A Daughter of the Renaissance: Marie le Jars de Gournay, Her life and Works* (The Hague, 1963); Elyane Dezon-Jones, *Fragments d'un discours féminin* (Paris, 1988) and "Marie de Gournay: le je / u / palimpseste," *L'esprit créateur* 23, no. 2 (Summer 1983): 26–36; Domna Stanton, "Woman as Object and Subject of Exchange: Marie de Gournay's *Le proumenoir (1594)*, *L'esprit créateur* 23, no. 2 (Summer 1983), 9–25, and "Autogynography: The Case of Marie de Gournay's 'Apologie pour celle qui escrit,' " in *Autobiography in French Literature*, French Literature Series 12 (Columbia, S.C., 1985); Tilde A. Sankovitch, *French Women Writers and the Book: Myths of Access and Desire* (Syracuse, 1988), 73–99; and Constance Jordan, *Renaissance Feminism: Literary Texts and Political Models* (Ithaca, 1990), 280–86.

3. Hélène Cixous, "Le rire de la Méduse," *L'arc* 61 (1975): 49.

4. Using the 1595 edition of the *Essais* in the Firestone Library at Princeton University, François Rigolot has republished the "Preface," with introduction, notes, and glossary in *Montaigne Studies* 1 (1989): 7–60. Page references in my text refer to this edition.

5. On the reactions to the *Essais* see Alan Boase, *The Fortunes of Montaigne: A History of the Essays in France, 1580–1669* (London, 1935; rep. New York, 1970).

6. On the 1595 "Preface" see Cathleen M. Bauschatz, "Marie de Gournay's 'Préface de 1595': A Critical Evaluation," *Bulletin de la Société des Amis de Montaigne*, nos. 3–4 (1986): 73–82.

7. Rigolot, "Préface de Marie de Gournay," points out the structural importance of what he calls "un double discours" that both defends Montaigne and legitimates Marie de Gournay. See his "Introduction," 17.

8. I have provided my own translations for the words of Marie de Gournay in this chapter. Her prose is often dense, and her syntax frequently complex, but I have not attempted to simplify in order to give some sense of her style.

9. Letter of May 2, 1596, written at Montaigne's château and quoted in full in Dezon-Jones, *Fragments*, 191.

10. Letter of Nov. 15, 1596, in Dezon-Jones, *Fragments*, 193. The text that follows, and that was sent to Justus Lipsius in manuscript form, prefaces the 1598 edition of the *Essais* (in the Firestone Library at Princeton) and is quoted in full by Rigolot, "Préface de Marie de Gournay," 12.

11. Boase, *The Fortunes of Montaigne*, 52.

12. Marie de Gournay recognizes and refuses this feminine "place" in "Egalité des hommes et des femmes" (1622). Cf. Dezon-Jones, *Fragments*, 113.

13. Marie de Gournay, *Copie de la vie de la Demoiselle de Gournay* (1616) in Dezon-Jones, *Fragments*, 139.

CHAPTER 3

1. On Montaigne's reading practice and his method of quotation see A. Compagnon, *La seconde main ou le travail de la citation* (Paris, 1979), esp. 279–312; Mary B. McKinley, *Words in a Corner: Studies in Montaigne's Latin Quotations* (Lexington, Ky., 1981); Terence Cave, "Problems of Reading in the *Essais*," in *Montaigne: Essays in Memory of Richard Sayce,* eds. I. D. McFarlane and Ian Maclean (Oxford, 1982), 133–66.

2. Terence Cave, "Problems of Reading in the *Essais*," 153. For readings of the "Au lecteur" see also Starobinski, *Montaigne en mouvement,* chap. 1, sec. 7; Fausta Garavini, *Monstres et chimères: Montaigne, le texte, et le fantasme,* trans. Isabel Picon (Paris, 1993), chap. 3; André Tournon, *Montaigne: La glose et l'essai* (Lyon, 1983); Michel Simonin, "Rhetorica ad lectorem: Lecture de l'avertissement des *Essais*," *Montaigne Studies* 1 (1989): 61–72.

3. Several critics have recognized the competing demands of both author (or text) and reader and have argued that they both must be respected. In *On Deconstruction* (Ithaca, 1982), 72–73, J. Culler speaks of the "divided quality of reading" that acknowledges textual completeness at the same time as it treats the text as something to be created in the process of reading. In his concept of the open text, which he elaborates in *The Role of the Reader* (Bloomington, 1984), U. Eco opens writing to numerous personal interventions on the part of the reader, but he maintains that in spite of reading the text remains the world intended by the author (p. 62). I place more stress on the tension between authorial intention and reading and argue that reading may (must?) in fact betray or misrepresent the world intended by the author. See also M. Charles, *Rhétorique de la lecture* (Paris, 1977), who posits the dynamic relationship between a text that both "permits" the reader's entry and constrains reading at the same time, between a reader who acts upon the text and who is acted on by it.

4. M. Foucault, *Les mots et les choses* (Paris, 1966), 50–59; Regosin, *The Matter of My Book,* 68–72; H. Friedrich, *Montaigne,* trans. Robert Rovini (Paris, 1968), 108–11.

5. For Ambrose's silent reading, see *The Confessions of St. Augustine,* book VI, 3.

6. R. Sebond, *La théologie naturelle,* trans. M. de Montaigne, in the *Oeuvres complètes de Michel de Montaigne,* ed. A. Armaingaud (Paris, 1932), 9:xi.

7. François Rabelais, *Oeuvres complètes,* ed. Pierre Jourda (Paris, 1962), vol. 1, p. 8. Translation is from *The Complete Works of François Rabelais,* trans. Donald M. Frame (Berkeley, 1991), 4.

8. See François Rigolot's chaps. 3 and 4 in *Les métamorphoses de Montaigne* on the thematic, structural, and stylistic significance of the letter in the *Essais.* Rigolot analyzes the letter as the expression of ideal friendship and contrasts it with the degraded essay written after the loss of the friend. My own observations on this subject reveal their debt to him.

9. On the effects of printing on the form and content of the *Essais* see

Barry Lydgate, "Mortgaging One's Work to the World: Publication and the Structure of Montaigne's *Essais*," *PMLA* 96 (1981): 210–223.

10. In his analysis of this passage and its context in the essay in *Rhétorique de la lecture* (289–98), Michel Charles privileges the painter as the only artist whose work exceeds his *intention* and concludes that Montaigne's writing represents a pictorial rather than an exegetical model, one characterized by anamorphic presentation. He argues that the essayist's reluctance to affirm his intention cunningly allows him to recuperate all readings as "intended" and to profit from the role that fortune might have played in the production of the text. While the pictorial metaphor based on the play of different configurations on the same surface or plane provides a richly suggestive perspective on the *Essais*, I would argue that elements of surface and depth, outside and inside (elements of what Charles calls the exegetical model), also function in the text to complicate and undermine Montaigne's efforts to write (be) an unequivocal, transparent surface, however diversely configured. Montaigne is both painter and poet, as Charles's own quotations from the *Essais* reveal. I also think that the essayist's ability to recuperate readings depends in large part on the fact that he has already inscribed "all" readings and readers in his text. Cf. my "Conceptions of the Text and the Generation(s) of Meaning: Montaigne's *Essais* and the Place(s) of the Reader," *Journal of Medieval and Renaissance Studies* 15, no. 1 (Spring 1985): 101–14.

11. Cave, "Problems of Reading in the *Essais*," 143. I am indebted to Cave's seminal essay, which touches on so many complex aspects of reading in the *Essais* both in terms of what he calls the moral and personal problems of reading (the text's status as a self-portrait) and intellectual and aesthetic problems concerning meaning and form in the work.

12. Montaigne's concept of man appears to include the "foreign" as an element of man's nature itself, that is, as something that he cannot escape without escaping from himself, no matter how close he comes to the ideal of knowing and being himself. To be human would thus not be to realize the dictum of the Delphic oracle but to strive toward it. Man is like his actions, which Montaigne characterizes in "De l'experience" (III, 13, 1,077) as "doubles et bigarrées à divers lustres." This is the doubleness that I have characterized as the monstrous. On the foreign as a psychological element in Montaigne, what Garavini calls "des monstres de l'inconscient," and on the essayist's efforts to neutralize it, see her *Monstres et chimères*.

13. I am indebted in this section to Cave's "Problems of Reading" and to his analysis of these same quotations from the *Essais*, which lead him to suggest that "Perhaps the first sense was *already* a particular reading, to which the author brought his own momentary preoccupations, and which was dissipated as the author-reader shifted his perspective. There would thus be no moment of perfect unity of text and meaning, presided over by a godlike author, only a set of words that can be read in various different ways by different readers" (156–57). Where Cave qualifies his observation by adding, "No doubt Montaigne does not go quite as far as this," I am inclined to

say that Montaigne's text does indeed allow us as readers to go as far as this, for "this" is precisely the nature of the obtrusive reader's text, which the *Essais* do go far enough to include.

14. Reacting to the intentional fallacy decried by American New Critics, Paul de Man seeks to restore the concept of structural intentionality to literary criticism. In terms of Heidegger's theory of hermeneutic circularity he explains literary interpretation as an effort at understanding that addresses the work of art as an intentional object rather than a natural or organic one and that produces a sense of literary "form" that is "the result of the dialectic interplay between the prefigurative structure of the foreknowledge [this foreknowledge is the text itself] and the intent at totality of the interpretative process" ("Form and Intent in the American New Criticism," in *Blindness and Insight: Essays in the Rhetoric of Contemporary Criticism*, rev. ed [Minneapolis, 1983], 31). De Man makes it clear that "form" is never absolute or absolutely or concretely in the work but is constituted in the mind of the interpreter as the work discloses itself to his endless questioning.

15. Charles recognizes this strategy in his epilogue on Montaigne in *Rhétorique de la lecture*, 297–98.

16. Georges Poulet, "Criticism and the Experience of Interiority," in *The Structuralist Controversy: The Languages of Criticism and the Sciences of Man*, eds. R. Macksey and E. Donato (Baltimore, 1970), 67. In his discussion of contemporary critics whose readings might be seen to realize the mysterious interrelationship among author, work, and reader that he has been describing, Poulet compares Jean Starobinski and his "optimism" to the Rousseau whom he characterizes in the terms I have quoted.

17. Ibid., 56–88. The quotation is from p. 63.

18. Georges Poulet, *Studies in Human Time*, trans. E. Coleman (Baltimore, 1956), 13. Poulet's image of Montaigne as detached yet still engaged with things strikes me as accurate, although I take issue with the way Poulet ultimately understates the resistance of things to the essayist's effort to reflect upon them, to integrate them within the mind, and, finally, to master them. Poulet recognizes the difficulty of Montaigne's task but insists on the ultimate triumph of the mind, a mind "forever free and forever faithful," and "faithful and identical to itself when it preserves and augments its power of apprehension" (48). My emphasis falls rather on the mind's occasional triumphs, on its equally frequent failures and lapses, and on its inability to succeed, to establish being and plenitude once and for all.

19. Thibaudet, *Montaigne*, 522.

20. W. Iser, *The Implied Reader: Patterns of Communication in Prose Fiction from Bunyan to Beckett* (Baltimore, 1974), 280 and *passim; The Act of Reading: A Theory of Aesthetic Response* (Baltimore, 1978), *passim.*

21. Iser, *The Act of Reading*, 34.

22. Iser, *The Implied Reader*, 279.

23. Ibid., 288.

24. Iser, *The Act of Reading*, 37.

25. Robert Holub sees this tension as reflecting inconsistencies in Iser's theory, his inability to decide how to weight the relationship between the freedom of the reader to produce meaning and the imposing determinacy of the text. See his *Reception Theory: A Critical Introduction* (London, 1984), 101–6. See also the exchange between Stanley Fish and Iser on the determinacy / indeterminacy question in *Diacritics* 11, nos. 1 and 3 (1981).

26. Iser, *The Act of Reading*, 167.

27. Cave, "Problems of Reading," 161.

28. See my "Conceptions of the Text and the Generation(s) of Meaning: Montaigne's *Essais* and the Place(s) of the Reader," where I explore the ways in which Montaigne's writing anticipates and authorizes its own readings.

29. See my "The Boundaries of Interpretation: Self, Text, Contexts in Montaigne's *Essais*," in *Renaissance Rereadings: Intertext and Context*, eds. Maryanne Horowitz, Anne Cruz, Wendy Furman (Urbana, 1988), 18–32.

30. Michel Charles insists upon the double activity of reading, the text acting upon the reader and the reader upon the text. See *Rhetorique de la lecture*, 63. He also draws our attention to the pertinence of Plato's *Ion* to the discussion of the complex relationship between the demands of the text to be heard and the need for the reader to have his say. The *Ion* situates in the singularity of the rhapsode as the hermeneut, the interpreter, the dual task of both reciting the poem of Homer and commenting upon it, as if both the poet's meaning and the listener / reader's understanding had to be given their due. In a note (p. 64) citing the article of Jean Pépin, "L'herméneutique ancienne," *Poétique* 23 (1975): 291–300, Charles attributes to Pépin the conclusion that "l'herméneute peut être le porte-parole ou l'exégète, avec un jeu possible sur les deux sens comme dans l'*Ion*, précisément, qui est cité [by Pépin] comme exemple: 'les deux sens principaux du verbe *hermeneuein*. ..s'entrelacent non sans subtilité avec les deux fonctions du rhapsode, sans que l'on sache toujours bien dans quel registre on se trouve' (p. 296)." In this figure of the rhapsode I find the simultaneous and competing demands of text and reader and the expression of their problematic relationship. Our discussion ultimately affirms Pépin's characterization of the rhapsode by suggesting how difficult it is to determine in any absolute way what finally belongs to the text and what to the reader.

CHAPTER 4

1. Montaigne's use of Pygmalion as a figure of the artist bringing the work to life and the relevance of that figure to the essayist himself have been examined by Mary McKinley in "Text and Context in Montaigne's Quotations: The Example of Ovid's *Metamorphoses*," *L'esprit créateur* 20 (Spring 1980): 46–65, and in *Words in a Corner*; Rigolot, *Les métamorphoses de Montaigne*, 20–26; Compagnon, *Nous, Michel de Montaigne*, 215–18, 222–27. In my story of Pygmalion the gods appear to reward the sculptor for his audacious love (self-love), but, if the story is pursued into future generations, we can

conclude that Pygmalion's presumption was punished after all, for its consequences seem to be visited on Galatea's granddaughter, Myrrha, who is
punished for falling in love with her own father (*Metamorphoses,* X.298–502).

2. See Mary McKinley's reading of the passage in the "Apologie" in "Text
and Context," 51–52.

3. Friedrich draws our attention to the ambivalent nature of folly in Erasmus ("Mais la folie apparaît aussi, et surtout, comme l'illusion dont la vie a
besoin") and to "l'illusion subjective salvatrice" of vanity in Montaigne. See
his *Montaigne,* 319–24.

4. On Narcissus and Pygmalion, see Leonard Barkan's analyses in *The
Gods Made Flesh: Metamorphosis and the Pursuit of Paganism* (New Haven,
1986), esp. 46–52, 75–78.

5. I am indebted to Paul de Man's essay on Nietzsche entitled "Rhetoric
of Tropes" in *Allegories of Reading* (New Haven, 1979) for its articulation of the
rhetorical relationship between self and text. See esp. 111–16.

6. In her chapter on "De la praesumption" Julia Watson analyzes in detail
the complex rhetorical strategies by which Montaigne presents himself as the
wise fool, the Simplex, and she explores the implications of the *nemo* as a
literary and iconographic persona and as a verbal joke, making use of Gerta
Calmann's "The Picture of Nobody: An Iconographical Study," *Journal of the
Warburg and Courtauld Institutes* no. 23 (1960): 60–104. See "The Strategy of
Self-Presentation in Montaigne's *Essais*" (Ph.D. diss., University of California, Irvine, 1979), chap. 3.

7. John Lyons quotes this maxim in his discussion of the witness in Marguerite de Navarre's *Heptaméron* in *Exemplum: The Rhetoric of Example in Early
Modern France and Italy* (Princeton, 1989), 82–83. I am indebted to his remarks
on the legal and rhetorical marginality of the witness.

8. Thibaudet, "Portrait français de Montaigne," *NRF,* 1933, 650, cited in
Hugo Friedrich, *Montaigne,* trans. R. Rovini (Paris, 1968), 63.

9. In his chapter on Montaigne in *Studies in Human Time* (Baltimore, 1956),
Georges Poulet raises the problem of the difficulty of seizing and mastering
the instant in itself: "The instant is the kingdom of the imperceptible. . . . It is
an instant which is an instant of passage, and which therefore is less an
instant than the passage from instant to instant" (45).

10. Ibid., 43.

11. For the rhetorical and narratological implications of Montaigne's
story of his fall from his horse and his "experience" of death, see my "The
Text of Memory: Experience as Narration in Montaigne's *Essais,*" in *The Dialectic of Discovery: Essays on the Teaching and Interpretation of Literature Presented to Lawrence E. Harvey,* eds. John D. Lyons and Nancy J. Vickers (Lexington, Ky., 1984), 145–58.

CHAPTER 5

1. Geoffrey Harpham describes the grotesque as defined by an "affinity / antagonism, by the co-presence of the normative, fully formed, 'high'

or ideal, and the abnormal, unformed, degenerate, 'low' or material" in *On the Grotesque*, 9.

2. The monstrous appears thirty-four times in the *Essais*—as "monstres," "monstrueuse," monstrueuses," "monstrueux"—although readers have tended to ignore or repress the term, its implications, and the threat to the rational (and the rational Montaigne) that it represents. The adjectival forms that dominate its appearances do function often as intensifiers, lending the meanings of "prodigious, "excessive," "extraordinary," "unnatural," "strange," even "miraculous" to customs, costumes, memory, war, and even to perfection when they are called "monstrous." My argument is that what connotes "prodigious" also has a literal, and shadowy, underside.

3. In *Monstres et chimères* Fausta Garavini examines the monstrous as the expression of the unconscious, the figure of its inexplicable and irrepressible fears and desires that leave their traces everywhere in the *Essais* in spite of reason's (writing's) efforts to repress or domesticate them. Writing about himself as the center of his discourse, as the reflection of his experience, Montaigne pursues what Garavini calls a therapy that confronts his tenacious phobias and oppressive phantasms (p. 220)—the repulsion of the body, the attraction to cruelty, the cadaver, suicide, and death itself—although it is a therapy that can never be fully successful or completely master its object. The terms of my approach to alterity in general and to the monstrous in particular differ dramatically from those of Garavini's psychological and psychoanalytical reading, although we are both concerned with what might be called forms and figures of otherness that operate in the *Essais*. Rather than consider the writing as a hedge against madness or neurosis, a form of therapy that seeks to overcome or to neutralize alterity, I read Montaigne's text as the profession and even the celebration of otherness, of difference, although I agree with Garavini that what is often most interesting in the *Essais* transpires without Montaigne's knowledge and in spite of him.

4. Numerous critics have considered monstrosity in the *Essais* in the context of Renaissance medical anthropology, inherited from Galen, which linked mind and body in the theory of humors. Montaigne's melancholy humor, to which he alludes in the opening of "De l'affection des peres aux enfans" as the origin of his text, would thus shed light on the essayist's inclination to solitude, his need to write and to read, his belief in the linkage of body and soul, and his inclination to what he calls "resverie" or that state of delirium or obsession that is equivalent to what produces monsters and chimeras in "De l'oisiveté." See Starobinski, *Montaigne en mouvement*, chap. 1, sec. 6; Michael Screech, *Montaigne and Melancholy: The Wisdom of the "Essays"* (London, 1983); Géralde Nakam, "Montaigne, la mélancolie et la folie," in *Etudes montaignistes en hommage à Pierre Michel*, eds. Claude Blum and François Moureau (Paris, 1984), 195–213; Pierre Lechenelle, *Montaigne et le mal de l'âme* (Paris, 1992); Olivier Pot, "L'inquiétante éstrangeté: La mélancolie de Montaigne," *Montaigne Studies* 3 (1991): 235–302.

5. Gisèle Mathieu-Castellani also reads the opening of "De l'oisiveté" in the light of its concluding paragraph to argue that, alongside the intellectual

subject responsible for opinions and judgments, Montaigne is seeking to present the subject who dreams and muses and gives himself over to the workings of the imagination. She recognizes the tension created by the essayist's problematic effort to recuperate dreams, fancy, and the unbridled imagination in the *Essais* and emphasizes the extent to which this becomes an obsessive topic of the writing itself. See *Montaigne: L'écriture de l'essai,* 25–43.

6. In *La nature et les prodiges* Jean Céard traces in detail the history of the debate about the significance of the monstrous from Aristotle and Augustine to the French sixteenth century.

7. Ambroise Paré, the essayist's contemporary, for example, naturalized the monster as nothing more or less than that which differs from nature's ordinary course and as the extreme example of its penchant for variety. And yet, Paré does not deny the possibility that monsters ultimately derive from God, that they are also in some way supernatural. He simply does not pursue this line of thinking and concentrates without apology on their natural causes. See the critical edition of *Des monstres et prodiges,* ed. Jean Céard (Geneva, 1971).

8. The belief in the ability of the female imagination to affect conception or the fetus during pregnancy and thus to lead to the birth of monsters also suggests that the potential to become either a model or a monster lies within the "same" seed. Unaffected, the seed develops into a normal child; acted upon by the imagination it can become a monster. See Marie-Hélène Huet, *Monstrous Imagination* (Cambridge, Mass., 1993).

9. Mathieu-Castellani also considers the "enfant monstrueux" to be an emblem of the structure of the writing and of its subject. She argues that in this essay Montaigne appropriates the differing positions on the monstrous of Augustine and Cicero (whom he paraphrases and quotes respectively) in order to naturalize it and bring it into the domain of reason. See *Montaigne: L'écriture de l'essai,* 221–235.

10. In *Exemplum,* John Lyons speaks about Montaigne's treatment of monstrosity as exemplary rarity and as the conversion of life into a spectacle (136–37). The enigma of the shepherd's monstrosity lies beyond the merely visual in the discrepancy between his desire inside and the apparent absence of its overdetermined sign outside. In fact, as we will see in the following chapter, the shepherd does show the outside sign that in the *Essais* becomes the most trustworthy indication of male desire, the beard.

11. Giving due weight to Montaigne's claims to be representing his "folie" and "songes," Mathieu-Castellani in *Montaigne: L'écriture de l'essai* also emphasizes the interiorization of monstrousness: "L'homme est un monstre qui s'ignore, Je est un monstre, les *Essais* ne sont que grotesques et corps monstrueux" (237). Cf. also her chaps. 1 and 2.

12. Citing the conclusion of "D'un enfant monstrueux" in *On the Grotesque,* Geoffrey Harpham states that "For Montaigne, there was no true grotesque, because no absolute incongruity. And this is the final paradox: really to understand the grotesque is to cease to regard it as grotesque" (76). He returns again to Montaigne in his conclusion: "Many works, such as

Montaigne's *Essays*, indulge in the grotesque only to leave it behind at the end out of an honorable belief that, although life would be poorer if there were no dragons to pass by, it would be a terrifying and bewildering affair if there were no Father of Souls to pass on to" (191). But my discussion has disclosed that the grotesque is not left behind in Montaigne's text or explained away as a meaningful element of God's hidden design. Nor can it be. In "Des boyteux" the monstrous does appear to vanish through greater understanding, but what vanishes is only a "false" monstrous. What seemed from afar to be strange turns out on closer inspection to have been familiar after all, to be nothing more than an illusion, an effect of faulty perception and of difficulties of perspective. When Montaigne argues in that essay and in "D'un enfant monstrueux" that the monstrous is a part of the variety of nature and the abundance of the divine order, he does not eliminate it or remove it as a cause of bewilderment. The monstrous does not terrify Montaigne because he can accept it as a part of the human condition, and in this sense we can say that he "understands" it. But recovering the monstrous in himself, understanding that it is in him, that it is him, the essayist finds that he does not and cannot master understanding either of the monstrous or of himself. Harpham does not read the lines from "Des boyteux" in which Montaigne states that the more he knows about himself, the more his deformity astonishes him, and the less he knows. Bewilderment and ignorance, as well as the knowledge and acceptance of that ignorance, accompany Montaigne's experience of the grotesque.

13. For the relation of Montaigne's profession of ignorance to the Pyrrhonism of the ancients and to Renaissance skepticism, see Friedrich, *Montaigne*, 141–48.

14. Friedrich distinguishes Montaigne from Augustine and advises reading confession in the *Essais* in its weaker sense as mere admission. He recognizes that the essayist shares the focus on the self and its unfathomable nature, and on self-analysis and self-abasement, but the absence of a desire for salvation, a teleological structure, and a movement toward God in which the self both loses and finds itself distinguish the *Essais* categorically from the Augustinian model. While I fully agree with the validity of this distinction and its significance for reading Montaigne, my position in this chapter is that "confession" remains a central, if understated, element of the lexical, semantic, and thematic network of the text and invites interpretation in its own right and in its own context. "Confession" and "profession" (which had the same meaning in the sixteenth century) are Montaigne's own terms, and I would argue for taking them in their strong sense as a discourse that avows, that acknowledges, and in some sense saves, rather than in the weaker sense, as most readers have done. My appreciation of monstrousness as a figure of the text depends on giving confession its due. See Friedrich, *Montaigne*, 229–30.

15. In *Words in a Corner*, Mary McKinley demonstrates how Montaigne both borrows from and subverts Horatian notions of subject matter and style to include monsters and the monstrous in his writing. See esp. chap. 2 for her

remarks on the ways in which the shift in emphasis in Renaissance aesthetics—both in literature and in the visual arts—from imitation to invention opens the way for this inclusion.

16. This dynamic of change, fluidity, and instability recalls Ovid's *Metamorphoses* and reminds us of the seminal role it plays thematically, structurally, and lexically as a subtext of the *Essais* and during the Renaissance and Baroque periods in general. See esp. McKinley, *Words in a Corner,* and Rigolot, *Les métamorphoses de Montaigne.* In *On the Grotesque* Geoffrey Harpham characterizes the grotesque as interval, a term that he uses both to capture the metamorphosing moment of the object and the moment between the observer's confusion and understanding. The grotesque, he states, is "the middle of a narrative of emergent comprehension" (15). My own emphasis on the irreducibility of the monstrous differs from that of Harpham in its implication not only that the monstrous ultimately and inevitably eludes comprehension but that it becomes the very sign of the incomprehensible.

17. In Montaigne's time this traditional view of the natural link of generations had important social consequences as well because patriarchal culture considered resemblance to be the father's mark, his signature imprinted on the offspring, a sign that determined important issues of paternity, of legitimacy, and of lineage and inheritance. Marie-Hélène Huet examines this issue in *Monstrous Imagination* and suggests how the birth of the monstrous child exposed the tenuousness of resemblance as the basis for paternity (31–35).

18. Paré, *Des monstres et prodiges,* 35–38. I am endebted to the discussion of Marie-Hélène Huet in *Monstrous Imagination,* 13–35.

CHAPTER 6

1. Sandra Gilbert and Susan Gubar in *The Madwoman in the Attic: The Woman Writer and the Nineteenth-Century Literary Imagination* (New Haven, 1979) discuss the implications for women writers of the patriarchal notion that the writer "fathers" his text, just as God fathered the world, in their seminal first chapter, 3–44.

2. See Susan Stanford Friedman, "Creativity and the Childbirth Metaphor: Gender Difference in Literary Discourse," in *Speaking of Gender,* ed. Elaine Showalter (New York, 1989), 73–100.

3. In "Gender Imprinting in Montaigne's *Essais,*" 85–96, Robert Cottrell analyzes the problematical and unstable nature of gender in Montaigne's essays and the implications of inscribing the writing, and all literature perhaps, as "womanly."

4. Michel de Montaigne, *Journal de voyage de Michel de Montaigne,* ed. François Rigolot (Paris, 1992), 6–7.

5. Thomas Laqueur examines the concept of the "one-sex model" and explores the complex relationships between sex and gender in *Making Sex: Body and Gender from the Greeks to Freud* (Cambridge, Mass., 1990). See also his "Orgasm, Generation, and the Politics of Reproductive Biology" in *The Mak-*

ing of the Modern Body: Sexuality and Society in the Nineteenth Century, eds. Catherine Gallagher and Thomas Laqueur (Berkeley, 1987), 1–41.

6. There is, of course, another way to read the story of Iphis, one I explore in "Montaigne's Memorable Stories of Gender and Sexuality," *Montaigne Studies* 6, nos. 1–2 (1994): 187–201. Instead of coding desire exclusively in heterosexual terms, as I have done here, one could speak of Iphis's love for Ianthe as the expression of lesbian desire. "Cows do not burn with love for cows, nor mares for mares," Iphis says, but her experience could be taken to prove that while they may not, women can love women and, in fact, they do, without having to be "men." The attribution of the penis and Iphis's transformation at the end would then merely be a way for her to consummate her love and to allow it to exist openly within a social and cultural context. This is a powerful alternative reading. I have chosen to read in heterosexual terms because both male and female appear to be inscribed in the character of Iphis from the beginning, as I tried to argue, and because I have read Iphis both from the vantage point of the single-sex theory and from that of Montaigne's essay, which is less hospitable to the lesbian interpretation. Both Ovid and Montaigne could be said from this perspective to reflect traditional gender ideology, which makes no place for two female sexual bodies outside of a heterosexual, male-oriented narrative. For insight on this issue see Valerie Traub, "Lesbian Desire in Early Modern England," in *Erotics Politics: Desire on the Renaissance Stage*, ed. Susan Zimmerman (New York, 1992), 150–67.

7. Pierre Villey, *Les sources des Essais: Annotations et éclaircissements*, vol. 4 of *Les Essais de Michel de Montaigne*, eds. Fortunat Strowski, François Gebelin, and Pierre Villey (Bordeaux, 1930), 48–49.

8. I am indebted in this discussion to Lawrence Kritzman, who speaks of the man within the woman's body as a psychic reality in "Montaigne's Fantastic Monsters and the Construction of Gender," 183–96.

9. Montaigne, *Journal de voyage*, 6. My translation.

10. See Traub, "Lesbian Desire in Early Modern England."

11. See Leonard Barkan's comments on Iphis in *The Gods Made Flesh*, 69–71. Thomas Laqueur makes the connection between Iphis and Mary in *Making Sex*, 139.

12. Laqueur makes the point in *Making Sex* that neither biological nor social sex "could be viewed as foundational or primary although gender divisions—the categories of social sex—were certainly construed as natural" (134). See esp. 124–34 for the discussion of what he refers to as "the one elastic sex" and the "open body."

13. Natalie Zemon Davis, "Women on Top," in *Society and Culture in Early Modern France* (Stanford, Calif., 1975), 124–51.

14. Ibid., 150.

15. The theme of male pregnancy in popular tales is the subject of Roberto Zapperi's *L'homme enceint: L'homme, la femme, et le pouvoir* (Paris, 1984). For the pregnant male as an aspect of carnival see Claude Gaignebet, *Le carnaval* (Paris, 1974), 48–49. The function and significance of male maternity in Rabelais's *Quart livre* is explored by Alice Berry in "Dark Births: Male

Maternity in Rabelais's *Quart livre*," *Journal of Medieval and Renaissance Studies* 22 (1992): 101–17. See also Samuel Kinser, *Rabelais's Carnival: Text, Context, Metatext* (Berkeley, 1990), 83–85.

16. Gilbert and Gubar, *The Madwoman in the Attic*, 6. See their argument about the implications of this metaphor for women writers in their opening chapter, "The Queen's Looking Glass: Female Creativity, Male Images of Women, and the Metaphor of Literary Paternity."

17. This appears to be the view of the neo-Aristotelians. The Galenists did believe that the woman possessed semen that contributed to the form and matter of the embryo. For reasons that reveal more about his thematic and rhetorical preoccupations than his medical opinions, Montaigne takes a position closer to the neo-Aristotelians. For the subject of woman as seen by physiologists, anatomists, and physicians in the Renaissance, see Ian Maclean, *The Renaissance Notion of Woman: A Study in the Fortunes of Scholasticism and Medical Science in European Intellectual Life* (Cambridge, 1980), chap. 3.

18. In terms of the traditional psychoanalytic opposition between a maternal order of nurturing and a paternal order of abstract signification where taking the position of the speaking subject requires a repudiation of continuity with the mother's body, we might see Montaigne collapsing or confounding the opposition by making the mother's body the origin of the speaking subject itself, or himself, in this case.

19. Elizabeth Harvey's *Ventriloquized Voices: Feminist Theory and English Renaissance Texts* (London, 1992) drew my attention to the figure of Socrates the midwife and to its implications both for the figure of the male writer giving birth to his own voice and for the complex question of the construction of gender. See esp. 76–115.

20. Patricia Parker, "Literary Fat Ladies and the Generation of the Text," in *Literary Fat Ladies: Rhetoric, Gender, Property* (London, 1987), 8–35.

21. Erasmus, *De duplici copia verborum ac rerum commentarii duo*, trans. Betty I. Knott, Book I, 1, in *Collected Works of Erasmus*, vol. 24 (Toronto, 1978), 295. In *The Cornucopian Text* Terence Cave has explored in detail the paradoxical tendencies of copia to both plenitude and emptiness.

22. Erasmus, *Ciceronianus*, trans. Betty I. Knott, in *Collected Works of Erasmus*, vol. 28 (Toronto, 1986), 404.

23. Cave, *The Cornucopian Text*, 3–34.

24. On gendered language, and on gender as a central rhetorical and thematic issue of the *Essais*, I am indebted to Robert Cottrell's "Gender Imprinting in Montaigne's *Essais*."

25. Robert Cottrell has demonstrated the richly suggestive semantic connections between *bas, molle*, and the feminine in the *Essais*. See his "Gender Imprinting in Montaigne's *Essais*," and "Croisement chiasmique dans le premier essai de Montaigne," *Bulletin de la société des amis de Montaigne*, 6e série, nos. 11–12 (July–Dec. 1982): 65–71.

26. Starobinski, *Montaigne en mouvement*, 227.

27. On the relation between sexual impotence and textual strength, see Robert Cottrell, *Sexuality/Textuality: A Study of the Fabric of Montaigne's Essais*,

146–66. Mathieu-Castellani demonstrates the presence and operation of the dynamic of seduction in the *Essais* and of Montaigne's rhetoric of seduction in her *Montaigne: L'écriture de l'essai,* 255–67.

28. I find it telling that two perceptive readers of the *Essais* attribute gender to the seducer and its object in opposite ways. Robert Cottrell pictures a feminine text seducing a masculine reader ("Gender Imprinting in Montaigne's *Essais*") and Gisèle Mathieu-Castellani portrays a masculine writer in the text seducing a feminine reader (*Montaigne: L'écriture de l'essai*). Rather than taking this as an either/or proposition that requires adjudication, I see the discrepancy as a sign of the diverse and divergent tendencies of Montaigne's text.

29. R. Howard Bloch describes the web of lexical and semantic elements that link the feminine and its dangerous deception to rhetoric, to literature, and even to the writer in medieval literature in "Medieval Misogyny," in *Misogyny, Misandry, and Misanthropy,* eds. R. Howard Bloch and Frances Ferguson (Berkeley, 1989), 1–24.

30. In "Gender Imprinting in Montaigne's *Essais*" Cottrell brings out the female side of the writing, although he does not speak to its doubleness: "the text itself is invested with intentions quite properly called female, for in the tradition in which the Montaignian text is located woman is associated with seduction, that is to say, with sophistry and the art of persuasion, with rhetoric" (88).

Bibliography

Ariès, Philippe. *L'enfant et la vie familiale sous l'ancien régime.* Paris, 1973.

Barkan, Leonard. *The Gods Made Flesh: Metamorphosis and the Pursuit of Paganism.* New Haven, 1986.

Barthes, Roland. "To Write: An Intransitive Verb?" In *The Structuralist Controversy: The Languages of Criticism and the Sciences of Man.* Eds. Richard Macksey and Eugenio Donato. Baltimore, 1970.

Bauschatz, Catherine. " 'Leur plus universelle qualité, c'est la diversité': Women as Ideal Readers in Montaigne's *Essais.*" *Journal of Medieval and Renaissance Studies* 19 (1989): 83–101.

———. "Marie de Gournay's 'Préface de 1595': A Critical Evaluation." *Bulletin de la société des amis de Montaigne,* nos. 3–4 (Jan.–June 1986): 73–82.

Beaujour, Michel. *Miroirs d'encre.* Paris, 1980.

Benveniste, Emile. "Actif et moyen dans le verbe." *Problèmes de linguistique générale,* vol. 1. Paris, 1966.

Berry, Alice. "Dark Births: Male Maternity in Rabelais's *Quart livre.*" *Journal of Medieval and Renaissance Studies* 22 (1992): 101–17.

Bloch, R. Howard. "Medieval Misogyny." In *Misogyny, Misandry, and Misanthropy.* Eds. R. Howard Bloch and Frances Ferguson. Berkeley, 1989.

Boase, Alan. *The Fortunes of Montaigne: A History of the Essays in France, 1580–1669.* London, 1935; rpt. New York, 1970.

Butor, Michel. *Essais sur les "Essais."* Paris, 1964.

Cave, Terence. *The Cornucopian Text: Problems of Writing in the French Renaissance.* Oxford, 1979.

———. "Problems of Reading in the *Essais.*" In *Montaigne: Essays in Memory of Richard Sayce.* Eds. I. D. McFarlane and Ian Maclean. Oxford, 1982.

Céard, Jean. *La nature et les prodiges: L'insolite au seizième siècle en France.* Geneva, 1977.

Charles, Michel. *Rhétorique de la lecture.* Paris, 1977.

Cixous, Hélène. "Le rire de la Méduse." *L'Arc* 61 (1975): 39–54.

Compagnon, Antoine. *Nous, Michel de Montaigne.* Paris, 1980.

———. *La seconde main ou le travail de la citation.* Paris, 1979.

Cottrell, Robert. "Croisement chiasmique dans le premier essai de Montaigne." *Bulletin de la société des amis de Montaigne,* 6e série, nos. 11–12 (July–Dec. 1982): 65–71.

———. "Gender Imprinting in Montaigne's *Essais.*" *L'esprit créateur* 30, no. 4 (Winter 1990): 85–96.

———. *Sexuality/Textuality: A Study of the Fabric of Montaigne's Essais.* Columbus, Ohio, 1981.

Culler, Jonathan. *On Deconstruction.* Ithaca, 1982.

Curtius, E. R. *European Literature and the Latin Middle Ages.* Trans. W. Trask. New York, 1953.

Davis, Natalie Zemon. "A Renaissance Text to the Historian's Eye." *Journal of Medieval and Renaissance Studies* 15 (1985): 47–56.

———. "Women on Top." In *Society and Culture in Early Modern France.* Stanford, Calif., 1975.

Defaux, Gérard. *Marot, Rabelais, Montaigne: L'écriture comme présence.* Paris, 1987.

de Man, Paul. "Form and Intent in the American New Criticism." In *Blindness and Insight: Essays in the Rhetoric of Contemporary Criticism.* Rev. ed. Minneapolis, 1983.

———. "Rhetoric of Tropes." In *Allegories of Reading.* New Haven, 1979.

Derrida, Jacques. "La pharmacie de Platon." *La dissémination.* Paris, 1972.

Dezon-Jones, Elyane. *Fragments d'un discours féminin.* Paris, 1988.

———. "Marie de Gournay: Le je/u/palimpseste." *L'esprit créateur* 23, no. 2 (Summer 1983): 26–36.

Eco, Umberto. *The Role of the Reader.* Bloomington, Ind., 1984.

Erasmus. *Ciceronianus.* Trans. Betty I. Knott. In *Collected Works of Erasmus.* Vol. 28. Toronto, 1978.

———. *De duplici copia verborum ac rerum commentarii duo.* Trans. Betty I. Knott. In *Collected Works of Erasmus.* Vol. 24. Toronto, 1978.

Fish, Stanley. "Why No One's Afraid of Wolfgang Iser." *Diacritics* 11 (1981): 2–13.

Foucault, Michel. "Language to Infinity." *Language, Counter-memory, Practice: Selected Essays and Interviews.* Ed. D. F. Bouchard. Trans. D. F. Bouchard and S. Simon. Ithaca, 1977.

———. *Les mots et les choses.* Paris, 1966.

Frame, Donald. *Montaigne's "Essais": A Study.* Englewood Cliffs, N.J., 1969.

Friedman, Susan Stanford. "Creativity and the Childbirth Metaphor: Gender Difference in Literary Discourse." In *Speaking of Gender.* Ed. Elaine Showalter. New York, 1989.

Friedrich, Hugo. *Montaigne.* Trans. Robert Rovini. Paris, 1968.

Gaignebet, Claude. *Le carnaval.* Paris, 1974.

Garavini, Fausta. *Monstres et chimères: Montaigne, le texte, et le fantasme.* Trans. Isabel Picon. Paris, 1993.

Gilbert, Sandra, and Susan Gubar. *The Madwoman in the Attic: The Woman Writer and the Nineteenth-Century Literary Imagination.* New Haven, 1979.

Gray, Floyd. *Le style de Montaigne.* Paris, 1958.

Harpham, Geoffrey. *On the Grotesque: Strategies of Contradiction in Art and Literature.* Princeton, 1982.

Harvey, Elizabeth. *Ventriloquized Voices: Feminist Theory and English Renaissance Texts.* London, 1992.

Holub, Robert. *Reception Theory: A Critical Introduction.* London, 1984.

Huet, Marie-Hélène. *Monstrous Imagination.* Cambridge, Mass., 1993.

Ilsley, M. H. *A Daughter of the Renaissance: Marie le Jars de Gournay, Her Life and Works.* The Hague, 1963.

Iser, Wolfgang. *The Act of Reading: A Theory of Aesthetic Response.* Baltimore, 1978.

———. *The Implied Reader: Patterns of Communication in Prose Fiction from Bunyan to Beckett.* Baltimore, 1974.

———. "Talk Like Whales." *Diacritics* 11 (1981): 82–87.

Jordan, Constance. *Renaissance Feminism: Literary Texts and Political Models.* Ithaca, 1990.

Kinser, Samuel. *Rabelais's Carnival: Text, Context, Metatext.* Berkeley, 1990.

Kritzman, Lawrence. *Destruction/Découverte: Le fonctionnement de la rhétorique dans les "Essais" de Montaigne.* Lexington, Ky., 1980.

———. "Montaigne's Family Romance." In *The Rhetoric of Sexuality and the Literature of the French Renaissance.* Cambridge, 1991.

———. "Montaigne's Fantastic Monsters and the Construction of Gender." In *Writing the Renaissance: Essays in Sixteenth-Century Literature in Honor of Floyd Gray.* Ed. Raymond C. La Charité. Lexington, Ky., 1992.

———. "Pedagogical Graffiti and the Rhetoric of Conceit." *Journal of Medieval and Renaissance Studies* 15 (1985): 69–83

Laqueur, Thomas. *Making Sex: Body and Gender from the Greeks to Freud.* Cambridge, Mass., 1990.

———. "Orgasm, Generation, and the Politics of Reproductive Biology." In *The Making of the Modern Body: Sexuality and Society in the* Nineteenth *Century.* Eds. Catherine Gallagher and Thomas Laqueur. Berkeley, 1987.

Leake, Roy E. *Concordance des "Essais" de Montaigne.* Geneva, 1981.

Lechenelle, Pierre. *Montaigne et le mal de l'âme.* Paris, 1992.

Lydgate, Barry. "Mortgaging One's Work to the World: Publication and the Structure of Montaigne's *Essais.*" *PMLA* 96 (1981): 210–23.

Lyons, John. *Exemplum: The Rhetoric of Example in Early Modern France and Italy.* Princeton, 1989.

Maclean, Ian. *The Renaissance Notion of Woman: A Study in the Fortunes of Scholasticism and Medical Science in European Intellectual Life.* Cambridge, 1980.

Mathieu-Castellani, Gisèle. *Montaigne: L'écriture de l'essai.* Paris, 1988.

Matoré, Georges. *Le vocabulaire et la société du seizième siècle.* Paris, 1988.

McKinley, Mary. *Words in a Corner: Studies in Montaigne's Latin Quotations.* Lexington, Ky., 1981.

———. "Text and Context in Montaigne's Quotations: The Example of Ovid's *Metamorphoses.*" *L'esprit créateur* 20 (Spring 1980): 46–65.

Montaigne, Michel de. *The Complete Essays of Montaigne.* Trans. D. Frame. Stanford, Calif., 1958.

———. *Les Essais de Michel de Montaigne.* Ed. Pierre Villey and V. L. Saulnier. Paris, 1965.

———. *Journal de voyage de Michel de Montaigne.* Ed. François Rigolot. Paris, 1992.

Nakam, Géralde. "Montaigne, la mélancolie, et la folie." In *Etudes montaig-*

nistes en hommage à Pierre Michel. Eds. Claude Blum and François Moureau. Paris, 1984.

Ong, Walter J., S.J. *Ramus, Method, and the Decay of Dialogue.* Cambridge, 1958.

Paré, Ambroise. *Des monstres et prodiges.* Ed. Jean Céard. Geneva, 1971.

Parker, Patricia. *Literary Fat Ladies: Rhetoric, Gender, Property.* London, 1987.

Pot, Olivier. "L'inquiétante estrangeté: La mélancolie de Montaigne." *Montaigne Studies* 3 (1991): 235–302.

Pouilloux, Jean-Yves. *Lire les "essais" de Montaigne.* Paris, 1969.

Poulet, Georges. "Criticism and the Experience of Interiority." In *The Structuralist Controversy: The Languages of Criticism and the Sciences of Man.* Eds. R. Macksey and E. Donato. Baltimore, 1970.

———. *Studies in Human Time.* Trans. Elliot Coleman. Baltimore, 1956.

Regosin, Richard L. "The Boundaries of Interpretation: Self, Text, Contexts in Montaigne's *Essais.*" In *Renaissance Rereadings: Intertext and Context.* Eds. Maryanne Horowitz, Anne Cruz, Wendy Furman. Urbana, 1988.

———. "Conceptions of the Text and the Generation(s) of Meaning: Montaigne's *Essais* and the Place(s) of the Reader." *Journal of Medieval and Renaissance Studies* 15 (1985): 101-14.

———. *The Matter of My Book: Montaigne's "Essais" as the Book of the Self.* Berkeley, 1977.

———. "Montaigne's Memorable Stories of Gender and Sexuality." *Montaigne Studies* 6 (1994): 187–201.

———. "The Text of Memory: Experience as Narration in Montaigne's *Essais.*" In *The Dialectic of Discovery: Essays on the Teaching and Interpretation of Literature Presented to Lawrence E. Harvey.* Eds. John D. Lyons and Nancy J. Vickers. Lexington, Ky., 1984.

Rendall, Steven. *Distinguo: Reading Montaigne Differently.* Oxford, 1992.

Rigolot, François. *Les métamorphoses de Montaigne.* Paris, 1988.

———. "Préface de Marie de Gournay à l'édition de 1595 des *Essais.*" *Montaigne Studies* 1 (1989): 7–60.

Sainte-Beuve, C. A. *Port-Royal.* Eds. René-Louis Doyon and Charles Marchesne. 10 vols. Paris, 1926–32.

Sankovitch, Tilde A. *French Women Writers and the Book: Myths of Access and Desire.* Syracuse, 1988.

Screech, Michael. *Montaigne and Melancholy: The Wisdom of the "Essays."* London, 1983.

Sebond, Raimond. *La théologie naturelle.* Trans. Michel de Montaigne in *Oeuvres complètes de Michel de Montaigne.* Ed. A. Armaingaud. Paris, 1932.

Simonin, Michel. "Rhetorica ad lectorem: Lecture de l'avertissement des *Essais.*" *Montaigne Studies* 1 (1989): 61–72.

Stanton, Domna. "Autogynography: The Case of Marie de Gournay's 'Apologie pour celle qui escrit.'" In *Autobiography in French Literature,* French Literature Series 12. Columbia, S.C., 1985.

———. "Woman as Object and Subject of Exchange: Marie de Gournay's *Le proumenoir* (1594)." *L'esprit créateur* 23, no. 2 (Summer 1983): 9–25.

Starobinski, Jean. *Montaigne en mouvement.* Paris, 1982.

Thibaudet, Albert. *Montaigne*. Ed. Floyd Gray. Paris, 1963.

Tournon, André. *Montaigne: La glose et l'essai*. Lyon, 1983.

Traub, Valerie. "Lesbian Desire in Early Modern England." In *Erotics Politics: Desire on the Renaissance Stage*. Ed. Susan Zimmerman. New York, 1992.

Valesio, Paulo. *Novantiqua: Rhetorics as a Contemporary Theory*. Bloomington, Ind., 1980.

Villey, Pierre. *Les sources des Essais: Annotations et éclaircissements*." Vol. 4 of *Les "Essais" de Michel de Montaigne*. Eds. Fortunat Strowski, François Gabelin, Pierre Villey. Bordeaux, 1930.

Watson, Julia. "The Strategy of Self-Presentation in Montaigne's Essais." Ph.D. diss., University of California, Irvine, 1979.

Wilden, Anthony. "Par divers moyens on arrive à pareille fin: A Reading of Montaigne." *Modern Language Notes* 83 (1968): 577–97.

Zapperi, Roberto. *L'homme enceint: L'homme, la femme, et le pouvoir*. Trans. Marie-Ange Maire Vigueur. Paris, 1983.

Index of Essays

Apologie de Raimond Sebond (II, 12), 85–92, 101, 130, 131–32, 207–210

Au lecteur, 13, 80–85, 175, 221

Consideration sur Ciceron (I, 40), 32, 92–93, 109, 110, 212

De l'affection des peres aux enfans (II, 8), 2, 4, 16, 17, 33, 35, 37, 39, 40, 43–44, 65, 75, 119, 124, 133, 152–53, 183, 184–85, 197, 205, 235n.4

De la force de l'imagination (I, 21), 185–90

De la gloire (II, 16), 33, 34, 39

De l'amitié (I, 28), 30, 41–42, 49, 55, 64, 66, 153–54, 177–78

De la phisionomie (III, 12), 19, 98, 117, 202, 217

De la praesumption (II, 17), 4, 10, 31, 49, 50–51, 52–57, 58–60, 120, 122–24, 126–28, 136–44, 213

De la punition de la couardise (I, 16), 161, 215

De la ressemblance des enfans aux peres (II, 37), 4, 25–26, 35, 44, 46–47, 64, 206

De l'art de conferer (III, 8), 19, 20, 97, 98, 99–100

De la solitude (I, 39), 34

De la vanité (III, 9), 18, 25, 27, 30, 34, 49, 51, 102–4, 108, 109, 134–35, 141, 142

De l'exercitation (II, 6), 26, 27, 38, 120–21, 140, 144–51, 157, 171, 172, 209, 221

De l'experience (III, 13), 38, 113–14, 117

De l'institution des enfans (I, 26), 3, 18, 21–22, 27, 35, 95, 97, 204, 205, 226n.3

De l'oisiveté (I, 8), 4, 32, 154–57, 159–63, 171, 181–82, 210, 235n.5

De mesnager sa volonté (III, 10), 203

Des boyteux (III, 11), 167–70, 171–73, 175, 222–23, 236n.12

Des livres (II, 10), 99, 101–2

De trois commerces (III, 3), 197, 216–22

Divers evenemens de mesme conseil (I, 24), 94–96, 231n.10

Du démentir (II, 18), 27, 121, 174

D'un enfant monstrueux (II, 30), 7, 84, 163–67, 176, 190, 236n.12

Du pedantisme (I, 25), 24, 217

Du repentir (III, 2), 118

Nos affections s'emportent au dela de nous (I, 3), 98

Sur des vers de Virgile (III, 5), 23, 27, 60, 131, 197–200, 202, 203, 214–15

General Index

Adages (Erasmus), 122, 222–23
anamorphosis, 219, 231n.10
androgyny, 185, 197, 200, 201, 203, 204, 213, 223. *See also* gender; sexual difference
Ariès, Philippe, 28
Aristotle, 45, 49, 182; on the monstrous, 178–79. *See also* metaphor
Austin, J. L., 191

Barkan, Leonard, 234n.4
Barthes, Roland, 35, 227n.12
Bauschatz, Cathleen, 225n.6, 228n.14, 229n.6
Benveniste, Emile, 35, 227n.12
Berry, Alice, 239n.15
Bloch, R. Howard, 241n.29
Boase, Alan, 229nn.5,11
Burke, Kenneth, 179

Cave, Terence, 213, 226n.1, 231nn.11,13, 240nn.21,23
Céard, Jean, 228n.19, 236n.6
Charles, Michel, 230n.3, 231n.10, 232n.15, 233n.30
Ciceronianus (Erasmus), 211–12
Cixous, Hélène, 59
Compagnon, Antoine, 225n.3, 226n.3, 228n.17
confession: as bearing witness, 139, 141; and being, 171; and the feminine, 220; of ignorance, 18, 123, 139, 172; paradox of, 127, 141–43, 173; of presumptuousness, 123, 173; and reading, 175, 176; as remedy, 127, 135, 141, 143, 170, 172–73; as secular, 171, 237n.14
copia: as dilation, 211–12
Cottrell, Robert, 225n.6, 238n.3, 240nn.24,25,27, 241nn.28,30
cross-dressing, 191, 195–96, 220–21; sodomy and, 192–93
Culler, Jonathan, 230n.3
culture. *See* gender; history; nature; rhetoric
Curtius, E. R., 225n.1

Davis, Natalie Zemon, 195, 228n.16, 239n.13
death: as absence, 37–39; and friendship, 37, 51; and narration, 149–50; practice of, 140, 144–46, 148–49; and self-reflexivity, 146; silence as, 32, 67; writing to confront, 39–42
De copia verborum (Erasmus), 211, 212
Defaux, Gérard, 226n.1
de Man, Paul, 232n.14, 234n.5
Derrida, Jacques, 225n.4, 228n.18
Dezon-Jones, Elyane, 229n.2

Eco, Umberto, 230n.12
enfant: definition of, 17, 18; as hybrid, 1, 3–4, 5, 42, 46; literal and figurative, 16–18, 119, 133; as monstrous, 163–67, 176; representing the father, 37, 40–41, 180; unsettled name of, 28
Erasmus, 93, 122; *Adages*, 122, 222–23; *Ciceronianus*, 211–12; *De copia verborum*, 211, 212
Essais: aesthetic (dis)order of, 7, 176; as child, 3, 16–17, 29–30, 134, 152–53; conversational style in, 18, 21, 34–35; feminine at conception, 181–82; origins of, 30–32, 38, 154–58, 206, 210; as process, 82–83; as public text, 31–33, 93–94, 120–21, 140; as self-portrait, 81–85, 98, 102, 116

fortune: and literary creation, 95–97, 100, 101, 103, 231n.10
Foucault, Michel, 39, 228n.15
Friedman, Susan Stanford, 238n.2
Friedrich, Hugo, 234n.3, 237nn.13, 14
friendship: and letter writing, 92–94; misreading, as hedge against, 41–42, 48–49, 51–52, 70–71, 92; and women, 55–57, 64, 66; and writing, 29–31, 65. *See also* Gournay, Marie de; La Boétie, Etienne de; reading; writing

Galatea, 126, 132. *See also* Pygmalion
Galen, 160, 187, 235n.4, 240n.17

Garavini, Fausta, 231n.12, 235n.3
gender, 12, 35–36, 180, 182; and art, 217, 223; and carnival, 195, 197; coding, ambivalence of, 198–99, 219, 221–22; as cultural construct, 134; and death, 192, 193, 194; and knowledge, 216, 218; and public performance, 191, 192, 195; sanctions of, social and legal, 191, 192, 193, 195; and sexual transformation, 185–90, 191, 194–95; as state of mind, 190; and writing, 201, 210–12, 213–16, 219–22. See also sexual difference
Gilbert, Sandra, 238n.1, 240n.16
Gournay, Marie de, 4, 8, 10, 92, 214, 223; as daughter ("fille d'alliance"), 50, 55, 59, 60, 62–63, 66, 75, 78–79; and friendship, 54–55, 57, 61, 64–69, 74; as guarantor of the *Essais*, 54, 60, 62–63, 70–71; as ideal reader, 105; and Mme de Montaigne, 71–75; and *Preface* to the *Essais*, 60–79; and selfhood, 67–68, 75; as textual figure, 50–51, 52–58; as woman writer, 55–57, 58–61, 67–70, 75–79
Gray, Floyd, 226n.1
grotesque, 158, 234n.1, 236n.12, 238n.16; as incongruity, 153, 177; as monstrous, 154
Gubar, Susan, 238n.1, 240n.16

Harpham, Geoffrey, 225n.5, 234n.1, 236n.12, 238n.16
Harvey, Elizabeth, 240n.19
hermaphrodite, 199, 213
history: and interpretation, 9–10, 118; of the monstrous, 158–59
Holob, Robert, 233n.25
Horace, 153, 176, 177, 183, 198
Huet, Marie-Hélène, 236n.8, 238n.17

ignorance, 139, 171, 173; as knowledge, 172; learned, 208; of self, 170. See also confession
imagination: and reading, 109; and sexual transformation, 181, 185, 188–90
Ion (Plato), 233n.30
Iphis, 185, 188–89, 193–94, 195, 199
Iser, Wolfgang: critique of, 111–115; and reader response, 109–11

Journal de voyage (Montaigne), 186, 191

Kritzman, Lawrence, 225n.6, 239n.8

La Boétie, Etienne de, 14, 31, 38, 51, 61, 105, 111, 223; death of, 29, 37, 48–49, 93;

and Marie de Gournay, 54–55, 64; Montaigne as surrogate for, 41–42, 48–49
language: acquisition of, 10, 19–22; and Babel, 30, 87; education, 10, 18, 19–22, 24–25; literal and figurative, 13–16, 42, 45–46; and moral action, 24–26; self-effacing, 23–24; and selfhood, 135, 150; and self-love, 135; self-reflexive, 142–43; and sexual transformation, 191; silent, 22–23, 32; as substance, 27–28, 29, 107. See also reading; rhetoric; writing
Laqueur, Thomas, 238n.5, 239nn.11, 12
lesbian desire, 191, 194, 239n.6
Lyons, John, 234n.7, 236n.10

Marie Germain, 186, 188, 189, 190, 199
maternity: elided by paternity, 35–36, 204, 205, 206, 209; as nurturing, 205; "sine patre," 206, 207; and writing, 206–7. See also *Essais*
Mathieu-Castellani, Gisèle, 227n.8, 235n.5, 236nn.9, 11, 240n.27, 241n.28
Matoré, Georges, 227n.9
McKinley, Mary, 233n.1, 234n.2, 237n.15
metaphor: as catachresis, 179, 184; defined in *Poetics*, 45; and metonymy, 26, 84, 179; and monstrousness, 179; and transfer of seed, 45–47
mimesis: seed as agent of, 46–47; of speech, 21
misogyny, 8, 185, 197, 202, 203, 204, 217, 219
monstrousness, 4, 7–8, 11; and conception of *Essais*, 154–56, 160; as difference and incongruity, 153, 166–67, 176; and female birth, 181, 206; and male birth, 184, 196; in man, 169–70, 173, 179, 231n.12; and melancholy, 235n.4; as miracle, 169; and nature, 158–60, 167; seed and, 46–47, 154, 156, 160–61, 173; shame of, 162–63; as showing, 163–67, 219–20; as sickness, 155, 171, 235n.3; textual child as, 153, 206; as the unfamiliar, 168, 169; and writing, ordered by, 157–58, 164, 207
Montaigne, Michel de: as father, 1, 3, 16–17, 50, 53, 125, 130, 134, 151, 184; as friend, 29, 48–49, 56; as monster, 7, 154, 157, 169–70, 180, 207; as *nemo*, 138–40, 150, 171; as woman, 35, 199, 204, 211, 220–21. See also *Essais*

Narcissus, 129–30, 136, 137, 151
nature: and art, 130–32, 137, 217–19, 221–22; book of, 86–89; conflict within, 161, 162; and culture, 20, 98,

201–4, 207; and ideal speech, 19–22, 22–25, 40; as monstrous, 154–57, 158–60, 164; ordered, 154; origin as unrecuperable, 200
nemo: as monstrous, 170; as "no one," 137–38; paradoxical status of, 138–39, 142; and self-knowledge, 138, 151; as witness, 139–40, 150–51

Ong, Walter J., 227n.6
oratio speculum animi, 226n.1
Ovid, 11, 133, 183, 205; Hermaphroditus, 213; Propoetides, 162–63. *See also* Iphis; Narcissus; Pygmalion

Paré, Ambroise, 186, 187, 188, 236n.7
Parker, Patricia, 211
passage: aesthetics of, 177–78; and death, 146, 148; portrayal of, 147, 148; temporality of, 146–47; and textuality, 149, 151
paternity, 8, 119, 134; and authority, 40, 43–44; erotic dimension of, 133–34; feminist criticism of, 183–84; and filial loyalty, 44–45, 75–76; as male birth ("sine matre"), 134, 180, 183–85, 196, 205–6, 207, 209, 210; parodied as male pregnancy, 196–97; and resemblance, 46, 64, 205; and spiritual offspring, 1–3, 16, 37, 53–54
Phaedrus (Plato), 5–7, 20, 42–43, 75, 112
Plato, 108, 183, 202; *Ion*, 233n.30; *Phaedrus*, 5–7, 20, 42–43, 75, 112; Platonic love, 1–2; *Symposium*, 1, 201; *Theaetetus*, 208
Poetics (Aristotle), 45
Poulet, Georges, 106–7, 148, 232nn.16, 18, 234n.9
Preface sur les Essais (Gournay), 60–79
presumption: as disease, 141, 143, 150; and humility, 123; and *nemo*, 137–38; and *philautia*, 122–23; and the public text, 120–21, 144. *See also* confession; writing
Pygmalion, 3, 124–26, 129, 130–32, 137, 151, 162, 180; and Myrrha, 133–34, 151

Ramus, Petrus, 24, 227n.6
reading: and friendship, 48–49, 64–65, 70, 80–85, 105, 109; and inscribed readers, 82–85, 94, 96, 102, 104, 108, 116; literal and figurative language and, 13–16, 42, 49; and misreading, 9, 41–42, 48–49, 51–57, 70–71, 80–85, 89–92, 102, 121; obtrusive, 11, 84–85, 89, 104, 111–18, 175–76, 231n.13, 233n.30;

as phenomenological union, 65, 105–8; as witnessing, 174
reason: attacked in *Apologie*, 90; and faith, 88; and pyrrhonism, 171, 207; vagaries of, 89, 168, 169–70, 181, 200
Renaissance: carnival and transvestism in, 195; *enfant* in, 28; grotesque in, 153; legal testimony in, 139; male pregnancy parodied in, 196; midwifery in, 209; monstrous in, 159; portrait in, 93; self-love in, 122; status of woman in, 61, 69, 73; stories of sexual change in, 189; sumptuary laws in, 191–93; theories of sexuality in, 187
Rendall, Steven, 225n.4, 228n.1
rhetoric, 14, 20, 23, 24, 25, 149, 173, 201, 202, 204, 220; and anti-rhetoric, 20–21, 25, 136, 217; as feminine, 216, 217; and miracles, 168; and monstrousness, 158; and seduction, 215, 216, 218, 219; and self-representation, 26, 136–37; and sexuality, 193. *See also* copia; metaphor
Rigolot, François, 77, 229nn.4, 7, 230n.8
Rousseau, Jean-Jacques, 105, 232n.16

Sainte-Beuve, C.-A., 226n.1
Sebond, Raimond: and authorial intention, 89–92; Montaigne as reader of, 87–89; as reader of the book of nature, 86–87; *Theologia naturalis*, 85
self-love: and artistic conception, 124–26, 130–34; and death, 130, 134; as incestuous, 3, 11, 124–26, 128, 133–34; paradoxical nature of, 127–29, 135; as *philautia*, 11, 122, 138; and self-knowledge, 127–28, 135. *See also* Narcissus
sexual difference, 187–88, 190, 203; and desire, 189, 191; and resemblance, 199, 200; single-sex theory of, 161, 187; as unstable, 187–88. *See also* Galen; Iphis; Marie Germain
Socrates, 1, 5, 38; and Delphic injunction, 140, 142; as midwife, 208–10; as model for Montaigne, 140, 172–73; and speech, 19; and writing, 112–13
Starobinski, Jean, 215, 232n.16
Symposium (Plato), 1, 201

textuality, 1, 6, 7, 46, 104, 116; and difference, 7, 42, 100–102, 161–62; and domination of the reader, 103, 112–13, 115–18; and errancy, 10, 51, 80, 85; and oral discourse, 35; and ownership, 11, 83, 95, 97, 113, 115; and sexuality, 198–200, 215; as site of dialogue, 34–35, 36–37, 108–17, 174

Theaetetus (Plato), 208
Theologia naturalis (Sebond), 85
Thibaudet, Albert, 107, 140, 226n.1
Traub, Valerie, 239n.10

Valesio, Paulo, 227nn.5, 7
Villey, Pierre, 189

Watson, Julia, 234n.6
witnessing: and confession, 139, 141;
credibility of, undermined, 168; and
Marie de Gournay, 67; and monstrousness, 165, 167, 168; and need for
"other," 33–34, 68–69; public, *Essais*
as, 31–33, 157; and self-abasement,
139, 140–41

writing: and absence, 36–38; and authority, 43–44, 85, 91; and being, 135, 171;
and borrowing, 97–100; and daughters, 4, 48–79, 134, 183; and death, 65–
67, 144–49; double gender of, 207, 210,
215–16, 222–23; and friendship, 29–
30, 48–51, 64–67, 69; formlessness of,
206–7; and intention, 100–102, 103,
231n.10, 232n.14; invention of, 5–7; in
Latin, 44, 213; as making, 25–28, 171;
and order, 157–58, 207; presumption
of, 11, 31–33, 120–51; as seduction,
197, 198, 215, 223, 241n.28

Zapperi, Roberto, 239n.15

Compositor:	Keystone Typesetting, Inc.
Text:	10 / 13 Palatino
Display:	Palatino
Printer and Binder:	Thomson-Shore, Inc.